CONTENTS

WHERE'S THE BAR? 1991/2
ISBN 1 872204 03 1
Printed and published by
Juma
44 Wellington Street
Sheffield 1

INTRODUCTION

As a parting shot to my introduction last year I suggested that the boom in non-league football is an artificial one created by the introduction of promotion to the Football League, and non-league football would only be successful in its own right when the winners of the GMVC one season declined promotion and opted to stay where they were. This prompted several letters, both agreeing and disagreeing, so I thought I might clarify my position. I've heard some non-league supporters (Wycombe and Kettering fans spring to mind, though I'm not claiming these attitudes are typical of those clubs) claim that nothing matters except the holy grail of promotion to Division Four. They dismiss not only the likes of the County cups and Bob Lord Trophy, but the F.A. Cup and F.A. Trophy too. They seem to miss the point that Wycombe and Kettering survived and thrived long before 1987. Indeed, there are clubs throughout the non-league sphere that have never won much and have little realistic prospect of changing that fact, but they nevertheless attract dedicated supporters, loyal players and officials and are run by people simply for the love of the game. They are not failures. So what when Division Four is a reality? Is all that matters then further promotion? Is any club which, ultimately, cannot compete with the Liverpools and Arsenals worthless? Perhaps this is the very attitude that distinguishes League from non-league. We all like to see our teams play well and win trophies, but competing is still the most important thing. Yes, I know the days of amateurism are long gone. Yes, I know there are financial pressures demanding success at many levels. But the fans on the terraces should be immune to all that.

And if my team were to win the GMVC? Would I want them to decline the step up? I don't know. Like Doran Garfunkel writing about Barnet in this edition, my feelings would be mixed. A week ago I travelled to the first qualifying round of the F.A. Cup. It was a glorious day; the match was played in a field with a wall round it; we outnumbered the home supporters by about three to one; the welcome was warm; there wasn't a policeman in evidence all day; and we won! Despite the fact that we never seem to qualify for the rounds we used to be exempt to I wouldn't want to give that up.

Unfortunately some people who one would want to be in the vanguard of protecting non-league ethics appear to be trying to impose this new compulsory ambitiousness instead. The name of the game is ground grading. Is it really justified to relegate a team attracting 3-400 spectators because their ground doesn't look like Wembley? Hard pressed clubs are being forced to spend money bringing grounds up to quite unnecessary standards. The GMVC wants to ensure all its clubs have the potential for promotion to the Football League. The Beazer Homes League wants all its Premier Division clubs to be promotable to the GMVC. Why? Three quarters of them are never going to get there.

My other moan for the year is the intrusion of sponsorship. We all know this is now an essential aspect of the game, and can understand companies wanting their names given the maximum prominence. But I'm losing count of the number of times I'm asked "Whatever happened to the old Southern League?", or "What eactly is the Diadora League?". I wouldn't mind betting you can find a few fans of Southern League teams who aren't even aware that the Larchimage Windows Cup.... sorry, Barclays Challenge Cup.... is the Southern League Cup under another name. In cases like this I believe strongly that the competitions themselves are devalued. Is it really too much to ask that the traditional (real) names of the competitions could be incorporated into the title along with the sponsors' name? Surely not?

Martin Lacey

VAUXHALL CONFERENCE TABLE 1990-91

	P	W	D	L	F	A	W	D	L	F	A	Pts	AVERAGE GATE 1990/91
BARNET	42	13	4	4	50	23	13	5	3	53	29	87	2,918
COLCHESTER UNITED	42	16	4	1	41	13	9	6	6	27	22	85	3,003
ALTRINCHAM	42	12	6	3	48	22	11	7	3	39	24	82	1,385
KETTERING TOWN	42	12	6	3	38	19	11	5	5	29	26	80	2,563
WYCOMBE WANDERERS	42	15	3	3	46	17	6	8	7	29	29	74	2,794
TELFORD UNITED	42	11	3	7	30	21	9	4	8	32	31	67	1,186
MACCLESFIELD TOWN	42	11	4	6	38	22	6	8	7	25	30	63	1,001
RUNCORN	42	12	4	5	44	29	4	6	11	25	38	58	729
MERTHYR TYDFIL	42	9	5	7	37	24	7	4	10	25	37	57	824
BARROW	42	10	8	3	34	24	5	4	12	25	41	57	1,427
WELLING UNITED	42	7	10	4	33	27	6	5	10	22	30	54	985
NORTHWICH VICTORIA	42	8	7	6	33	30	5	6	10	32	45	52	748
KIDDERMINSTER H.	42	8	5	8	33	30	6	5	10	23	37	52	1,197
YEOVIL TOWN	42	9	5	7	38	29	4	6	11	20	29	50	2,634
STAFFORD RANGERS	42	7	9	5	30	26	5	5	11	18	25	50	1,174
CHELTENHAM TOWN	42	8	6	7	29	25	4	6	11	25	47	48	1,029
GATESHEAD	42	10	3	8	32	38	4	3	14	20	54	48	586
BOSTON UNITED	42	9	4	8	40	31	3	7	11	15	38	47	1,372
SLOUGH TOWN	42	9	4	8	31	29	4	2	15	20	51	45	1,168
BATH CITY	42	9	4	8	39	27	1	8	12	16	34	42	883
SUTTON UNITED	42	6	6	9	29	33	4	3	14	33	49	39	874
FISHER ATHLETIC	42	3	9	9	22	30	2	6	13	16	49	30	651

VAUXHALL CONFERENCE LEADING GOALSCORERS 1990-91

Conf.			FA	BL	FT
30	GARY BULL (BARNET)	+	2	–	–
24	MARK WEST (WYCOMBE WANDERERS)	+	6	–	3
22	KEN McKENNA (ALTRINCHAM)	+	3	2	3
19	MARK CARTER (BARNET)	+	–	1	1
	PAUL RANDALL (BATH CITY)	+	–	–	3
18	COLIN COWPERTHWAITE (BARROW)	+	–	2	1
	TERRY ROBBINS (WELLING UNITED)	+	2	1	–
17	MARIO WALSH (COLCHESTER UNITED)	+	–	–	1
16	PAUL CAVELL (BOSTON UNITED)	+	5	1	2
	NICKY EVANS (BARNET)	+	5	–	–
15	CHARLIE BUTLER (GATESHEAD)	+	–	1	–
	PETER HOWELL (KIDDERMINSTER HARRIERS)	+	–	1	4
14	JOHN ASKEY (MACCLESFIELD TOWN)	+	–	–	–
	JOHN BRADY (ALTRINCHAM)	+	1	–	2
	KIM CASEY (CHELTENHAM TOWN)	+	2	–	1

GM VAUXHALL CONFERENCE RESULTS 1990-91

	ALTRINCHAM	BARNET	BARROW	BATH CITY	BOSTON UNITED	CHELTENHAM TOWN	COLCHESTER UNITED	FISHER ATHLETIC	GATESHEAD	KETTERING TOWN	KIDDERMINSTER H.	MACCLESFIELD TOWN	MERTHYR TYDFIL	NORTHWICH VICTORIA	RUNCORN	SLOUGH TOWN	STAFFORD RANGERS	SUTTON UNITED	TELFORD UNITED	WELLING UNITED	WYCOMBE WANDERERS	YEOVIL TOWN
ALTRINCHAM	X	4-1	1-1	2-0	1-1	3-0	2-2	0-0	4-1	3-2	1-2	5-2	9-2	0-2	1-0	3-0	0-0	4-1	2-1	0-1	1-0	2-2
BARNET	0-0	X	3-1	2-0	5-0	2-1	1-3	8-1	1-1	0-1	2-3	3-1	2-3	1-1	2-0	6-1	2-0	1-0	0-0	3-2	3-2	3-2
BARROW	1-0	4-2	X	1-1	1-1	0-0	2-2	3-1	3-1	0-1	1-3	1-1	0-2	2-2	2-1	2-1	2-0	3-1	2-1	1-1	2-2	1-0
BATH CITY	2-3	1-4	1-1	X	1-0	2-0	1-2	0-1	3-0	3-3	4-1	0-2	0-0	4-1	6-1	4-0	0-1	2-2	0-1	2-1	1-2	2-1
BOSTON UNITED	2-6	1-3	0-2	3-0	X	2-1	1-3	4-1	5-1	1-2	3-1	1-1	3-0	4-1	2-2	0-1	0-2	2-2	2-1	0-0	0-1	4-0
CHELTENHAM TOWN	1-4	1-4	3-1	0-0	5-0	X	1-2	0-0	1-0	2-2	0-0	2-2	0-1	1-1	1-3	2-0	1-2	3-2	0-1	3-0	1-0	1-0
COLCHESTER UNITED	1-1	0-0	1-0	2-0	3-1	3-1	X	2-1	3-0	3-1	2-0	1-0	3-1	4-0	2-2	2-1	2-0	1-0	2-0	2-1	2-2	0-1
FISHER ATHLETIC	0-0	2-4	1-2	0-3	1-2	1-1	0-0	X	0-2	0-0	1-1	1-2	0-0	5-2	0-1	1-1	1-3	1-1	2-0	1-1	2-3	2-1
GATESHEAD	0-3	1-3	5-1	2-0	0-1	3-3	1-2	1-0	X	1-2	2-1	1-1	1-0	0-4	3-1	1-0	2-1	0-9	5-1	0-3	2-1	1-1
KETTERING TOWN	1-1	1-3	2-0	1-1	1-1	5-1	1-0	3-2	1-0	X	4-1	2-0	2-0	1-0	3-0	0-0	2-0	5-2	2-5	0-0	0-1	1-1
KIDDERMINSTER H.	0-1	0-3	3-1	3-2	3-3	2-0	0-0	3-3	2-3	3-0	X	0-0	1-2	3-1	3-1	1-2	2-1	1-0	1-3	1-2	1-2	0-0
MACCLESFIELD TOWN	0-1	3-2	3-0	3-1	2-0	5-1	1-0	1-1	4-0	1-2	0-0	X	0-1	1-2	2-1	1-2	2-1	4-2	1-2	2-1	0-0	2-1
MERTHYR TYDFIL	0-2	1-1	0-2	0-0	2-0	3-0	3-0	7-0	3-1	1-3	1-2	0-2	X	3-2	0-0	3-0	1-1	3-0	2-3	1-0	2-4	1-1
NORTHWICH VICTORIA	1-1	0-2	2-2	2-0	3-1	5-2	2-2	0-0	3-2	0-1	1-1	4-1	0-3	X	1-4	1-0	1-1	1-0	2-4	1-2	1-1	2-0
RUNCORN	1-3	3-2	3-1	1-1	2-1	2-2	0-3	5-1	2-0	2-1	5-1	1-2	2-1	2-1	X	3-1	1-0	5-1	0-0	2-3	1-1	0-3
SLOUGH TOWN	3-3	1-3	3-0	2-0	2-0	0-3	0-2	1-0	1-1	0-3	0-0	0-1	1-2	2-4	2-1	X	2-1	1-2	2-0	3-0	3-3	2-0
STAFFORD RANGERS	2-1	2-2	2-2	2-1	1-2	2-2	0-2	2-0	0-1	0-0	3-1	2-2	2-0	0-0	1-1	3-4	X	1-2	1-1	1-0	2-1	1-1
SUTTON UNITED	1-2	0-1	2-1	1-1	0-0	2-3	0-1	3-1	3-3	1-2	1-2	3-1	1-1	2-2	1-3	5-2	0-3	X	0-3	1-1	1-0	1-0
TELFORD UNITED	1-2	1-1	0-1	2-2	1-0	1-2	2-0	3-1	1-2	0-1	1-0	1-2	3-1	1-0	2-0	2-1	0-0	4-2	X	2-1	1-0	1-2
WELLING UNITED	2-2	1-4	4-2	2-1	0-0	0-0	1-1	1-1	6-0	0-0	1-0	0-0	2-1	4-5	2-2	2-0	2-1	1-2	1-1	X	1-1	0-3
WYCOMBE WANDERERS	3-0	1-3	2-1	0-0	3-0	0-2	1-0	2-0	4-0	5-1	2-3	0-0	2-1	3-0	1-1	2-1	3-0	4-1	3-2	4-1	X	2-0
YEOVIL TOWN	2-3	1-4	0-3	3-2	1-1	4-0	2-0	0-1	4-1	0-1	2-0	2-1	3-3	1-1	1-0	7-2	0-0	2-1	1-2	0-1	2-2	X

BEAZER HOMES LEAGUE 1990/1 TABLES

PREMIER DIVISION

	P	W	D	L	F	A	W	D	L	F	A	F	A	Pts
Farnborough Town	42	13	3	5	47	26	13	4	4	32	17	79	43	85
Gloucester City	42	15	6	0	56	24	8	8	5	30	25	86	49	83
Cambridge City	42	14	4	3	41	20	7	10	4	22	23	63	43	77
Dover Athletic	42	10	7	4	27	16	11	4	6	29	21	56	37	74
Bromsgrove Rovers	42	14	4	3	45	21	6	7	8	23	28	68	49	71
Worcester City	42	10	7	4	32	17	8	5	8	23	25	55	42	66
Burton Albion	42	11	6	4	31	15	4	9	8	28	33	59	48	60
Halesowen Town	42	8	6	7	35	28	9	3	9	38	39	73	67	60
V.S. Rugby	42	10	3	8	35	22	6	8	7	21	24	56	46	59
Bashley	42	8	5	8	30	27	7	7	7	26	25	56	52	57
Dorchester Town	42	12	4	5	29	23	3	8	10	18	31	47	54	57
Wealdstone	42	9	4	8	31	29	7	4	10	26	29	57	58	56
Dartford	42	13	4	4	45	22	2	5	14	16	42	61	64	54
Rushden Town	42	10	6	5	42	23	4	5	12	22	43	64	66	53
Atherstone United	42	7	5	9	27	27	7	5	9	28	31	55	58	52
Moor Green	42	10	2	9	38	34	5	4	12	26	41	64	75	51
Poole Town	42	8	4	9	29	33	4	9	8	27	36	56	69	49
Chelmsford City	42	3	11	7	23	31	8	4	9	34	37	57	68	48
Crawley Town	42	7	9	5	28	27	5	3	13	17	40	45	67	48
Waterlooville	42	5	8	8	25	29	6	5	10	26	41	51	70	46
Gravesend & Northfleet	42	7	6	8	28	31	2	1	18	18	60	46	91	34
Weymouth	42	3	8	10	25	30	1	4	16	25	58	50	88	24

MIDLAND DIVISION

(*1,*3,*4 denotes points deducted)

	P	W	D	L	F	A	W	D	L	F	A	F	A	Pts
Stourbridge	42	18	2	1	45	17	10	4	7	35	31	80	48	90
Corby Town	42	16	2	3	54	16	11	2	8	45	32	99	48	85
Hednesford Town	42	13	3	5	40	23	12	4	5	39	24	79	47	82
Tamworth	42	14	1	6	43	24	11	4	6	41	21	84	45	80
Nuneaton Borough	42	13	6	2	42	23	8	5	8	32	28	74	51	70*4
Barry Town	42	13	3	5	38	21	7	4	10	23	27	61	48	67
Newport A.F.C.	42	10	3	8	28	24	9	3	9	26	22	54	46	63
King's Lynn	42	11	4	6	27	25	6	5	10	26	37	53	62	60
Grantham Town	42	8	4	9	28	27	9	3	9	34	29	62	56	58
Redditch United	42	9	6	6	35	34	7	4	10	31	41	66	75	58
Hinckley Town	42	8	6	7	43	34	8	3	10	29	34	72	68	57
Sutton Coldfield Town	42	9	5	7	28	29	6	6	9	28	36	56	65	56
Bedworth United	42	10	4	7	30	31	5	5	11	27	42	57	73	54
Bilston Town	42	9	5	7	47	37	5	4	12	22	42	69	79	51
Leicester United	42	9	7	5	33	32	5	3	13	32	45	65	77	51*1
Racing Club Warwick	42	7	6	8	32	32	5	7	9	24	33	56	65	49
Bridgnorth Town	42	8	4	9	36	35	5	5	11	26	39	62	74	48
Stroud	42	8	5	8	27	27	3	9	9	24	37	51	64	47
Dudley Town	42	6	7	8	24	37	5	6	10	24	36	48	73	46
Alvechurch	42	6	5	10	32	44	4	3	14	22	48	54	92	38
Willenhall Town	42	6	6	9	31	32	4	4	13	27	37	58	69	37*3
Spalding United	42	5	4	12	16	32	3	5	13	19	38	35	70	33

SOUTHERN DIVISION

(*1 denotes point deducted)

	P	W	D	L	F	A	W	D	L	F	A	F	A	Pts
Buckingham Town	40	14	2	4	35	18	11	6	3	38	20	73	38	83
Trowbridge Town	40	14	6	0	43	11	8	6	6	24	20	67	31	78
Salisbury	40	14	5	1	39	14	8	6	6	24	25	63	39	77
Baldock Town	40	14	3	3	40	20	7	6	7	26	32	66	52	72
Ashford Town	40	14	3	3	51	19	8	2	10	31	33	82	52	71
Yate Town	40	12	3	5	42	23	9	5	6	34	25	76	48	71
Hastings Town	40	13	3	4	39	16	5	8	7	27	30	66	46	65
Hythe Town	40	10	5	5	32	18	7	4	9	23	26	55	44	59*1
Andover	40	9	4	7	40	37	7	2	11	29	39	69	76	54
Margate	40	9	5	6	30	25	5	6	9	22	30	52	55	53
Burnham	40	10	6	4	35	17	2	10	8	22	32	57	49	52
Bury Town	40	10	2	8	34	33	5	3	12	24	41	58	74	50
Sudbury Town	40	7	6	7	34	29	6	4	10	26	39	60	68	49
Newport I.O.W.	40	6	5	9	20	26	7	4	9	36	36	56	62	48
Gosport Borough	40	4	7	9	20	26	8	4	8	27	32	47	58	47
Witney Town	40	8	6	6	36	35	4	5	11	21	40	57	75	47
Dunstable	40	2	10	8	22	29	7	5	8	26	34	48	63	42
Canterbury City	40	8	2	10	37	41	4	4	12	23	42	60	83	42
Erith & Belvedere	40	6	4	10	26	31	4	2	14	20	42	46	73	36
Fareham Town	40	7	5	8	26	35	2	4	14	20	39	46	74	36
Corinthian	40	4	8	8	21	33	1	4	15	13	45	34	78	27

(Records of Folkestone Town (1990) expunged)

FACTS

BEAZER HOMES LEAGUE 1990/1 RESULTS

Beazer Homes League 1990/91

PREMIER DIVISION

PREMIER DIVISION	ATHERSTONE UNITED	BASHLEY	BROMSGROVE ROVERS	BURTON ALBION	CAMBRIDGE CITY	CHELMSFORD CITY	CRAWLEY TOWN	DARTFORD	DORCHESTER TOWN	DOVER ATHLETIC	FARNBOROUGH TOWN	GLOUCESTER CITY	GRAVESEND & N'FLEET	HALESOWEN TOWN	MOOR GREEN	POOLE TOWN	RUSHDEN TOWN	V.S. RUGBY	WATERLOOVILLE	WEALDSTONE	WEYMOUTH	WORCESTER CITY
ATHERSTONE UNITED		1-0	0-1	1-1	1-1	0-1	1-0	3-0	0-3	3-2	1-2	2-2	3-4	2-0	0-2	1-1	4-0	0-1	1-1	1-2	1-0	1-3
BASHLEY	0-0		1-1	2-1	2-2	2-1	0-1	0-1	2-2	0-3	1-1	0-1	3-1	1-2	4-1	1-0	3-1	0-2	5-1	0-1	3-2	0-2
BROMSGROVE ROVERS	2-0	2-4		3-3	2-2	1-0	3-2	4-0	4-0	1-2	3-2	0-1	3-0	2-1	1-1	1-1	2-0	4-1	3-0	1-0	2-1	1-0
BURTON ALBION	1-0	0-0	1-0		2-0	1-1	2-0	3-0	1-0	1-2	2-0	1-2	2-1	1-2	5-0	1-1	0-1	0-0	1-1	3-2	3-2	0-0
CAMBRIDGE CITY	4-3	2-2	0-0	2-1		4-0	4-1	2-1	3-1	0-0	0-0	1-2	1-0	1-3	2-1	1-0	1-4	2-0	3-0	2-1	5-0	1-0
CHELMSFORD CITY	3-4	2-2	1-2	2-2	0-0		1-4	1-1	0-0	1-1	1-2	0-2	1-0	2-2	3-4	1-1	0-3	1-0	1-1	0-0	2-0	0-0
CRAWLEY TOWN	1-0	1-0	3-2	1-1	1-1	2-3		2-2	0-1	0-1	0-1	3-3	2-1	2-2	1-0	2-4	2-2	0-0	1-0	1-0	2-2	1-1
DARTFORD	1-1	1-0	2-1	2-0	2-0	1-1	6-1		3-0	1-0	1-2	2-1	3-0	3-3	2-1	0-0	1-2	2-0	5-1	1-2	5-3	1-3
DORCHESTER TOWN	1-2	2-1	1-0	1-0	0-2	1-1	2-0	1-1		1-0	2-1	1-0	4-1	2-1	3-0	2-1	0-0	0-3	0-3	1-1	1-3	3-2
DOVER ATHLETIC	1-0	0-1	4-2	0-0	0-1	3-2	1-1	0-2	3-0		1-0	3-0	3-1	2-1	0-0	0-0	1-0	0-0	1-0	1-2	2-2	1-1
FARNBOROUGH TOWN	3-1	1-3	0-2	1-0	0-0	3-1	2-0	2-2	2-1	1-3		1-1	5-0	2-1	2-1	3-2	4-0	1-3	7-0	2-3	3-2	2-0
GLOUCESTER CITY	2-2	3-0	3-1	2-1	1-1	3-2	5-0	2-0	1-1	4-1	1-1		6-3	2-1	3-2	4-0	3-2	2-2	3-1	2-1	1-1	3-1
GRAVESEND & NORTHFLEET	4-1	2-1	1-1	1-1	2-2	0-2	0-1	3-1	1-1	0-1	1-2	0-4		3-1	2-1	2-4	0-0	0-1	0-3	1-1	3-1	2-1
HALESOWEN TOWN	0-1	2-4	1-1	1-3	3-0	1-4	1-2	2-1	0-0	2-2	1-2	0-0	3-0		0-2	3-3	3-0	2-1	2-2	1-0	5-0	2-0
MOOR GREEN	1-2	0-1	1-2	3-6	0-1	1-0	2-1	3-1	1-3	1-0	0-2	3-2	3-1	1-2		5-4	4-0	2-2	0-1	2-0	4-2	1-1
POOLE TOWN	1-4	2-2	0-0	2-3	1-3	1-2	2-0	1-0	2-0	1-1	0-4	1-2	2-0	0-2	1-0		4-2	1-1	0-3	3-2	3-0	1-2
RUSHDEN TOWN	2-1	1-1	4-1	1-1	4-1	6-1	3-1	4-2	1-0	0-1	1-1	1-1	4-0	4-3	1-2	0-1		1-1	3-1	0-1	1-1	0-1
V.S. RUGBY	2-0	1-1	2-2	2-3	0-1	0-1	0-1	3-0	2-1	0-1	0-1	0-1	4-2	3-1	2-2	3-0	2-1		1-2	2-1	3-0	3-0
WATERLOOVILLE	1-1	0-1	0-1	2-0	0-1	3-3	0-0	1-0	1-1	0-4	0-2	2-2	3-0	2-3	2-3	0-0	1-1	1-0		2-2	2-1	2-3
WEALDSTONE	1-3	1-1	0-1	0-0	1-1	0-3	2-0	2-1	2-1	2-3	0-2	2-1	3-0	1-2	2-1	4-1	2-1	1-1	1-3		4-2	0-1
WEYMOUTH	0-2	0-1	1-1	0-0	1-1	2-5	1-1	0-0	1-1	0-1	0-2	1-1	1-2	2-3	4-1	2-3	5-1	3-0	1-1	0-2		0-1
WORCESTER CITY	0-0	1-0	2-1	4-1	0-1	2-0	2-0	3-0	1-1	2-0	1-2	1-1	1-1	1-2	1-1	0-0	1-1	1-2	2-1	3-2	3-0	

BEAZER HOMES LEAGUE 1990/1 RESULTS

FACTS

Beazer Homes League 1990/91 — Midland Division

1990/91 MIDLAND DIVISION	ALVECHURCH	BARRY TOWN	BEDWORTH UNITED	BILSTON TOWN	BRIDGNORTH TOWN	CORBY TOWN	DUDLEY TOWN	GRANTHAM TOWN	HEDNESFORD TOWN	HINCKLEY TOWN	KING'S LYNN	LEICESTER UNITED	NEWPORT A.F.C.	NUNEATON BOROUGH	RACING CLUB WARWICK	REDDITCH UNITED	SPALDING UNITED	STOURBRIDGE	STROUD	SUTTON COLDFIELD TOWN	TAMWORTH	WILLENHALL TOWN
ALVECHURCH	X	1-0	2-1	3-0	1-0	0-4	2-2	1-2	1-1	0-2	2-4	1-5	0-0	1-2	1-1	7-2	2-1	1-2	1-3	2-4	0-5	3-3
BARRY TOWN	4-2	X	0-1	5-1	0-2	2-1	4-1	2-1	3-2	3-0	0-0	1-0	1-0	1-1	1-1	1-3	2-0	1-3	2-0	1-2	1-0	3-0
BEDWORTH UNITED	3-0	2-1	X	1-1	0-2	0-4	0-0	2-1	1-3	3-0	1-0	0-1	4-2	0-5	0-2	2-1	0-2	3-1	2-1	2-0	3-3	1-1
BILSTON TOWN	2-2	0-2	5-3	X	3-1	6-2	0-2	2-1	0-2	1-2	2-0	2-2	1-2	4-0	1-0	2-2	5-2	2-3	4-4	2-2	1-2	2-1
BRIDGNORTH TOWN	3-0	1-2	2-1	5-0	X	1-1	2-1	0-2	0-4	0-1	3-1	3-2	0-2	1-3	1-2	3-1	3-3	0-1	2-2	2-2	1-2	3-2
CORBY TOWN	2-1	3-2	6-0	2-0	2-2	X	2-1	0-2	2-3	2-1	5-0	6-0	2-1	0-1	4-0	1-1	3-1	3-0	2-0	5-0	1-0	1-0
DUDLEY TOWN	2-1	1-0	2-2	2-1	0-2	1-4	X	1-1	1-3	2-1	1-1	2-2	1-0	2-2	2-1	0-2	0-2	1-2	1-1	0-3	0-4	2-2
GRANTHAM TOWN	1-1	0-1	1-2	2-0	0-0	0-2	0-0	X	2-0	3-3	3-2	2-0	0-2	0-3	2-1	2-3	5-1	2-1	3-0	0-1	0-3	0-1
HEDNESFORD TOWN	3-4	1-3	0-2	1-2	2-0	2-0	5-0	1-0	X	3-0	3-1	1-0	3-1	3-2	0-0	2-1	0-0	2-2	3-2	2-0	3-2	0-1
HINCKLEY TOWN	3-1	4-1	1-2	3-3	5-1	1-3	3-2	3-2	3-4	X	0-0	2-4	0-1	2-0	2-2	6-0	1-0	1-1	2-2	1-1	0-2	0-2
KING'S LYNN	2-0	2-1	1-1	1-2	2-1	0-6	2-2	0-1	1-0	1-0	X	2-3	2-1	2-0	2-0	3-2	1-1	0-2	0-0	2-0	0-2	1-0
LEICESTER UNITED	5-0	0-2	3-2	3-2	1-0	3-3	2-2	2-2	1-1	1-1	1-0	X	0-2	0-3	1-1	0-0	4-2	0-3	3-1	1-0	0-4	2-1
NEWPORT A.F.C.	1-1	1-0	2-0	1-0	4-1	1-2	0-1	1-3	0-0	0-3	1-3	2-1	X	4-1	1-2	0-1	2-0	1-0	0-1	2-1	1-1	3-2
NUNEATON BOROUGH	4-0	2-0	1-0	3-0	3-2	3-2	0-2	2-2	1-1	1-4	2-0	3-1	2-1	X	3-3	2-1	2-0	4-1	2-2	1-1	0-0	1-0
RACING CLUB WARWICK	3-2	1-1	2-1	2-0	3-4	1-2	1-1	0-1	1-2	0-0	1-2	4-2	1-3	1-0	X	0-2	0-0	3-2	1-1	3-1	2-3	2-2
REDDITCH UNITED	0-1	2-1	1-0	0-0	1-1	2-0	1-2	3-2	1-4	2-3	1-1	4-2	1-0	1-1	2-2	X	2-1	3-3	1-3	3-2	2-4	2-1
SPALDING UNITED	1-0	0-1	2-3	0-2	0-2	0-1	1-2	1-5	1-3	1-3	1-2	2-1	0-0	0-0	1-0	2-1	X	0-2	0-0	2-1	0-0	1-3
STOURBRIDGE	3-0	2-0	1-1	3-2	3-0	2-0	3-1	4-3	3-1	1-0	3-0	2-1	2-0	1-0	3-2	1-4	1-0	X	2-0	1-1	2-0	2-1
STROUD	0-1	2-2	2-2	1-1	3-0	0-2	3-1	1-0	2-1	3-1	0-2	0-0	0-1	0-3	2-0	0-0	2-3	0-2	X	1-2	2-1	3-2
SUTTON COLDFIELD TOWN	3-2	1-1	2-2	1-0	1-1	3-2	1-0	1-2	0-1	4-1	0-4	1-0	0-2	3-2	1-2	2-4	0-0	0-1	0-0	X	2-1	2-1
TAMWORTH	2-0	0-1	3-0	3-4	3-2	3-1	3-1	2-0	0-1	1-0	4-0	2-4	1-4	2-2	2-0	3-0	2-0	2-1	1-0	1-2	X	3-1
WILLENHALL TOWN	1-3	1-1	3-1	0-1	2-2	1-3	1-0	0-1	0-2	2-3	3-3	3-1	1-1	0-1	1-2	2-0	1-0	2-2	5-1	2-2	0-2	X

Beazer Homes League 1990/91 — Southern Division

1990/91 SOUTHERN DIVISION	ANDOVER	ASHFORD TOWN	BALDOCK TOWN	BUCKINGHAM TOWN	BURNHAM	BURY TOWN	CANTERBURY CITY	CORINTHIAN	DUNSTABLE	ERITH & BELVEDERE	FAREHAM TOWN		GOSPORT BOROUGH	HASTINGS TOWN	HYTHE TOWN	MARGATE	NEWPORT I.O.W.	SALISBURY	SUDBURY TOWN	TROWBRIDGE TOWN	WITNEY TOWN	YATE TOWN
ANDOVER	X	1-4	2-2	0-5	2-1	2-0	4-2	0-0	3-2	0-1	2-0		8-1	2-2	3-3	2-1	1-3	0-1	2-1	0-2	4-1	2-5
ASHFORD TOWN	5-1	X	1-1	5-1	2-3	3-1	3-1	5-0	3-0	1-4	4-0		1-0	1-1	1-0	2-1	3-0	2-2	4-1	0-1	3-1	2-0
BALDOCK TOWN	2-1	1-0	X	1-2	5-1	4-0	2-0	2-0	1-3	2-3	2-1		2-2	2-1	2-1	1-0	3-2	0-0	2-0	2-1	1-1	3-1
BUCKINGHAM TOWN	1-0	0-2	0-0	X	2-1	4-1	4-2	2-1	3-0	2-1	2-0		2-2	2-0	1-0	4-1	2-1	0-1	0-2	0-1	2-1	2-1
BURNHAM	3-0	2-0	0-1	1-1	X	2-1	3-0	2-2	5-0	3-0	3-1		0-0	2-1	0-1	2-2	1-1	1-1	1-2	3-1	1-0	0-2
BURY TOWN	1-5	4-1	3-3	0-3	3-0	X	3-1	2-1	0-1	4-1	0-2		2-0	0-3	1-2	1-0	2-1	2-0	0-3	2-1	3-4	1-1
CANTERBURY CITY	1-2	4-1	0-2	5-3	1-1	2-4	X	3-1	1-2	2-0	4-2		1-0	1-3	1-3	0-3	3-1	3-1	3-4	1-1	0-3	1-4
CORINTHIAN	0-4	0-0	1-1	0-0	2-2	0-2	0-0	X	1-5	2-1	1-0		1-2	3-3	1-3	4-2	3-2	0-2	0-1	1-2	0-0	1-1
DUNSTABLE	0-1	1-3	2-2	2-2	0-0	2-0	0-2	2-2	X	1-1	1-1		0-1	2-1	2-2	0-0	1-2	2-3	0-0	2-3	0-1	2-2
ERITH & BELVEDERE	4-1	1-2	2-1	0-1	1-1	1-0	1-1	0-0	0-1	X	2-1		1-3	1-2	0-4	3-0	1-2	0-1	2-2	1-2	4-2	1-4
FAREHAM TOWN	2-1	1-0	3-1	2-5	2-1	1-3	2-1	2-1	1-1	0-0	X		1-3	1-1	0-0	1-2	0-5	1-1	5-2	0-3	0-2	1-2
												X										
GOSPORT BOROUGH	0-1	4-2	0-1	1-1	1-1	0-1	2-3	1-0	0-2	2-0	0-2		X	1-3	1-1	0-1	2-2	1-1	2-1	1-1	1-1	0-1
HASTINGS TOWN	3-0	0-0	4-1	0-2	3-2	0-2	1-0	2-0	1-1	4-2	2-1		2-1	X	5-0	0-1	1-2	2-1	3-0	0-0	4-0	2-0
HYTHE TOWN	1-2	3-2	0-1	0-0	0-0	2-1	1-1	4-0	4-0	0-1	2-1		3-0	3-1	X	1-1	2-4	0-1	2-0	1-0	1-1	2-1
MARGATE	2-1	1-3	0-1	0-1	2-2	1-0	0-0	3-1	1-2	4-2	2-1		1-2	1-1	1-0	X	1-1	1-0	3-2	2-2	3-1	1-2
NEWPORT I.O.W.	1-1	3-1	2-1	0-2	0-2	3-3	1-3	4-0	0-0	2-1	2-1		0-4	0-2	0-1	0-0	X	1-2	0-1	1-0	0-0	0-1
SALISBURY	3-1	1-0	2-0	2-0	1-0	1-1	6-2	0-1	3-1	2-0	1-1		1-1	4-1	3-1	2-2	2-1	X	1-1	1-0	2-0	1-0
SUDBURY TOWN	4-1	2-3	5-1	0-3	1-1	2-2	3-2	1-0	3-3	4-1	1-1		0-1	0-0	0-1	0-3	2-2	3-0	X	0-1	3-0	0-3
TROWBRIDGE TOWN	1-1	1-0	3-1	0-0	2-2	2-0	2-0	3-0	1-0	3-1	3-1		2-1	0-0	2-0	3-0	2-0	2-2	5-1	X	5-0	1-1
WITNEY TOWN	1-3	2-5	0-2	0-2	1-0	5-1	1-2	5-2	2-1	1-0	3-3		3-1	1-1	1-0	2-2	3-2	1-4	1-1	1-1	X	2-2
YATE TOWN	4-2	1-2	2-3	1-4	1-1	4-1	3-0	2-1	1-1	3-0	2-0		1-2	3-0	1-0	2-0	1-2	3-0	3-1	1-1	3-2	X

FACTS

BEAZER HOMES LEAGUE ATTENDANCES 1990/1

Lge. Pos.	Team	Agg.	Average	Last Seas.	%change	Highest	Lowest
	PREMIER DIVISION						
4	DOVER ATHLETIC	25822	1230	1227	+0.24	2065 v. Cambridge City	519 v. Moor Green
8	+ HALESOWEN TOWN	24719	1177	1087	+8.28	2507 v. Worcester City	768 v. Crawley Town
6	WORCESTER CITY	19921	949	786	+20.74	1663 v. Burton Albion	262 v. Waterlooville
2	GLOUCESTER CITY	19880	947	678	+39.68	2550 v. VS Rugby	512 v. Moor Green
5	BROMSGROVE ROVERS	18295	871	628	+38.69	1780 v. Gloucester City	555 v. Waterlooville
11	DORCHESTER TOWN	16453	784	377	+107.96	1860 v. Weymouth	482 v. Waterlooville
18	CHELMSFORD CITY	15984	761	947	−19.64	1240 v. Dover Athletic	391 v. Weymouth
22	WEYMOUTH	14282	680	666	+2.10	1400 v. Dorchester Town	401 v. Farnborough Town
7	BURTON ALBION	14137	673	890	−24.38	1065 v. Halesowen Town	258 v. Rushden Town
13	DARTFORD	13032	621	953	−34.84	1061 v. Gravesend & N.	326 v. Rushden Town
1	* FARNBOROUGH TOWN	12390	590	937	−37.03	1202 v. Gloucester City	366 v. Poole Town
12	WEALDSTONE	10987	523	482	+8.51	820 v. Cambridge City	338 v. Crawley Town
9	VS RUGBY	10224	487	531	−8.29	932 v. Burton Albion	289 v. Dover Athletic
21	GRAVESEND & N'FLEET	10198	486	562	−13.52	1263 v. Dartford	292 v. Bashley
19	CRAWLEY TOWN	9338	445	436	+2.06	826 v. Dover Athletic	325 v. Bromsgrove Rovers
17	+ POOLE TOWN	9093	433	350	+23.71	1160 v. Weymouth	141 v. VS Rugby
3	CAMBRIDGE CITY	8989	428	339	+26.25	1046 v. Dover Athletic	207 v. Wealdstone
15	ATHERSTONE UNITED	8458	403	488	−17.42	738 v. Halesowen Town	206 v. Bashley
10	+ BASHLEY	8392	400	373	+7.24	836 v. Poole Town	160 v. Gravesend & N.
16	MOOR GREEN	8045	383	368	+4.08	602 v. Burton Albion	243 v. Dorchester Town
14	+ RUSHDEN TOWN	7847	374	388	−0.04	540 v. Burton Albion	218 v. Dorchester Town
20	WATERLOOVILLE	6659	317	278	+14.03	593 v. Bashley	178 v. Chelmsford City
	TOTAL	293145	635	565	+12.39		
	MIDLAND DIVISION						
4	TAMWORTH	22031	1049	1044	+0.48	2011 v. Nuneaton Borough	638 v. Stroud
7	+ NEWPORT	19606	934	n/a	n/a	2271 v. Redditch United	502 v. Alvechurch
5	NUNEATON BOROUGH	15362	732	779	−6.03	1604 v. Tamworth	435 v. Stroud
3	HEDNESFORD TOWN	9308	443	288	+53.82	1292 v. Tamworth	171 v. Bilston
1	STOURBRIDGE	8403	400	256	+56.25	1003 v. Tamworth	153 v. Bilston
8	KINGS LYNN	7900	376	348	+8.05	903 v. Tamworth	219 v. Nuneaton Borough
2	* CORBY TOWN	6535	311	210	+48.10	568 v. Stroud	172 v. Hednesford Town
6	BARRY TOWN	6419	306	272	+12.50	933 v. Newport	110 v. Grantham Town
15	LEICESTER UNITED	5245	250	169	+47.92	1058 v. Hinckley Town	80 v. Dudley Town
13	BEDWORTH UNITED	5103	243	245	−0.82	906 v. Nuneaton Borough	127 v. Bridgnorth Town
11	+ HINCKLEY TOWN	5011	239	n/a	n/a	1022 v. Nuneaton Borough	70 v. Bedworth United
19	DUDLEY TOWN	4779	228	289	−21.11	617 v. Tamworth	114 v. Bridgnorth Town
22	SPALDING UNITED	4669	222	309	−28.16	407 v. Nuneaton Borough	123 v. Barry Town
9	GRANTHAM TOWN	4636	221	359	−38.44	427 v. Corby Town	71 v. Willenhall Town
10	REDDITCH UNITED	4412	210	218	−3.67	523 v. Tamworth	122 v. Spalding United
12	SUTTON COLDFIELD T.	4187	199	220	−9.55	797 v. Tamworth	95 v. Redditch United
14	BILSTON TOWN	3687	176	192	−9.90	355 v. Stourbridge	93 v. Stroud
20	* ALVECHURCH	3614	172	282	−39.01	327 v. Nuneaton Borough	50 v. Grantham
17	BRIDGNORTH TOWN	3536	168	200	−16.00	480 v. Tamworth	95 v. Willenhall Town
21	WILLENHALL TOWN	3275	156	187	−16.58	391 v. Tamworth	54 v. Kings Lynn
16	RACING CLUB WARWICK	3231	154	186	−17.20	419 v. Tamworth	70 v. Barry Town
18	STROUD	2577	123	152	−19.08	310 v. Tamworth	70 v. Bridgnorth Town/ Redditch United
	TOTAL	153526	332	341	−2.64		
	SOUTHERN DIVISION						
13	+ SUDBURY TOWN	10608	530	n/a	n/a	904 v. Bury Town	360 v. Ashford Town
2	TROWBRIDGE TOWN	10072	504	372	+35.48	860 v. Yate Town	355 v. Newport IOW
12	BURY TOWN	6985	349	479	−27.14	650 v. Sudbury Town	196 v. Newport IOW
14	+ NEWPORT IOW	6807	340	n/a	n/a	490 v. Margate	178 v. Gosport Borough
7	HASTINGS TOWN	6672	334	317	+5.36	442 v. Newport IOW	253 v. Hythe Town
5	* ASHFORD TOWN	6211	311	442	−29.64	475 v. Hastings Town	202 v. Bury Town
10	MARGATE	5903	295	277	+6.50	475 v. Ashford Town	201 v. Andover
3	SALISBURY	5814	291	286	+1.75	469 v. Trowbridge Town	198 v. Canterbury City
8	HYTHE TOWN	5812	291	355	−18.03	465 v. Hastings Town	143 v. Buckingham Town
4	BALDOCK TOWN	5446	272	235	+15.75	417 v. Burnham	203 v. Andover
6	YATE TOWN	4788	237	242	−2.07	522 v. Trowbridge Town	142 v. Newport IOW
9	ANDOVER	4263	213	172	+23.84	464 v. Salisbury	118 v. Burnham
1	BUCKINGHAM TOWN	4010	201	180	+11.67	317 v. Ashford Town	146 v. Hythe T./Trowbridge
19	ERITH & BELVEDERE	3527	176	170	+3.53	359 v. Ashford Town	85 v. Dunstable
15	* GOSPORT BOROUGH	3354	168	213	−21.13	403 v. Fareham Town	90 v. Newport IOW
16	WITNEY TOWN	3251	163	164	−0.61	266 v. Trowbridge Town	110 v. Erith & Belvedere
20	FAREHAM TOWN	3233	162	165	−1.82	375 v. Gosport Borough	113 v. Hythe T./Bury T.
17	DUNSTABLE	2759	138	147	−6.12	234 v. Sudbury Town	91 v. Corinthian
18	CANTERBURY CITY	2321	116	122	−4.92	329 v. Ashford Town	44 v. Andover
11	BURNHAM	1894	95	91	+4.40	172 v. Sudbury Town	54 v. Hythe Town
21	CORINTHIAN	1715	86	79	+8.86	188 v. Sudbury Town	45 v. Witney T./Yate Town
	TOTAL	105445	251	230	+9.13		

* = Relegated team 1990   + = Promoted team 1990

Compiled by Sudhir Rawal

VAUXHALL LEAGUE 1990/1 TABLES

PREMIER DIVISION

		Home					Away					Totals					
	Pl	W	D	L	Gf	Ga	W	D	L	Gf	Ga	W	D	L	Gf	Ga	Pts.
Redbridge Forest	42	17	1	3	41	19	12	5	4	33	24	29	6	7	74	43	93
Enfield	42	14	6	1	45	12	12	5	4	38	18	26	11	5	83	30	89
Aylesbury United	42	17	1	3	52	17	8	9	4	39	30	25	10	7	91	47	85
Woking	42	13	6	2	41	11	11	4	6	43	28	24	10	8	84	39	82
Kingstonian	42	14	6	1	56	22	7	6	8	30	35	21	12	9	86	57	75
Grays Athletic	42	12	3	6	38	25	8	5	8	28	28	20	8	14	66	53	68
Marlow	42	10	7	4	37	20	8	6	7	35	29	18	13	11	72	49	67
Carshalton Athletic	42	10	5	6	38	32	9	2	10	42	35	19	7	16	80	67	64
Hayes	42	11	4	6	34	19	9	0	12	26	39	20	4	18	60	58	64
Wivenhoe Town	42	6	8	7	38	35	10	3	8	31	31	16	11	15	69	66	59
Wokingham Town	42	9	6	6	30	22	6	7	8	28	32	15	13	14	58	54	58
Windsor & Eton	42	12	0	9	31	33	3	10	8	17	30	15	10	17	48	63	55
Bishop's Stortford	42	9	5	7	29	26	5	7	9	25	23	14	12	16	54	49	54
Dagenham	42	6	9	6	36	32	7	2	12	26	36	13	11	18	62	68	50
Hendon	42	5	7	9	23	28	7	3	11	25	34	12	10	20	48	62	46
St. Albans City	42	5	4	12	27	38	6	8	7	33	36	11	12	19	60	74	45
Bognor Regis Town	42	4	6	11	19	30	8	2	11	25	41	12	8	22	44	71	44
Basingstoke Town	42	6	4	11	27	47	6	3	12	30	48	12	7	23	57	95	43
Staines Town	42	6	5	10	28	40	4	5	12	18	39	10	10	22	46	79	39*
Harrow Borough	42	5	4	12	34	45	5	4	12	23	39	10	8	24	57	84	38
Barking	42	3	7	11	17	42	5	3	13	24	43	8	10	24	41	85	34
Leyton-Wingate	42	5	1	15	23	45	2	6	13	21	46	7	7	28	44	91	28

*1pt. Deducted by Vauxhall League

DIVISION ONE:

		Home					Away					Totals					
	Pl	W	D	L	Gf	Ga	W	D	L	Gf	Ga	W	D	L	Gf	Ga	Pts.
Chesham United	42	13	4	4	57	22	14	4	3	45	15	27	8	7	102	37	89
Bromley	42	13	6	2	38	16	9	8	4	24	21	22	14	6	62	37	80
Yeading	42	14	3	4	42	21	9	5	7	33	24	23	8	11	75	45	77
Aveley	42	9	7	5	36	21	12	2	7	40	22	21	9	12	76	43	72
Hitchin Town	42	13	2	6	48	22	8	7	6	30	28	21	9	12	78	50	72
Tooting & Mitcham Utd.	42	8	8	5	38	28	12	4	5	33	20	20	12	10	71	48	72
Walton & Hersham	42	12	5	4	43	23	9	3	9	30	25	21	8	13	73	48	71
Molesey	42	13	3	5	32	16	9	2	10	33	30	22	5	15	65	46	71
Whyteleafe	42	10	4	7	36	26	11	2	8	26	27	21	6	15	62	53	69
Dorking	42	11	3	7	42	30	9	2	10	36	37	20	5	17	78	67	65
Chalfont St. Peter	42	12	3	6	28	21	7	2	12	28	42	19	5	18	56	63	62
Dulwich Hamlet	42	7	5	9	32	24	9	6	6	35	30	16	11	15	67	54	59
Harlow Town	42	10	4	7	37	31	7	4	10	36	33	17	8	17	73	64	59
Boreham Wood	42	10	3	8	32	27	5	5	11	14	26	15	8	19	46	53	53
Wembley	42	6	5	10	29	27	7	7	7	33	32	13	12	17	62	59	51
Uxbridge	42	5	3	13	20	32	10	2	9	25	29	15	5	22	45	61	50
Croydon	42	8	2	11	21	42	7	3	11	23	43	15	5	22	44	85	50
Heybridge Swifts	42	6	5	10	22	27	7	5	9	24	32	13	10	19	46	59	49
Southwick	42	10	3	8	37	30	3	5	13	12	45	13	8	21	49	75	47
Lewes	42	5	4	12	30	40	5	4	12	19	42	10	8	24	49	82	38
Metropolitan Police	42	5	2	14	28	38	4	4	13	27	38	9	6	27	55	76	33
Worthing	42	2	3	16	13	57	0	1	20	15	100	2	4	36	28	157	10

DIVISION TWO NORTH:

		Home					Away					
	Pl	W	D	L	Gf	Ga	W	D	L	Gf	Ga	Pts.
Stevenage Borough	42	21	0	0	75	11	13	5	3	47	18	107
Vauxhall Motors	42	14	4	3	46	22	10	6	5	36	28	82
Billericay Town	42	12	3	6	42	23	10	5	6	28	18	74
Ware	42	13	3	5	38	18	9	5	7	40	33	74
Berkhamsted Town	42	10	9	2	29	15	9	2	10	31	36	68
Witham Town	42	12	3	6	43	29	7	7	7	27	30	67
Purfleet	42	8	7	6	32	29	9	7	5	36	28	65
Rainham Town	42	11	4	6	30	22	8	3	10	27	24	64
Hemel Hempstead	42	7	10	4	25	23	9	4	8	37	33	62
Barton Rovers	42	10	6	5	33	17	7	4	10	28	41	61
Saffron Walden Town	42	10	7	4	45	36	6	6	9	27	41	61
Collier Row	42	8	5	8	33	34	8	6	7	30	29	59
Kingsbury Town	42	10	4	7	33	31	7	4	10	31	41	59
Edgware Town	42	12	2	7	49	26	5	5	11	24	39	58
Hertford Town	42	8	4	9	31	34	8	6	7	38	36	58
Royston Town	42	8	7	6	42	33	6	8	7	36	29	57
Tilbury	42	6	5	10	35	32	8	1	12	35	47	48
Basildon United	42	6	7	8	29	39	5	3	13	32	51	43
Hornchurch	42	6	5	10	33	44	4	4	13	20	43	39
Clapton	42	5	6	10	33	42	4	4	13	21	51	34*
Finchley	42	2	2	17	25	64	4	5	12	25	48	25
Tring Town	42	1	3	17	13	49	0	6	15	17	50	12

* 3pts. Deducted by Vauxhall League

DIVISION TWO SOUTH:

		Home					Away					
	Pl	W	D	L	Gf	Ga	W	D	L	Gf	Ga	Pts.
Abingdon Town	42	15	2	4	53	10	14	5	2	42	18	94
Maidenhead Utd.	42	16	2	3	47	13	12	6	3	38	20	92
Egham Town	42	13	4	4	44	17	14	2	5	56	29	87
Malden Vale	42	13	3	5	40	23	13	2	6	32	21	83
Ruislip Manor	42	14	2	5	53	20	11	3	7	40	24	80
Southall	42	14	4	3	50	20	9	6	6	34	23	79
Harefield United	42	14	5	2	47	26	9	5	7	34	30	79
Newbury Town	42	10	5	6	36	27	13	3	5	35	18	77
Hungerford Town	42	10	4	7	45	33	6	9	6	39	36	61
Leatherhead	42	9	6	6	43	24	8	3	10	39	31	60
Banstead Athletic	42	8	6	7	31	32	7	7	7	27	30	58
Hampton	42	6	9	6	32	23	8	6	7	30	20	57
Epsom & Ewell	42	9	5	7	30	23	6	7	8	19	27	57
Chertsey Town	42	8	6	7	36	35	7	3	11	40	37	54
Horsham	42	8	4	9	36	26	6	3	12	22	41	49
Flackwell Heath	42	5	8	8	26	33	6	3	12	30	45	44
Bracknell Town	42	5	4	12	26	38	6	3	12	34	59	40
Feltham	42	8	4	9	32	34	2	4	15	13	46	38
Cove	42	6	2	13	29	41	4	5	12	22	53	37
Eastbourne Utd.	42	9	3	9	36	44	1	4	16	17	65	37
Petersfield United	42	3	3	15	19	52	3	0	18	16	67	21
Camberley Town	42	1	2	18	17	75	0	4	17	10	68	9

FACTS

VAUXHALL LEAGUE 1990/1 RESULTS

Vauxhall League Premier Division

		H\A	1	2	3	4	5	6	7	8	9	10	11	12	13	14	15	16	17	18	19	20	21	22
1	Aylesbury Utd	1	*	2-1	3-0	1-0	4-1	3-2	2-1	1-0	1-0	6-1	4-0	2-0	3-0	3-0	2-0	3-1	3-0	2-2	1-2	1-2	2-3	3-1
2	Barking	2	3-2	*	4-2	0-5	0-2	0-2	0-2	1-1	0-1	0-2	2-1	1-1	0-2	0-0	0-8	0-1	3-3	1-1	1-1	1-4	0-1	0-0
3	Basingstoke	3	1-1	3-2	*	3-2	2-5	0-4	4-0	0-4	2-1	1-1	2-4	2-4	2-0	0-1	0-2	1-2	0-4	1-0	1-1	0-1	0-6	2-2
4	Bishops Stort	4	0-2	3-2	1-1	*	0-2	3-2	1-0	0-0	1-1	2-0	4-2	0-0	1-1	3-1	1-4	1-2	0-1	3-0	1-3	1-2	2-0	1-0
5	Bognor Regis	5	1-1	0-1	3-1	1-0	*	1-1	2-0	1-2	0-3	1-1	0-1	1-1	1-3	0-0	1-2	2-4	1-2	1-2	1-1	0-2	0-2	1-0
6	Carshalton	6	3-5	4-0	2-4	3-1	4-0	*	0-3	0-2	3-1	2-2	2-0	1-0	3-2	2-2	0-0	1-1	0-4	2-0	1-0	2-1	2-2	1-2
7	Dagenham	7	3-2	0-0	5-2	0-0	0-2	1-3	*	1-3	2-2	1-3	4-0	3-2	2-2	1-0	1-2	1-1	2-2	4-0	2-2	2-2	0-1	1-1
8	Enfield	8	1-1	2-2	2-0	0-0	4-0	2-0	1-1	*	3-0	6-1	3-1	4-0	3-0	3-1	3-0	0-3	1-1	0-0	1-0	2-0	2-0	2-1
9	Grays Ath	9	4-1	5-1	5-3	1-2	2-0	1-0	3-2	0-2	*	0-2	1-0	2-0	2-1	1-1	3-1	0-2	3-0	1-3	1-0	2-2	1-1	0-1
10	Harrow Borough	10	2-2	3-4	0-1	2-1	1-3	1-3	4-1	2-4	1-3	*	1-2	1-3	0-2	2-1	2-0	2-3	1-1	2-1	3-3	1-3	0-1	3-3
11	Hayes	11	2-2	2-1	2-3	2-0	0-0	1-1	1-0	0-3	0-2	2-0	*	3-1	0-0	3-0	0-0	2-0	1-2	2-0	3-0	0-1	4-1	4-1
12	Hendon	12	1-1	0-1	1-2	1-1	0-3	0-2	1-2	1-1	0-1	1-1	1-0	*	3-1	3-3	0-2	2-0	2-2	0-1	0-0	2-3	3-1	1-0
13	Kingstonian	13	0-0	5-1	5-2	2-2	4-1	3-1	2-0	4-1	5-1	2-0	0-1	2-1	*	3-1	1-1	2-2	5-2	2-0	1-1	3-1	4-2	1-1
14	Leyton-Wingate	14	0-4	2-0	1-2	0-3	3-1	1-3	1-4	1-4	1-2	1-0	1-2	0-2	2-2	*	0-2	1-2	3-0	1-2	2-0	1-2	0-4	1-4
15	Marlow	15	3-3	3-1	2-0	3-1	5-0	5-1	3-0	1-1	1-0	3-1	0-2	1-3	1-1	1-0	*	1-2	0-0	2-1	0-0	1-1	1-1	0-1
16	Redbridge F	16	0-4	2-1	2-0	1-0	1-0	2-1	1-0	2-1	1-1	1-0	1-0	2-0	2-0	7-4	5-1	*	2-1	2-0	3-0	2-0	0-1	2-4
17	St. Albans	17	1-2	1-2	1-1	2-3	1-1	2-1	2-4	0-1	0-3	1-0	1-2	3-0	3-4	2-1	0-4	1-2	*	2-2	0-1	1-0	1-2	2-2
18	Staines	18	0-1	1-2	2-1	0-0	1-2	0-4	5-1	1-1	1-3	2-0	2-3	1-2	0-3	2-1	2-2	2-1	3-3	*	1-0	1-2	0-7	1-1
19	Windsor & Eton	19	1-2	2-1	1-0	1-0	2-0	3-2	1-2	0-3	1-0	0-5	1-4	0-1	1-3	6-2	1-0	1-2	2-0	2-1	*	3-2	2-1	0-2
20	Wivenhoe Town	20	1-1	2-1	3-3	0-4	1-2	1-3	1-1	0-1	3-1	2-3	3-0	1-3	6-1	1-1	1-1	0-1	1-1	3-0	2-2	*	4-4	2-1
21	Woking	21	3-1	0-0	0-2	0-0	3-0	2-4	1-0	2-1	1-1	4-0	4-0	2-0	0-0	3-0	4-1	0-0	2-0	5-1	0-0	1-0	*	4-0
22	Wokingham	22	0-0	1-0	3-0	0-0	3-0	3-2	0-2	0-2	1-1	1-0	2-1	2-1	0-2	0-1	2-2	1-1	1-4	1-1	5-0	4-0	0-2	*

PREMIER DIVISION ATTENDANCES

	1	2	3	4	5	6	7	8	9	10	11	12	13	14	15	16	17	18	19	20	21	22
1. AYLESBURY UNITED	+	851	1023	825	938	723	732	1383	562	1006	630	617	1148	1031	1137	1231	640	851	1061	915	1542	1030
2. BARKING	255	+	140	121	112	103	451	289	233	190	137	182	227	112	137	218	179	114	154	207	352	181
3. BASINGSTOKE TOWN	623	185	+	368	315	498	312	270	395	294	341	321	412	328	413	344	253	378	249	361	905	432
4. BISHOPS STORTFORD	355	220	215	+	207	427	410	598	174	310	317	158	410	283	197	355	393	205	287	215	593	389
5. BOGNOR REGIS TOWN	241	285	268	232	+	190	170	220	198	170	252	210	325	210	202	236	240	203	210	228	320	309
6. CARSHALTON ATHLETIC	424	305	319	242	455	+	383	400	345	279	254	254	312	254	350	333	350	279	364	284	768	463
7. DAGENHAM	441	444	403	388	333	355	+	540	416	307	477	304	383	388	350	639	367	469	481	291	840	340
8. ENFIELD	914	507	926	658	609	493	904	+	611	735	351	724	1001	526	520	2003	524	506	528	598	1268	472
9. GRAYS ATHLETIC	467	372	357	442	330	402	547	711	+	341	477	407	648	481	357	456	449	379	480	414	778	342
10. HARROW BOROUGH	331	254	189	232	252	232	225	422	192	+	395	325	469	273	237	207	325	234	231	246	719	295
11. HAYES	335	301	252	340	285	235	219	570	209	333	+	219	411	251	239	282	316	301	281	309	554	240
12. HENDON	445	213	252	254	206	207	269	741	283	295	282	+	386	211	251	282	409	281	235	253	731	268
13. KINGSTONIAN	1091	811	551	627	758	718	601	1148	851	687	835	701	+	856	875	589	854	620	903	739	2507	601
14. LEYTON-WINGATE	224	159	145	150	152	192	288	311	164	131	148	241	271	+	123	263	222	82	177	168	395	160
15. MARLOW	701	242	245	235	222	319	310	280	220	280	284	210	386	160	+	266	365	204	325	288	897	315
16. REDBRIDGE FOREST	316	242	243	305	141	218	1052	729	294	209	192	220	354	207	183	+	207	201	220	468	828	240
17. ST.ALBANS CITY	761	429	416	258	301	285	425	920	410	429	337	336	525	316	332	401	+	257	310	382	937	457
18. STAINES TOWN	526	292	335	303	273	252	163	396	294	264	343	300	614	276	288	275	325	+	333	241	736	368
19. WINDSOR & ETON	266	196	272	174	217	218	209	320	196	239	417	379	495	191	350	272	284	215	+	214	575	312
20. WIVENHOE TOWN	308	288	700	372	304	229	301	402	367	124	329	347	386	354	236	539	324	673	489	+	519	405
21. WOKING	1584	1455	1871	1026	1551	1084	1779	1713	1816	1246	1067	1402	1681	1048	1544	1595	2367	1334	1023	1187	+	1512
22. WOKINGHAM TOWN	413	210	335	296	203	316	178	387	274	416	148	266	335	127	157	368	304	360	470	386	783	+

VAUXHALL LEAGUE 1990/1 RESULTS

FACTS

Vauxhall League Division One

	Team	H\A	1	2	3	4	5	6	7	8	9	10	11	12	13	14	15	16	17	18	19	20	21	22
1	Aveley	1	*	0-0	1-1	4-1	1-1	1-2	4-1	2-2	2-2	2-1	1-1	1-2	2-1	0-1	2-0	0-1	3-0	2-0	1-1	1-2	5-1	1-0
2	Boreham Wood	2	0-2	*	1-2	1-0	2-3	0-1	1-2	2-2	0-0	3-1	1-2	3-1	3-0	3-2	0-0	1-0	4-1	2-1	0-2	0-2	3-2	2-1
3	Bromley	3	2-4	3-0	*	1-1	2-0	3-0	0-3	0-0	3-2	0-0	3-1	5-1	2-0	1-0	1-1	1-1	2-1	1-0	3-0	1-1	3-0	1-0
4	Chalfont St P.	4	1-0	3-1	0-0	*	1-0	2-1	4-2	1-0	2-1	1-1	0-3	3-0	2-0	0-1	1-0	1-1	0-2	0-1	2-1	0-1	3-1	1-4
5	Chesham Utd	5	3-1	2-1	0-1	3-2	*	4-0	2-0	2-0	2-1	5-1	0-0	5-2	1-3	0-2	8-1	0-0	0-1	2-1	1-1	7-2	8-0	2-2
6	Croydon	6	0-5	1-2	0-0	2-1	0-4	*	2-0	1-3	2-4	1-0	1-1	1-0	0-5	0-3	1-0	0-4	0-2	1-3	2-1	3-0	2-1	1-3
7	Dorking	7	0-3	1-0	0-0	5-0	0-3	0-0	*	2-4	1-0	4-0	5-2	3-0	4-2	4-3	2-1	2-4	0-1	2-2	0-2	0-1	4-0	3-2
8	Dulwich Hamlet	8	1-1	1-0	0-1	1-0	1-3	1-2	4-1	*	1-3	1-2	0-2	0-0	2-1	0-0	4-0	0-1	3-0	0-2	3-3	0-2	9-0	0-0
9	Harlow Town	9	4-1	2-0	3-0	0-1	0-3	0-2	0-3	1-1	*	1-1	1-3	3-2	2-0	4-1	1-0	1-1	1-1	3-1	0-4	4-3	6-2	0-1
10	Heybridge Swts	10	0-2	0-0	0-2	2-1	0-2	2-2	1-2	0-1	0-4	*	1-4	5-0	1-1	1-2	0-0	3-0	1-2	1-0	0-1	2-0	0-0	2-1
11	Hitchin Town	11	2-0	1-2	0-0	2-0	1-1	6-3	1-4	2-3	1-0	3-1	*	2-0	2-1	2-0	6-1	0-2	4-0	0-1	2-1	2-0	9-1	0-1
12	Lewes	12	1-2	0-0	3-4	1-2	1-4	1-2	3-2	5-2	2-2	0-2	1-1	*	1-3	2-1	0-0	1-2	0-1	2-3	0-1	1-0	4-1	1-5
13	Met Police	13	0-4	0-1	3-1	1-2	0-3	5-1	2-3	1-3	0-2	0-2	0-2	0-1	*	1-1	4-0	1-3	1-2	1-1	2-3	0-2	2-0	4-1
14	Molesey	14	0-1	3-1	1-2	2-0	1-3	1-0	3-0	0-1	4-2	1-0	0-0	2-0	1-0	*	4-1	1-0	1-0	0-3	1-1	2-0	3-0	1-1
15	Southwick	15	0-2	2-0	1-0	2-1	1-0	2-0	3-5	1-1	1-2	0-2	3-0	0-0	2-2	2-4	*	1-3	1-0	0-2	5-2	0-1	8-3	2-0
16	Tooting & M	16	0-0	1-0	2-2	2-5	1-1	1-2	1-1	2-1	0-0	2-0	2-1	1-1	2-1	1-3	5-1	*	5-0	4-4	1-1	0-1	5-1	0-2
17	Uxbridge	17	0-3	0-1	1-1	0-2	0-3	3-0	1-4	0-1	1-0	3-3	1-0	1-2	1-1	1-2	0-1	1-3	*	1-0	1-2	0-1	4-1	0-1
18	Walton & Hersh	18	3-1	2-1	1-1	2-0	0-0	4-0	2-1	2-2	3-1	0-2	4-0	3-1	3-0	3-1	2-1	1-3	0-2	*	3-3	0-2	4-0	1-1
19	Wembley	19	1-2	0-1	0-1	2-3	3-4	3-0	0-0	3-1	1-3	0-0	0-2	0-1	2-1	2-1	0-1	3-0	1-1	1-2	*	2-2	4-0	1-1
20	Whyteleafe	20	2-1	1-1	1-3	2-4	0-2	3-0	1-0	1-2	3-1	0-1	1-1	1-0	2-1	2-1	1-1	0-2	2-1	1-0	1-1	*	10-0	1-3
21	Worthing	21	0-4	1-1	2-0	2-2	0-4	0-4	1-2	0-5	0-3	1-3	0-0	1-3	2-3	0-4	0-1	0-2	0-6	0-3	3-2	0-2	*	0-3
22	Yeading	22	2-1	2-1	1-2	5-0	0-1	1-1	1-0	2-0	4-3	4-1	3-4	2-2	1-1	1-0	3-1	2-0	0-1	1-0	1-0	2-1	4-1	*

FIRST DIVISION ATTENDANCES

	1	2	3	4	5	6	7	8	9	10	11	12	13	14	15	16	17	18	19	20	21	22
1. AVELEY	+	115	255	95	180	95	175	185	120	196	165	156	995	145	165	155	105	165	102	155	135	95
2. BOREHAM WOOD	183	+	212	122	225	108	113	200	149	122	196	114	124	117	109	119	125	152	142	157	101	145
3. BROMLEY	619	772	+	442	484	640	476	680	415	503	520	535	478	451	377	731	420	392	454	426	451	387
4. CHALFONT ST.PETER	195	108	306	+	563	158	226	150	165	166	163	135	165	125	106	175	185	123	185	105	134	304
5. CHESHAM UNITED	503	419	802	523	+	309	513	369	261	329	789	235	520	280	523	320	511	547	375	190	649	481
6. CROYDON	82	75	344	163	132	+	113	144	101	130	110	85	117	121	108	126	95	95	111	153	90	67
7. DORKING	224	210	387	225	186	152	+	134	195	151	189	192	199	259	273	284	207	224	203	227	180	223
8. DULWICH HAMLET	188	135	269	151	208	188	220	+	194	191	193	150	213	177	155	303	187	183	134	252	165	229
9. HARLOW TOWN	129	82	183	136	195	68	112	100	+	111	98	80	86	113	110	114	157	128	89	120	99	92
10. HEYBRIDGE SWIFTS	151	151	241	148	321	173	165	164	218	+	158	153	156	198	142	178	176	148	147	131	153	106
11. HITCHIN TOWN	490	318	309	350	612	339	230	307	295	360	+	390	194	700	427	376	408	358	304	285	429	432
12. LEWES	182	155	231	118	206	157	172	170	159	122	185	+	146	104	168	202	109	197	158	161	198	124
13. METROPOLITAN POLICE	90	88	160	88	160	85	145	132	92	130	97	106	+	127	86	131	80	197	81	83	102	91
14. MOLESEY	90	84	180	70	203	73	86	119	56	66	80	82	102	+	76	125	85	198	85	75	75	96
15. SOUTHWICK	77	105	154	145	208	56	157	206	129	124	106	168	90	114	+	101	123	110	79	159	131	116
16. TOOTING & MITCHAM U	125	148	282	98	312	145	147	251	174	87	176	167	135	242	132	+	138	186	139	169	244	152
17. UXBRIDGE	121	94	194	103	234	98	169	97	108	91	171	149	58	130	107	93	+	130	105	113	92	179
18. WALTON & HERSHAM	130	220	357	114	347	223	352	202	156	158	150	105	145	292	180	210	109	+	255	148	147	147
19. WEMBLEY	105	85	121	90	155	82	110	105	102	89	102	71	96	85	81	110	120	102	+	85	91	95
20. WHYTELEAFE	81	155	255	211	211	134	241	153	173	133	163	149	82	118	101	106	103	163	94	+	107	72
21. WORTHING	132	59	286	61	172	131	103	128	109	101	344	247	208	98	232	141	104	79	112	128	+	74
22. YEADING	116	140	197	130	205	106	117	76	92	79	110	95	183	78	117	158	230	130	131	120	93	+

FACTS

VAUXHALL LEAGUE 1990/1 RESULTS

Vauxhall League Division Two (North)

		H\A	1	2	3	4	5	6	7	8	9	10	11	12	13	14	15	16	17	18	19	20	21	22
1	Barton Rovers	1	*	5-0	1-2	0-1	2-0	0-0	3-1	5-1	2-1	0-0	0-1	3-0	1-1	2-1	1-1	2-1	0-2	2-2	0-0	0-1	2-0	2-1
2	Basildon Utd	2	1-0	*	0-4	0-0	3-2	0-0	1-3	3-2	1-1	1-1	2-0	3-4	2-2	2-0	1-5	0-1	2-2	2-3	3-2	2-2	0-4	0-1
3	Berkhamsted	3	2-0	1-1	*	1-0	1-1	2-1	1-2	2-1	2-1	0-1	0-0	1-0	2-2	1-0	1-1	7-1	0-0	1-0	1-0	1-1	1-1	1-1
4	Billericay	4	2-0	1-0	3-0	*	1-1	0-1	3-1	0-1	2-2	4-2	4-0	3-1	1-3	1-1	1-2	4-2	0-1	1-2	5-0	3-2	1-0	2-1
5	Clapton	5	0-1	1-4	4-2	0-1	*	1-1	2-3	4-2	1-4	2-3	1-2	1-2	0-0	1-1	3-2	2-2	0-5	5-2	1-0	0-0	1-2	3-3
6	Collier Row	6	1-3	3-1	4-1	1-1	3-0	*	1-0	1-0	3-1	1-1	1-1	1-2	0-2	1-4	1-1	1-3	0-3	3-0	3-3	1-4	1-3	2-0
7	Edgware Town	7	3-1	4-0	0-2	1-1	3-0	6-1	*	6-3	2-3	0-3	2-0	2-0	1-2	0-1	1-1	3-0	1-4	5-3	5-0	3-0	1-0	0-1
8	Finchley	8	1-3	0-4	1-3	0-2	4-1	0-2	0-1	*	0-3	4-3	0-4	2-5	1-2	1-2	1-5	1-3	0-6	1-4	1-1	3-3	2-4	2-3
9	Hemel Hempstead	9	0-0	3-1	1-1	1-0	1-1	1-1	2-1	4-0	*	0-3	1-0	1-0	2-2	0-1	1-4	1-1	2-1	1-3	0-0	1-1	2-2	0-0
10	Hertford Town	10	2-4	5-2	1-0	0-1	3-1	0-2	0-0	2-1	0-1	*	3-2	0-1	1-3	2-1	0-1	2-2	0-0	0-2	3-2	1-3	2-1	4-4
11	Hornchurch	11	3-1	0-0	1-3	0-1	2-2	0-4	3-3	2-2	1-2	2-3	*	4-2	1-3	0-2	2-1	1-1	1-3	1-0	2-1	1-4	2-5	4-1
12	Kingsbury Town	12	1-1	3-2	1-0	0-3	0-2	0-1	1-0	1-3	3-1	2-4	3-1	*	3-2	1-0	1-1	3-1	2-2	5-2	1-1	0-2	0-1	2-1
13	Purfleet	13	2-2	0-2	1-2	1-1	2-1	3-1	3-0	1-0	1-3	4-0	1-1	3-1	*	1-0	2-2	0-0	1-3	0-2	2-2	0-3	3-3	1-0
14	Rainham Town	14	2-0	0-1	0-1	5-4	1-0	2-1	0-1	0-0	2-1	2-0	4-2	1-2	1-1	*	1-0	1-0	0-1	2-1	2-1	1-2	2-2	1-1
15	Royston Town	15	1-2	3-3	2-2	1-2	3-0	2-2	1-1	2-2	0-3	2-1	4-2	1-1	1-2	3-2	*	2-2	2-3	3-1	5-0	2-1	2-0	0-1
16	Saffron Walden	16	4-4	3-2	5-1	2-0	0-3	4-4	4-1	1-0	1-1	3-3	1-0	4-4	2-1	0-3	1-1	*	1-0	0-2	3-1	3-1	2-3	1-1
17	Stevenage Boro	17	3-0	3-1	4-0	2-0	7-1	2-1	3-2	7-0	6-0	1-0	7-0	2-1	3-0	3-2	2-1	3-1	*	4-0	5-1	4-0	2-0	2-0
18	Tilbury	18	6-0	6-1	2-1	0-1	0-1	1-2	1-1	2-2	1-3	1-1	1-2	2-3	2-1	1-0	2-2	0-2	2-3	*	1-0	1-1	3-4	0-1
19	Tring Town	19	1-3	0-3	2-4	0-5	1-2	0-2	1-1	0-1	0-3	1-2	1-1	2-2	0-3	0-2	1-3	0-1	0-3	1-3	*	0-2	1-0	1-3
20	Vauxhall Motors	20	4-1	5-2	2-1	1-3	6-1	2-0	1-0	1-2	2-1	2-1	2-1	0-0	1-1	2-0	1-0	2-0	2-2	4-1	3-1	*	2-2	1-2
21	Ware	21	0-2	3-1	0-1	1-1	6-0	2-0	3-0	2-0	2-1	2-2	2-0	2-0	2-1	0-2	3-1	2-3	2-0	2-1	1-0	0-1	*	1-1
22	Witham Town	22	2-0	2-1	1-0	1-0	2-1	1-3	5-2	2-2	1-1	2-4	3-0	3-0	1-2	2-2	2-1	4-0	0-3	4-1	3-1	1-2	1-3	*

Vauxhall League Division Two (South)

		H\A	1	2	3	4	5	6	7	8	9	10	11	12	13	14	15	16	17	18	19	20	21	22
1	Abingdon Town	1	*	2-0	0-1	11-0	1-0	4-0	3-0	2-1	4-0	4-0	2-1	2-0	3-0	3-0	6-1	1-1	0-1	0-0	2-1	2-0	0-1	1-2
2	Banstead Ath	2	3-3	*	5-1	3-0	2-0	3-1	0-0	1-5	0-2	2-1	0-0	1-1	1-2	0-3	2-5	2-0	0-0	2-1	0-2	4-1	0-4	0-0
3	Bracknell	3	1-2	0-2	*	3-0	0-3	2-2	1-0	0-2	1-5	0-0	3-1	0-1	2-2	4-0	1-1	1-2	0-3	0-1	1-3	3-1	3-6	0-1
4	Camberley	4	0-4	0-1	4-5	*	0-8	2-1	0-3	1-3	1-1	0-1	1-2	0-5	1-4	2-2	0-5	0-7	1-4	1-4	0-6	0-3	2-3	1-3
5	Chertsey Town	5	0-1	2-2	2-4	1-1	*	5-2	1-1	0-4	2-0	3-1	1-1	1-0	2-2	0-1	2-2	4-3	4-3	1-2	1-3	2-1	0-1	2-0
6	Cove	6	1-2	1-3	4-1	3-0	1-3	*	1-0	0-4	0-1	1-0	3-5	1-3	4-1	0-2	2-3	0-5	1-1	0-2	1-2	4-0	1-1	0-2
7	Eastbourne Utd	7	1-1	1-1	4-3	3-1	1-7	3-2	*	0-4	2-0	3-1	4-2	0-2	0-4	2-0	2-2	2-1	2-4	0-1	1-2	3-1	1-2	1-3
8	Egham Town	8	1-1	1-3	0-1	8-1	1-0	4-0	2-2	*	3-0	1-0	3-2	1-2	1-0	2-0	2-1	2-0	0-2	2-0	1-1	7-0	1-0	1-1
9	Epsom & Ewell	9	0-1	3-2	1-2	0-0	1-0	2-2	4-0	1-3	*	1-1	1-0	3-2	2-0	1-3	2-2	2-0	1-2	1-2	0-1	3-0	1-0	0-0
10	Feltham	10	2-3	0-0	4-0	2-1	1-4	0-2	3-1	3-4	0-4	*	3-2	1-0	0-2	1-1	1-1	2-1	3-4	0-1	1-2	2-0	1-1	2-0
11	Flackwell Hth	11	1-3	2-0	1-1	1-0	2-2	0-2	5-1	1-4	0-0	1-2	*	0-0	2-3	1-1	2-2	2-2	0-1	0-3	2-1	2-0	1-5	0-0
12	Hampton	12	1-4	1-1	2-2	0-0	3-1	0-1	11-1	1-1	0-0	2-1	1-1	*	0-1	0-2	1-1	0-2	1-1	1-0	0-0	5-0	0-2	2-1
13	Harefield	13	2-2	2-0	7-1	2-0	2-2	2-2	3-1	4-2	0-0	2-1	4-1	0-3	*	3-0	2-1	2-1	0-3	2-1	2-1	3-2	1-0	2-2
14	Horsham	14	0-3	0-0	3-2	5-0	0-1	5-0	5-0	2-3	3-0	3-0	0-1	1-1	0-2	*	1-2	2-1	0-1	1-4	1-0	1-2	2-2	1-1
15	Hungerford	15	1-2	1-2	3-2	4-1	1-1	6-1	3-0	2-2	1-1	4-2	4-1	2-1	1-2	5-2	*	1-0	1-1	1-3	1-3	1-3	2-0	0-3
16	Leatherhead	16	1-2	2-2	4-0	5-1	5-0	1-1	2-0	1-2	1-1	4-0	0-1	0-0	1-2	2-0	3-2	*	1-1	1-1	1-0	5-1	2-3	1-4
17	Maidenhead Utd	17	1-3	2-0	2-1	2-0	1-0	5-1	2-0	2-1	4-0	3-0	5-0	1-2	2-2	2-0	3-1	1-2	*	3-0	0-0	3-0	2-0	1-0
18	Malden Vale	18	1-0	2-2	2-1	2-0	3-1	5-0	3-1	0-3	2-0	3-0	1-0	2-1	1-1	2-0	2-3	3-3	0-2	*	1-2	2-0	1-0	2-3
19	Newbury	19	0-0	1-2	1-2	5-1	2-3	2-0	2-2	2-0	0-2	1-1	0-4	0-0	2-1	3-0	0-0	2-0	3-2	2-0	*	3-1	1-3	4-3
20	Petersfield	20	0-3	1-3	2-2	3-1	4-2	0-1	5-3	1-4	0-1	0-0	0-4	0-4	1-1	1-3	0-3	0-2	0-2	1-2	0-1	*	0-6	0-4
21	Ruislip Manor	21	0-2	4-0	3-1	3-0	4-1	1-1	2-0	2-3	2-0	7-1	3-0	2-0	3-2	3-2	0-0	0-1	2-0	2-3	1-2	7-0	*	2-1
22	Southall	22	1-0	2-1	5-1	2-2	2-1	1-0	7-1	3-1	1-1	1-0	6-1	2-2	1-0	4-0	2-1	2-5	0-0	0-1	1-2	5-0	2-0	*

SECOND DIVISION NORTH (21 MATCHES)

CLUB	AGG 90/91	AVE 90/91	AVE 89/90
BARTON ROVERS	29/9	142	134
BASILDON UNITED	1954	93	118
BERKHAMPSTEAD TOWN	2029	97	86
BILLERICAY TOWN	5082	242	249
CLAPTON	1466	70	99
COLLIER ROW	2291	109	115
EDGWARE TOWN	3010	143	*RNK
FINCHLEY	960	46	58
HEMEL HEMPSTEAD	2206	105	97
HERTFORD TOWN	2279	109	126
HORNCHURCH	1633	78	80
KINGSBURY TOWN	1470	70	67
PURFLEET	1948	93	94
RAINHAM TOWN	1445	69	60
ROYSTON TOWN	3763	179	175
SAFFRON WALDEN TOWN	2866	136	119
STEVENAGE BOROUGH	10194	485	344
TILBURY	1831	87	181
TRING TOWN	1890	90	113
VAUXHALL MOTORS	1969	94	85
WARE	3089	147	109
WITHAM TOWN	2271	108	120

SECOND DIVISION SOUTH (21 MATCHES)

CLUB	AGG 90/91	AVE 90/91	AVE 89/90
ABINGDON TOWN	5902	281	262
BANSTEAD ATHLETIC	931	44	45
BRACKNELL TOWN	1776	85	67
CAMBERLEY TOWN	1208	58	69
CHERTSEY TOWN	2349	112	111
COVE	1505	72	*RNK
EASTBOURNE UTD	1565	75	86
EGHAM TOWN	2380	113	93
EPSOM & EWELL	1942	92	105
FELTHAM	1939	92	97
FLACKWELL HEATH	1340	64	77
HAMPTON	3022	144	173
HAREFIELD UNITED	2101	100	107
HORSHAM	2211	105	76
HUNGERFORD TOWN	2256	107	116
LEATHERHEAD	2329	111	140
MAIDENHEAD UNITED	5158	246	154
MALDEN VALE	2223	106	93
NEWBURY TOWN	2366	113	112
PETERSFIELD UNITED	1590	76	86
RUISLIP MANOR	4194	200	170
SOUTHALL	1757	84	75

HFS LOANS LEAGUE PREMIER DIVISION 1990/1

FACTS

	TEAM	P	HOME					AWAY					TOTAL		
			W	D	L	F	A	W	D	L	F	A	F	A	pts
1	WITTON ALBION	40	15	4	1	48	16	13	5	2	33	15	81	31	93
2	STALYBRIDGE CELTIC	40	14	5	1	29	8	8	6	6	15	18	44	26	77
3	MORECAMBE	40	12	7	1	49	26	7	9	4	23	18	72	44	73
4	FLEETWOOD TOWN	40	9	6	5	33	20	11	3	6	36	24	69	44	69
5	SOUTHPORT	40	11	5	4	32	20	7	9	4	34	28	66	48	68
6	MARINE	40	11	3	6	36	20	7	8	5	20	19	56	39	65
7	BISHOP AUCKLAND	40	10	3	7	28	22	7	7	6	34	34	62	56	61
8	BUXTON	40	10	7	3	36	22	7	4	9	30	39	66	61	59
9	LEEK TOWN	40	7	8	5	27	23	8	3	9	21	21	48	44	56
10	FRICKLEY ATHLETIC	40	9	2	9	36	33	7	4	9	28	29	64	62	54
11	HYDE UNITED	40	10	4	6	52	29	4	7	9	21	34	73	63	53
12	GOOLE TOWN	40	9	4	7	34	27	5	6	9	34	47	68	74	52
13	DROYLSDEN	40	7	7	6	40	33	5	4	11	27	37	67	70	47
14	CHORLEY	40	8	4	8	32	27	4	6	10	23	28	55	55	46
15	MOSSLEY	40	9	7	4	31	25	4	3	13	24	43	55	68	45
16	HORWICH	40	7	6	7	35	29	6	0	14	27	52	62	81	45
17	MATLOCK TOWN	40	6	5	9	29	31	6	2	12	23	39	52	70	43
18	BANGOR CITY	40	6	4	10	21	28	3	8	9	31	42	52	70	39
19	SOUTH LIVERPOOL	40	5	4	11	29	44	5	5	10	29	48	58	92	39
20	GAINSBOROUGH TRINI	40	6	7	7	35	38	3	4	13	22	46	57	84	38
21	SHEPSHED CHOUSE	40	3	4	13	18	34	3	3	14	20	49	38	83	25

	Ba	BA	Bx	Ch	Dr	Fl	Fr	Ga	Go	Ho	Hy	Le	Ma	Mt	Mr	My	Sh	SL	So	St	Wi
Bangor		01	02	13	13	24	10	00	23	31	10	11	11	10	12	21	12	11	21	01	01
B Auckland	30		12	10	21	01	10	31	30	12	20	03	00	11	11	10	31	20	34	01	04
Buxton	11	22		43	11	12	21	43	31	51	00	02	03	21	00	10	40	10	00	11	40
Chorley	13	11	01		30	22	13	53	22	12	40	02	10	10	12	21	11	31	12	20	01
Droylsden	22	34	11	00		13	22	30	42	31	20	11	40	12	01	12	42	32	22	22	14
Fleetwood T	31	01	01	10	32		50	20	11	32	41	00	41	13	11	00	11	12	00	31	02
Frickley A	22	01	12	14	54	20		31	32	01	31	10	00	12	10	23	23	51	14	31	01
Gainsboro	11	21	44	01	00	04	13		42	41	23	21	23	24	22	42	32	11	13	00	00
Goole T	43	03	22	21	20	01	43	22		41	00	41	01	12	00	31	21	31	01	01	12
Horwich	41	22	40	11	21	02	11	21	13		20	03	00	50	11	24	30	24	22	01	12
Hyde U	45	32	50	10	10	11	20	12	12	03		02	00	53	31	62	70	91	13	11	11
Leek Town	02	02	10	00	21	12	21	40	11	12	11		23	10	11	33	31	22	11	10	00
Marine	11	12	02	31	11	10	13	30	20	21	30	41		20	01	31	30	31	23	01	11
Matlock T	22	31	33	31	01	11	13	23	12	21	13	10	13		12	40	10	11	00	01	13
Morecambe	11	33	21	11	61	32	21	44	53	52	11	31	00	41		02	30	21	21	00	20
Mossley	20	11	32	11	33	21	00	01	20	53	22	10	32	00	10		10	02	22	01	24
Shepshed Ch	11	41	10	12	02	14	01	10	22	12	14	01	02	01	23	00		12	22	02	02
S. L'pool	21	22	14	22	34	24	14	11	24	30	23	01	01	32	04	10	03		22	20	02
Southport	32	31	31	21	02	21	01	10	33	20	11	10	00	10	00	40	31	34		00	02
Stalybridge	31	10	31	21	10	20	00	10	11	30	10	01	10	20	00	10	31	11	20		11
Witton A	21	33	41	10	10	01	21	40	40	41	11	20	00	51	21	32	11	41	21	30	
	Ba	BA	Bx	Ch	Dr	Fl	Fr	Ga	Go	Ho	Hy	Le	Mn	Mt	Mr	Ms	Sh	SL	So	St	Wi

LEADING GOALSCORERS.

COLEMAN (Morecambe)	32
THOMAS (Witton Alb)	30
CLARKE (Buxton)	29
HOLDEN (Southport)	28
WHITEHALL (Southport)	19
BLACKHURST (Southport)	19
KIRKHAM (Hyde Utd)	19
GREEN (S.Liverpool)	18
LUTKEVITCH (Hyde Utd)	18
WAKENSHAW(Fleetwood T)	18
CLARKSON (Fleetwood T)	17
ROSS (Chorley)	17
COLLIER (Goole T)	16
GRIMSHAW (Witton Alb)	15
HURLSTONE (Goole Town)	14
CAIN (Morecambe)	14
SHAW (B. Auckland)	14

FACTS

HFS LOANS LEAGUE DIVISION ONE 1990/1

	TEAM	P	HOME W	D	L	F	A	AWAY W	D	L	F	A	TOTAL F	A	pts
1	WHITLEY BAY	42	17	4	0	67	15	8	6	7	28	23	95	38	85
2	EMLEY	42	13	5	3	47	20	11	7	3	31	17	78	37	84
3	WORKSOP TOWN	42	15	3	3	49	20	10	4	7	36	36	85	56	82
4	ACCRINGTON STANLEY	42	12	6	3	46	22	9	7	5	37	35	83	57	76
5	RHYL	42	15	2	4	38	24	6	5	10	24	39	62	63	70
6	EASTWOOD TOWN	42	10	5	6	37	25	7	6	8	33	35	70	60	62
7	WARRINGTON TOWN	42	12	5	4	43	15	5	5	11	25	37	68	52	61
8	LANCASTER CITY	42	13	4	4	38	17	6	4	11	20	40	58	57	61
9	BRIDLINGTON TOWN	42	9	5	7	43	26	6	10	5	29	26	72	52	60
10	CURZON ASHTON	42	7	7	7	28	29	7	7	7	21	28	49	57	56
11	CONGLETON TOWN	42	10	8	3	36	28	4	4	13	21	43	57	71	54
12	NETHERFIELD	42	8	7	6	36	26	6	4	11	31	40	67	66	53
13	NEWTOWN	42	8	8	5	39	30	5	4	12	29	45	68	75	51
14	CAERNARFON TOWN	42	12	3	6	41	25	1	7	13	10	39	51	64	49
15	ROSSENDALE UNITED	42	8	5	8	42	33	4	8	9	25	34	67	67	48
16	RADCLIFFE BOROUGH	42	8	6	7	32	31	4	6	11	18	38	50	69	48
17	IRLAM TOWN	42	6	7	8	27	31	6	4	11	28	45	55	76	47
18	WINSFORD UNITED	42	5	10	6	23	27	6	3	12	28	39	51	66	46
19	HARROGATE TOWN	42	7	9	5	27	23	4	4	13	28	50	55	73	46
20	WORKINGTON	42	9	7	5	31	19	2	4	15	23	48	54	67	41
21	FARSLEY CELTIC	42	6	3	12	28	37	5	6	10	21	41	49	78	39
22	ALFRETON TOWN	42	6	4	11	24	40	1	8	12	17	44	41	84	33

	Ac	Al	Br	Ca	Co	Cu	Ea	Em	Fa	Ha	Ir	La	Ne	Nw	Ra	Rh	Ro	Wa	WB	Wl	Wo	Ws
Accrington..		22	00	30	52	01	21	00	20	41	23	21	11	53	33	30	40	00	02	41	21	20
Alfreton T..	11		01	11	11	31	05	03	12	14	32	02	01	26	10	21	31	02	00	01	43	12
Bridlington.	51	02		01	41	41	22	12	40	40	23	11	23	00	11	30	01	22	21	12	21	31
Caernarfon..	30	63	11		12	01	31	10	03	14	51	40	40	10	10	20	12	31	14	11	21	00
Congleton...	33	22	11	10		33	11	10	00	22	21	10	21	12	31	21	21	21	11	02	31	34
Curzon Ash..	11	11	03	20	11		00	01	31	01	02	11	31	41	21	24	11	00	02	32	32	13
Eastwood T..	02	10	11	21	20	03		23	50	52	20	10	31	12	00	22	11	11	21	30	23	12
Emley.......	03	11	20	51	60	00	42		31	10	12	30	31	21	31	30	22	41	10	12	11	11
Farsley C...	03	40	03	11	10	02	11	03		41	00	12	13	34	12	02	32	03	23	20	40	02
Harrogate T.	12	00	15	21	20	11	01	22	11		00	01	00	41	02	11	11	21	10	22	41	20
Irlam Town..	12	20	22	32	21	00	02	11	11	21		11	01	41	33	13	11	01	13	21	01	03
Lancaster C.	12	00	40	11	00	10	22	01	01	21	21		23	21	31	40	21	31	20	20	30	21
Netherfield.	22	51	22	21	20	11	13	12	12	11	20	20		40	40	02	00	02	11	13	10	33
Newtown.....	12	21	02	00	42	22	00	11	33	41	50	22	43		12	11	20	10	23	21	00	24
Radcliffe B.	21	11	22	30	20	10	12	13	00	42	02	01	14	11		12	11	21	11	43	21	23
Rhyl........	23	31	10	00	31	21	32	11	21	21	12	20	21	20	30		06	20	02	21	31	20
Rossendale..	22	11	51	10	13	12	23	03	71	02	22	32	20	11	10	01		41	22	24	51	01
Warrington..	20	20	11	00	20	00	31	12	20	40	61	50	32	22	01	20	01		20	30	22	12
Whitley Bay.	20	31	10	70	22	30	20	42	31	30	10	60	21	20	60	22	41	51		11	22	61
Winsford U..	22	20	00	00	03	01	12	00	12	11	43	23	11	21	20	00	22	04	00		10	22
Workington..	22	40	02	30	12	01	31	00	11	22	31	02	22	01	00	20	30	11	10	10		21
Worksop T...	23	20	22	20	10	60	41	01	10	31	22	31	21	21	00	62	10	51	12	21	21	
	Ac	Al	Br	Ca	Co	Cu	Ea	Em	Fa	Ha	Ir	La	Ne	Nw	Ra	Rh	Ro	Wa	WB	Wl	Wo	Ws

BARKER (Whitley Bay) 33
CHANDLER(" ") 29
CLARK (Worksop T) 29
FLEMING (Netherfield) 27
RICHARDSON (EastwoodT) 26
BECK (Accrington S) 25
WYLIE (Rossendale U) 24
LLOYD (Rhyl) 24
BIDDLE (Congleton T) 24
ARCHER (Bridlington T) 19
PRIEST (Curzon Ashton) 19
MOSS (Worksop T) 18
EDWARDS (Newtown) 18
GASCOIGNE (Bridlington) 18
DUNN (Warrington T) 17
DOWNING (Harrogate T) 17
McDONALD (Radcliffe B) 16
CURLEY (Radcliffe B) 16
NICHOLSON (Workington) 16

WHO'S WON WHAT FACTS

ALLIANCE PREMIER LEAGUE - CHAMPIONS/Runners-up

1979/80 ALTRINCHAM/Weymouth; 1980/81 ALTRINCHAM/Kettering Town; 1981/82 RUNCORN/Enfield; 1982/83 ENFIELD/Maidstone United; 1983/84 MAIDSTONE UNITED/Nuneaton Borough; 1984/85 WEALDSTONE/Nuneaton Borough; 1985/86 ENFIELD/Frickley Athletic; 1986/87 SCARBOROUGH/Barnet; 1987/88 LINCOLN CITY/Barnet; 1988/89 MAIDSTONE UNITED/Kettering Town; 1989/90 DARLINGTON/Barnet; 1990/91 BARNET/Colchester United.

BOB LORD TROPHY - WINNERS/Finalists

1979/80 NORTHWICH VICTORIA/Altrincham; 1980/81 ALTRINCHAM/Kettering Town; 1981/82 WEYMOUTH/Enfield; 1982/83 RUNCORN/Scarborough; 1983/84 SCARBOROUGH/Barnet; 1984/85 RUNCORN/Maidstone United; 1985/86 STAFFORD RANGERS/Barnet; 1989/90 YEOVIL TOWN/Kidderminster Harriers; 1990/91 SUTTON UNITED/Barrow.

SOUTHERN LEAGUE - CHAMPIONS/Runners-up

1945/46 CHELMSFORD CITY/Hereford United; 1946/47 GILLINGHAM/Guildford City; 1947/48 MERTHYR TYDFIL/Gillingham; 1948/49 GILLINGHAM/Chelmsford City; 1949/50 MERTHYR TYDFIL/Colchester United; 1950/51 MERTHYR TYDFIL/Hereford United; 1951/52 MERTHYR TYDFIL/Weymouth; 1952/53 HEADINGTON UNITED/Merthyr Tydfil; 1953/54 MERTHYR TYDFIL/Headington United; 1954/55 YEOVIL TOWN/Weymouth; 1955/56 GUILDFORD CITY/Cheltenham Town; 1956/57 KETTERING TOWN/Bedford Town; 1957/58 GRAVESEND & NORTHFLEET/Bedford Town; 1958/59 BEDFORD TOWN/Hereford United; 1959/60 BATH CITY/Headington United; 1960/61 OXFORD UNITED/Chelmsford City; 1961/62 OXFORD UNITED/Bath City; 1962/63 CAMBRIDGE CITY/Cambridge United; 1963/64 YEOVIL TOWN/Chelmsford City; 1964/65 WEYMOUTH/Guildford City; 1965/66 WEYMOUTH/Chelmsford City; 1966/67 ROMFORD/Nuneaton Borough; 1967/68 CHELMSFORD CITY/Wimbledon; 1968/69 CAMBRIDGE UNITED/Hillingdon Borough; 1969/70 CAMBRIDGE UNITED/Yeovil Town; 1970/71 YEOVIL TOWN/Cambridge City; 1971/72 CHELMSFORD CITY/Hereford United; 1972/73 KETTERING TOWN/Yeovil Town; 1973/74 DARTFORD/Grantham; 1974/75 WIMBLEDON/Nuneaton Borough; 1975/76 WIMBLEDON/Yeovil Town; 1976/77 WIMBLEDON/Minehead; 1977/78 BATH CITY/Weymouth; 1978/79 WORCESTER CITY/Kettering Town; 1979/80 BRIDGEND TOWN/Dorchester Town; 1980/81 ALVECHURCH/Dartford; 1981/82 WEALDSTONE/Nuneaton Borough; 1982/83 AP LEAMINGTON/Kidderminster Harriers; 1983/84 DARTFORD/Fisher Athletic; 1984/85 CHELTENHAM TOWN/Kings Lynn; 1985/86 WELLING UNITED/Chelmsford City; 1986/87 FISHER ATHLETIC/Bromsgrove Rovers; 1987/88 AYLESBURY UNITED/Dartford; 1988/89 MERTHYR TYDFIL/Dartford; 1989/90 DOVER ATHLETIC/Bath City; 1990/91 FARNBOROUGH TOWN/Gloucester City.

SOUTHERN LEAGUE CUP - WINNERS/Finalists

1945/46 CHELMSFORD CITY/Worcester City; 1946/47 GILLINGHAM/Yeovil Town; 1947/48 MERTHYR TYDFIL/Colchester United; 1948/49 YEOVIL TOWN/Colchester United; 1949/50 COLCHESTER UNITED/Bath City; 1950/51 MERTHYR TYDFIL/Guildford City; 1951/52 HEREFORD UNITED/Guildford City; 1952/53 HEADINGTON UNITED/Weymouth; 1953/54 HEADINGTON UNITED/Lovells Athletic; 1954/55 YEOVIL TOWN/Tonbridge; 1955/56 GLOUCESTER CITY/Yeovil Town; 1956/57 HEREFORD UNITED/Tonbridge; 1957/58 CHELTENHAM TOWN/Gravesend & Northfleet; 1958/59 HEREFORD UNITED/Bath City; 1959/60 CHELMSFORD CITY/Worcester City; 1960/61 YEOVIL TOWN/Chelmsford City; 1961/62 CAMBRIDGE CITY/Margate; 1962/63 GUILDFORD CITY/Nuneaton Borough; 1963/64 BURTON ALBION/Weymouth; 1964/65 CAMBRIDGE UNITED/Weymouth; 1965/66 YEOVIL TOWN/Guildford City; 1966/67 GUILDFORD CITY/Barnet; 1967/68 MARGATE/Ramsgate Athletic; 1968/69 CAMBRIDGE UNITED/Cheltenham Town; 1969/70 WIMBLEDON/Romford; 1970/71 TELFORD UNITED/Weymouth; 1971/72 BARNET/Hereford United; 1972/73 WEYMOUTH/Hillingdon Borough; 1973/74 AP LEAMINGTON/Bromsgrove Rovers; 1974/75 KETTERING TOWN/Margate; 1975/76 WIMBLEDON/Yeovil Town; 1976/77 DARTFORD/Yeovil Town; 1977/78 GRAVESEND & NORTHFLEET/Weymouth; 1978/79 BATH CITY/Yeovil Town; 1979/80 KIDDERMINSTER HARRIERS/Dartford; 1980/81 BEDFORD TOWN/Bognor Regis Town; 1981/82 WEALDSTONE/Gloucester City; 1982/83 ALVECHURCH/Waterlooville; 1983/84 AP LEAMINGTON/Dartford; 1984/85 FISHER ATHLETIC/Cheltenham Town; 1985/86 BROMSGROVE ROVERS/Cheltenham Town; 1986/87 WATERLOOVILLE/Hednesford Town; 1987/88 DARTFORD/Bromsgrove Rovers; 1988/89 DARTFORD/Burton Albion; 1989/90 VS RUGBY/Dartford; 1990/91 CHELMSFORD CITY/Hythe Town.

ISTHMIAN LEAGUE - CHAMPIONS/Runners-up

1945/46 WALTHAMSTOW AVENUE/Oxford City; 1946/47 LEYTONSTONE/Dulwich Hamlet; 1947/48 LEYTONSTONE/Kingstonian; 1948/49 DULWICH HAMLET/Walthamstow Avenue; 1949/50 LEYTONSTONE/Wimbledon; 1950/51 LEYTONSTONE/Walthamstow Avenue; 1951/52 LEYTONSTONE/Wimbledon; 1952/53 WALTHAMSTOW AVENUE/Bromley; 1953/54 BROMLEY/Walthamstow Avenue; 1954/55 WALTHAMSTOW AVENUE/St. Albans City; 1955/56 WYCOMBE WANDERERS/Bromley; 1956/57 WYCOMBE WANDERERS/Woking; 1957/58 TOOTING & MITCHAM UNITED/Wycombe Wanderers; 1958/59 WIMBLEDON/Dulwich Hamlet; 1959/60 TOOTING & MITCHAM UNITED/Wycombe Wanderers; 1960/61 BROMLEY/Walthamstow Avenue; 1961/62 WIMBLEDON/Leytonstone; 1962/63 WIMBLEDON/Kingstonian; 1963/64 WIMBLEDON/Hendon; 1964/65 HENDON/Enfield; 1965/66 LEYTONSTONE/Hendon; 1966/67 SUTTON UNITED/Walthamstow Avenue; 1967/68 ENFIELD/Sutton United; 1968/69 ENFIELD/Hitchin Town; 1969/70 ENFIELD/Wycombe Wanderers; 1970/71 WYCOMBE WANDERERS/Sutton United; 1971/72 WYCOMBE WANDERERS/Enfield; 1972/73 HENDON/Walton & Hersham; 1973/74 WYCOMBE WANDERERS/Hendon; 1974/75 WYCOMBE WANDERERS/Enfield; 1975/76 ENFIELD/Wycombe Wanderers; 1976/77 ENFIELD/Wycombe Wanderers; 1977/78 ENFIELD/Dagenham; 1978/79 BARKING/Dagenham; 1979/80 ENFIELD/Walthamstow Avenue; 1980/81 SLOUGH TOWN/Enfield; 1981/82 LEYTONSTONE & ILFORD/Sutton United; 1982/83 WYCOMBE WANDERERS/Leytonstone & Ilford; 1983/84 HARROW BOROUGH/Worthing; 1984/85 SUTTON UNITED/Worthing; 1985/86 SUTTON UNITED/Yeovil Town; 1986/87 WYCOMBE WANDERERS/Yeovil Town; 1987/88 YEOVIL TOWN/Bromley; 1988/89 LEYTONSTONE-ILFORD/Farnborough Town; 1989/90 SLOUGH TOWN/Wokingham Town; 1990/91 REDBRIDGE FOREST/Enfield.

F.A. TROPHY FINALS (at Wembley unless otherwise stated)

1970 Macclesfield Town 2 Telford United 0; 1971 Telford United 3 Hillingdon Borough 2; 1972 Stafford Rangers 3 Barnet 0; 1973 Scarborough 2 Wigan Athletic 1; 1974 Morecambe 2 Dartford 1; 1975 Matlock Town 4 Scarborough 0; 1976 Scarborough 3 Stafford Rangers 2; 1977 Scarborough 2 Dagenham 1; 1978 Altrincham 3 Leatherhead 1; 1979 Stafford Rangers 2 Kettering Town 0; 1980 Dagenham 2 Mossley 1; 1981 Bishops Stortford 1 Sutton United 0; 1982 Enfield 1 Altrincham 0; 1983 Telford United 2 Northwich Victoria 1; 1984 Northwich Victoria 1 Bangor City 1, Replay (Stoke City) Northwich Victoria 2 Bangor City 1; 1985 Wealdstone 2 Boston United 1; 1986 Altrincham 1 Runcorn 0; 1987 Kidderminster Harriers 0 Burton Albion 0, Replay (West Brom.) Kidderminster Harriers 2 Burton Albion 1; 1988 Enfield 0 Telford United 0, Replay (West Brom.) Enfield 3 Telford United 2; 1989 Telford United 1 Macclesfield Town 0; 1990 Barrow 3 Leek Town 0; 1991 Wycombe Wanderers 2 Kidderminster Harriers 1.

NORTHERN PREMIER LEAGUE - CHAMPIONS/Runners-up

1968/69 MACCLESFIELD TOWN/Wigan Athletic; 1969/70 MACCLESFIELD TOWN/Wigan Athletic; 1970/71 WIGAN ATHLETIC/Stafford Rangers; 1971/72 STAFFORD RANGERS/Boston United; 1972/73 BOSTON UNITED/Scarborough; 1973/74 BOSTON UNITED/Wigan Athletic; 1974/75 WIGAN ATHLETIC/Runcorn; 1975/76 RUNCORN/Stafford Rangers; 1976/77 BOSTON UNITED/Northwich Victoria; 1977/78 BOSTON UNITED/Wigan Athletic; 1978/79 MOSSLEY/Altrincham; 1979/80 MOSSLEY/Witton Albion; 1980/81 RUNCORN/Mossley; 1981/82 BANGOR CITY/Mossley; 1982/83 GATESHEAD/Mossley; 1983/84 BARROW/Matlock Town; 1984/85 STAFFORD RANGERS/Macclesfield Town; 1985/86 GATESHEAD/Marine; 1986/87 MACCLESFIELD TOWN/Bangor City; 1987/88 CHORLEY/Hyde United; 1988/89 BARROW/Hyde United; 1989/90 COLNE DYNAMOES/Gateshead; 1990/91 WITTON ALBION/Stalybridge Celtic.

NORTHERN PREMIER LEAGUE CHALLENGE CUP - WINNERS/Finalists

1968/69 BANGOR CITY/Runcorn; 1969/70 ALTRINCHAM/Macclesfield Town; 1970/71 FLEETWOOD/Macclesfield Town; 1971/72 WIGAN ATHLETIC/Gainsborough Trinity; 1972/73 NORTHWICH VICTORIA/Wigan Athletic; 1973/74 BOSTON UNITED/Altrincham; 1974/75 RUNCORN/Stafford Rangers; 1975/76 BOSTON UNITED/Mossley; 1976/77 SCARBOROUGH/Runcorn; 1977/78 MATLOCK TOWN/Boston United; 1978/79 MOSSLEY/Northwich Victoria; 1979/80 RUNCORN/Lancaster City; 1980/81 RUNCORN/Marine; 1981/82 GAINSBOROUGH TRINITY/Mossley; 1982/83 BURTON ALBION/Macclesfield Town; 1983/84 SOUTH LIVERPOOL/Hyde United; 1984/85 MARINE/Goole Town; 1985/86 HYDE UNITED/Marine; 1986/87 MACCLESFIELD TOWN/Burton Albion; 1987/88 GOOLE TOWN/Barrow; 1988/89 MOSSLEY/Fleetwood Town; 1989/90 HYDE UNITED/Gateshead; 1990/91 SOUTHPORT/Buxton.

NORTHERN PREMIER LEAGUE PRESIDENTS CUP - WINNERS/Finalists

1981/82 BUXTON/Goole Town; 1982/83 KINGS LYNN/Burton Albion; 1983/84 WORKINGTON/Marine; 1984/85 RHYL/Macclesfield Town; 1985/86 WORKSOP TOWN/Burton Albion; 1986/87 MACCLESFIELD TOWN/Marine; 1987/88 SOUTH LIVERPOOL/Southport; 1988/89 BANGOR CITY/South Liverpool; 1989/90 FLEETWOOD TOWN/Witton Albion; 1990/91 WITTON ALBION/Fleetwood Town.

FACTS

F.A. CUP 1990/1

PRELIMINARY ROUND - 1 SEPTEMBER 1990

				RESULT	ATT
1	Willington	v	Cleator Moor Celtic	0-1	48
2	Ashington	v	Prudhoe East End	1-4	22
3	Shildon	v	Garforth Town	3-1	129
4	North Shields	v	Whickham	2-0	132
5	West Auckland Town	v	Annfield Plain	4-2	57
6	Bedlington Terriers	v	Norton & Stockton Ancients	0-4	60
7	Blackpool (wren) Rovers	v	Accrington Stanley	2-4	104
8	Billingham Town	v	Brandon United	1-0	80
9	Netherfield	v	Murton	0-3	160
10	Chester-le-Street Town	v	Easington Colliery	0-2	69
11	Penrith	v	Harrogate Railway	0-5	75
12	Langley Park	v	Washington	2-0	47
13	Ferryhill Athletic	v	Blackpool Mechanics	3-1	63
14	Shotton Comrades	v	Esh Winning	1-2	12
15	Crook Town	v	Horden CW	1-2	39
16	Great Harwood Town	v	Harrogate Town	2-2	121
	Harrogate Town	v	Great Harwood Town	2-1	352
17	Northallerton Town	v	Clitheroe	4-2	120
18	Darwen	v	Peterlee Newtown	2-0	94
19	Darlington CB	v	Evenwood Town	0-1	17
20	Lancaster City	v	Thackley	2-0	129
21	Hebburn	v	Ryhope CA	0-2	52
	(at Washington FC)				
22	Whitby Town	v	Leyland DAF	2-0	213
23	Irlam Town	v	Formby	2-0	38
24	Ashton United	v	Denaby United	0-2	160
25	Bridgnorth Town	v	Vauxhall GM	1-1	125
	Vauxhall GM	v	Bridgnorth Town	4-1	80
26	Knowsley United	v	Ossett Town	1-1	75
	Ossett Town	v	Knowsley United	2-3 (aet)	190
27	Glossop	v	Skelmersdale United	1-1	290
	Skelmersdale United	v	Glossop	0-2	190
28	Atherton LR	v	Rossendale United	3-1	208
29	Burscough	v	Maine Road	0-3	92
30	Farsley Celtic	v	Ossett Albion	1-1	196
	Ossett Albion	v	Farsley Celtic	0-2	146
31	Prescot AFC	v	Emley	1-1	237
	Emley	v	Prescot AFC	2-1 (aet)	417
32	Bootle	v	Winsford United	1-0	60
33	Chadderton	v	Radcliffe Borough	1-2	91
34	Armthorpe Welfare	v	Sheffield	3-0	45
35	Hednesford Town	v	Guiseley	2-0	338
36	Salford City	v	Warrington Town	0-3	121
37	Newtown	v	Eastwood Town	1-1	230
	Eastwood Town	v	Newtown	2-1	241
38	Belper Town	v	St Helens Town	2-3	158
39	Oakham United	v	Long Eaton United	1-1	48
	(at Long Eaton United)				
	Long Eaton United	v	Oakham United	0-1	61
40	Sutton Town	v	Rocester	2-2	154
	Rocester	v	Sutton Town	1-0	223
41	Borrowash Victoria	v	Gresley Rovers	1-2	176
42	North Ferriby United	v	Leicester United	1-2	136
43	Willenhall Town	v	Brigg Town	1-1	119
	Brigg Town	v	Willenhall Town	1-1	150
	Brigg Town	v	Willenhall Town	1-3	240
44	Louth United	v	Princes End United	1-1	61
	Princes End United	v	Louth United	1-0	54
45	Alfreton Town	v	Rushall Olympic	2-2	96
	Rushall Olympic	v	Alfreton Town	3-0	243
46	Paget Rangers	v	Boldmere St Michaels	2-0	95
47	Nuneaton Borough	v	Hinckley Town	4-1	834
48	Wellingborough Town	v	Tividale	1-0	65
49	Arnold Town	v	Wednesfield	1-1	180
	Wednesfield	v	Arnold Town	1-0	65
50	Alvechurch	v	Desborough Town	2-1	154
51	Stratford Town	v	Highgate United	3-1	80
52	Solihull Borough	v	Banbury United	0-0	147
	Banbury United	v	Solihull Borough	1-1	229
	Solihull Borough	v	Banbury United	2-2	155
	Banbury United	v	Solihull Borough	3-4	263
53	Heanor Town	v	Halesowen Harriers	0-4	134
54	Dudley Town	v	Corby Town	1-1	201
	Corby Town	v	Dudley Town	1-0	254
55	Hinckley Athletic	v	Friar Lane OB	3-1	183
56	Eastwood Hanley	v	West Midlands Police	0-2	65
57	Irthlingborough Diamonds	v	Buckingham Town	3-4	51
58	Chasetown	v	Evesham United	0-2	84
59	Brackley Town	v	Walsall-Wood	1-0	102
60	Oldbury United	v	Wolverton	0-0	87
	Wolverton	v	Oldbury United	2-1	31
61	Mile Oak Rovers	v	Stourbridge	0-5	51
62	Sandwell Borough	v	Northampton Spencer	4-1	25
63	Holbeach United	v	Potton United	1-2	105
64	Boston	v	Kings Lynn	2-0	332
65	Malvern Town	v	Soham Town Rangers	3-0	83
66	Rothwell Town	v	Stamford	7-2	65
67	Welwyn GC	v	Chalfont St Peter	1-2	33
68	Wisbech Town	v	Barton Rovers	1-1	358
	Barton Rovers	v	Wisbech Town	2-1	156
69	Baker Perkins	v	Letchworth GC	5-2	57
70	Lowestoft Town	v	Mirrless Blackstone	1-0	187
71	Boreham Wood	v	Gorleston	2-0	85
72	Haverhill Rovers	v	Eynesbury Rovers	1-1	101
	Eynesbury Rovers	v	Haverhill Rovers	0-2	200
73	Leighton Town	v	Spalding United	0-1	160
74	Bourne Town	v	Ely City	3-0	137
75	Great Yarmouth Town	v	Langford	2-2	160
	Langford	v	Great Yarmouth Town	0-1 (aet)	230
76	Wembley	v	Bury Town	1-0	73
77	Newmarket Town	v	Cheshunt	2-1	66
78	Tiptree United	v	Harlow Town	0-1	75
79	Braintree Town	v	Collier Row	1-0	212
80	Rayners Lane	v	Hoddesdon Town	2-1	43
81	Clapton	v	Felixstowe Town	5-2	54
82	Ford United	v	Kingsbury Town	3-1	13
83	Ruislip Manor	v	Northwood	2-1	197
84	Halstead Town	v	Canvey Island	1-1	247
	Canvey Island	v	Halstead Town	1-7	147
85	Cray Wanderers	v	Waltham Abbey	3-1	86
86	Stowmarket Town	v	Saffron Walden Town	1-1	120
	Saffron Walden Town	v	Stowmarket Town	2-1	120
87	Hemel Hempstead	v	Metropolitan Police	1-2	110
88	Clacton Town	v	Hertford Town	0-1	156
89	Burnham Ramblers	v	Hornchurch	0-2	94
90	Chesham United	v	Baldock Town	4-1	195
91	Arlesey Town	v	Walthamstow Pennant	0-4	89
92	Witham Town	v	Basildon United	2-3	137
93	Harwich & Parkeston	v	Berkhamsted Town	4-1	221
94	Wootton Blue Cross	v	Hounslow	1-3	52
95	Barkingside	v	Aveley	2-1	55
96	East Thurrock United	v	Stevenage Borough	0-1	225
97	Molesey	v	Vauxhall Motors	1-1	60
	Vauxhall Motors	v	Molesey	0-5	75
98	Flackwell Heath	v	Tring Town	5-0	45
99	Banstead Athletic	v	Malden Vale	1-0	51
100	Ware	v	Corinthian Casuals	0-0	70
	Corinthian Casuals	v	Ware	1-0	85
	(at Ware)				
101	Alma Swanley	v	Purfleet	1-2	40
102	Billericay Town	v	Hanwell Town	4-0	228
103	Croydon	v	Egham Town	0-4	71
104	Eton Manor	v	Edgware Town	0-2	80
105	Tilbury	v	Southall	0-0	77
	Southall	v	Tilbury	1-3	86
106	Horsham YMCA	v	Darenth Heathside	3-2	36
107	Harefield United	v	Merstham	0-1	41
108	Croydon Athletic	v	Andover	2-2	47
	Andover	v	Croydon Athletic	7-1	292
109	Royston Town	v	Rainham Town	1-1	71
	Rainham Town	v	Royston Town	1-2	75
110	Chertsey Town	v	Walton & Hersham	0-3	207
111	Horsham	v	Epsom & Ewell	2-0	88
112	Slade Green	v	Ringmer	2-0	36
113	Tooting & Mitcham United	v	Hastings Town	1-1	230
	Hastings Town	v	Tooting & Mitcham United	0-2	338
114	Tonbridge AFC	v	Shoreham	2-1	311
115	Chipstead	v	Littlehampton Town	2-3	70
116	Southwick	v	Corinthians	1-0	104
117	Steyning Town	v	Whitehawk	1-2	66
118	Peacehaven & Telscombe	v	Selsey	8-1	126
119	Ramsgate	v	Margate	0-1	560
120	Camberley Town	v	Oakwood	0-5	26
	(at Oakwood FC)				
121	Ashford Town	v	Leatherhead	3-1	345
122	Sheppey United	v	Pagham	0-2	102
123	Sittingbourne	v	Burgess Hill Town	2-0	434
124	Cove	v	Haywards Heath Town	4-0	52
125	Canterbury City	v	Dorking	0-0	127
	Dorking	v	Canterbury City	4-1	280
126	Arundel	v	Chatham Town	2-3	61
127	Three Bridges	v	Wick	1-3	121
128	Eastbourne United	v	Tunbridge Wells	6-5	97
129	Langney Sports	v	Portfield	3-0	130
130	Lancing	v	Lewes	0-3	125
131	Havant Town	v	Horndean	3-0	203
132	Bracknell Town	v	Hampton	2-3	70
133	Hungerford Town	v	Fareham Town	1-0	105
134	Feltham	v	Thame United	2-0	30
135	Salisbury	v	Uxbridge	1-1	199
	Uxbridge	v	Salisbury	1-2	134
136	Sholing Sports	v	Abingdon United	1-3	47
137	Bournemouth	v	Thatcham Town	1-0	39
138	Newbury Town	v	Eastleigh	2-1	74
139	Chichester City	v	Lymington AFC	1-5	55
140	Trowbridge Town	v	Clandown	7-1	326
141	Totton AFC	v	Warminster Town	2-3	35
142	Calne Town	v	Paulton Rovers	2-0	86
143	Romsey Town	v	Frome Town	1-0	67
144	Melksham Town	v	Keynsham Town	2-1	80
145	Westbury United	v	Stroud	1-1	92
	Stroud	v	Westbury United	3-0	90
146	Clevedon Town	v	Dawlish Town	3-3	72
	Dawlish Town	v	Clevedon Town	2-3	80
147	Swanage Town & Herston	v	Devizes Town	4-0	95
148	Barry Town	v	Minehead	2-1	276
149	Shortwood United	v	St Blazey	1-2	128
150	Cwmbran Town	v	Mangotsfield United	0-4	152
	(at Mangotsfield United)				
151	Maesteg Park	v	Sharpness		
	(Walk-over for Maesteg Park - Sharpness withdrawn				
152	Bridgend Town	v	Ton Pentre	2-1	61
153	Radstock Town	v	Weston-Super-Mare	0-3	120
154	Yate Town	v	Glastonbury	4-0	164
155	Ilfracombe Town	v	Barnstaple Town	4-0	220
156	Wimborne Town	v	Bideford	3-2	120
157	Tiverton Town	v	Welton Rovers	4-1	217
158	St Austell	v	Falmouth Town	0-4	210
159	Saltash United	v	Torrington	1-1	147
	Torrington	v	Saltash United	2-5	87

F.A. CUP 1990/1 FACTS

FIRST ROUND QUALIFYING - 15 SEPTEMBER 1990				RESULT	ATTENDANCE
1	Shildon	v	Cleator Moor Celtic	2-1	91
2	Alnwick Town	v	Fleetwood Town	0-5	80
3	North Shields	v	Gateshead	1-1	423
	Gateshead	v	North Shields	0-1	441
4	Durham City	v	Prudhoe East End	0-3	40
5	Accrington Stanley	v	West Auckland Town	3-0	537
6	Blyth Spartans	v	Bridlington Town	2-0	368
7	Billingham Town	v	Guisborough Town	1-2	150
8	Gretna	v	Norton & Stockton Ancients	5-1	169
9	Harrogate Railway	v	Murton	2-0	110
10	Ferryhill Athletic	v	South Bank	1-1	125
	South Bank	v	Ferryhill Athletic	1-0	105
11	Langley Park	v	Tow Law Town	2-1	144
12	Colne Dynamoes	v	Easington Colliery		
	(Walkover for Easington Colliery - Colne Dynamoes disbanded)				
13	Harrogate Town	v	Esh Winning	1-3	170
14	Stockton	v	Spennymoor United	0-2	145
	(at Spennymoor United)				
15	Northallerton Town	v	Billingham Synthonia	2-0	83
16	Workington	v	Horden CW	1-1	201
	Horden CW	v	Workington	2-1	159
17	Lancaster City	v	Darwen	1-0	194
18	Whitby Town	v	Newcastle Blue Star	4-7	275
19	Ryhope CA	v	Consett	1-2	33
20	Seaham Red Star	v	Evenwood Town	1-1	111
	Evenwood Town	v	Seaham Red Star	0-1	52
21	Vauxhall GM	v	Irlam Town	0-2	58
22	Morecambe	v	Horwich RMI	2-2	285
	Horwich RMI	v	Morecambe	3-0	249
23	Knowsley United	v	Colwyn Bay	0-0	313
	Colwyn Bay	v	Knowsley United	3-0	529
24	Caernarfon Town	v	Denaby United		
	(tie awarded to Caernarfon Town as Denaby United unable to fulfil fixture)				
25	Maine Road	v	Glossop	1-0	108
26	Altrincham	v	Rhyl	3-2	817
27	Farsley Celtic	v	Bangor City	0-0	157
	Bangor City	v	Farsley Celtic	3-0	298
28	Harworth CI	v	Atherton LR	1-2	30
29	Radcliffe Borough	v	Emley	0-0	280
	Emley	v	Radcliffe Borough	1-0 (aet)	478
30	Chorley	v	Mossley	4-0	470
31	Armthorpe Welfare	v	Southport	1-2	168
32	Ilkeston Town	v	Bootle	2-3	296
33	Eastwood Town	v	Hednesford Town	1-1	236
	Hednesford Town	v	Eastwood Town	1-1	470
	Eastwood Town	v	Hednesford Town	2-3	316
34	Oakham United	v	Hyde United	1-2	158
35	St Helens Town	v	Curzon Ashton	0-3	202
36	South Liverpool	v	Warrington Town	2-0	237
37	Leicester United	v	Rocester	1-0	248
38	Droylsden	v	Stalybridge Celtic	1-1	530
	Stalybridge Celtic	v	Droylsden	1-2	549
39	Willenhall Town	v	Marine	0-0	164
	Marine	v	Willenhall Town	2-2	245
	Marine	v	Willenhall Town	4-1	202
40	Worksop Town	v	Gresley Rovers	2-1	161
41	Paget Rangers	v	Princes End United	1-2	59
42	Frickley Athletic	v	Gainsborough Trinity	4-3	317
43	Nuneaton Borough	v	Goole Town	1-0	872
44	Blakenall	v	Rushall Olympic	3-2	319
45	Alvechurch	v	Wellingborough Town	4-1	129
46	Witton Albion	v	Congleton Town	2-0	611
47	Stratford Town	v	Buxton	1-4	164
48	Bilston Town	v	Wednesfield	6-0	145
49	Corby Town	v	Solihull Borough	3-0	295
50	West Midlands Police	v	Matlock Town	0-6	85
51	Hinckley Athletic	v	Grantham Town	2-1	219
52	Burton Albion	v	Halesowen Harriers	2-0	767
53	Brackley Town	v	Buckingham Town	1-1	303
	Buckingham Town	v	Brackley Town	1-1	376
	Buckingham Town	v	Brackley Town	2-0	401
54	Shepshed Charterhouse	v	Lye Town	3-1	362
55	Wolverton AFC	v	Atherstone United	2-2	200
	Atherstone United	v	Wolverton AFC	4-1	377
56	Racing Club Warwick	v	Evesham United	0-0	128
	Evesham United	v	Racing Club Warwick	5-1	486
57	Potton United	v	Stourbridge	1-1	106
	Stourbridge	v	Potton United	7-0	401
58	Bedworth United	v	Sutton Coldfield Town	1-5	131
59	Boston	v	Bromsgrove Rovers	0-3	95
60	March Town United	v	Sandwell Borough	1-1	154
	Sandwell Borough	v	March Town United	2-2	137
	Sandwell Borough	v	March Town United	1-0	125
61	Chalfont St Peter	v	Malvern Town	2-6	125
62	Moor Green	v	Tamworth	1-2	865
63	Barton Rovers	v	Redditch United	0-2	138
64	Histon	v	Rothwell Town	2-1	101
65	Boreham Wood	v	Baker Perkins	0-0	112
	Baker Perkins	v	Boreham Wood	1-2	120
66	Spalding United	v	Rushden Town	0-3	302
67	Haverhill Rovers	v	VS Rugby	1-1	214
	VS Rugby	v	Haverhill Rovers	5-0	475
68	Boston United	v	Lowestoft Town	7-0	1135
69	Wembley	v	Bourne Town	4-1	77
70	Sudbury Town	v	Heybridge Swifts	1-3	665
71	Newmarket Town	v	Cambridge City	1-2	437
72	Finchley	v	Great Yarmouth Town	1-2	60
73	Rayners Lane	v	Harlow Town	0-3	80
74	Ford United	v	St Albans City	3-1	116
75	Clapton	v	Barnet	0-2	764
	(at Dagenham FC - 16-9-90)				
76	Hitchin Town	v	Braintree Town	0-1	410
77	Cray Wanderers	v	Ruislip Manor	2-3	117
78	Metropolitan Police	v	Hendon	1-3	90
79	Saffron Walden Town	v	Wealdstone	0-4	270
80	Wivenhoe Town	v	Halstead Town	3-1	309
81	Chesham United	v	Hertford Town	0-0	265
	Hertford Town	v	Chesham United	1-5	210
82	Enfield	v	Barking	4-1	579
83	Walthamstow Pennant	v	Chelmsford City	0-3	240
84	Biggleswade Town	v	Hornchurch	2-2	53
	Hornchurch	v	Biggleswade Town	3-1	122
85	Hounslow	v	Basildon United	4-3	78
86	Stevenage Borough	v	Bishops Stortford	2-3	476
87	Barkingside	v	Redbridge Forest	1-3	174
88	Fisher Athletic	v	Harwich & Parkeston	0-0	157
	Harwich & Parkeston	v	Fisher Athletic	2-1	550
89	Banstead Athletic	v	Molesey	3-3	67
	Molesey	v	Banstead Athletic	2-0	76
90	Dagenham	v	Burnham	1-1	413
	Burnham	v	Dagenham	1-2	155
91	Corinthian Casuals	v	Grays Athletic	1-5	114
92	Beckenham Town	v	Flackwell Heath	0-2	110
93	Egham Town	v	Purfleet	2-1	93
94	Tilbury	v	Witney Town	1-1	76
	Witney Town	v	Tilbury	2-1	202
95	Edgware Town	v	Harrow Borough	1-0	401
96	Leyton Wingate	v	Billericay Town	0-0	176
	Billericay Town	v	Leyton Wingate	1-0	404
97	Andover	v	Horsham YMCA	3-0	251
98	Walton & Hersham	v	Bromley	2-3	376
99	Royston Town	v	Yeading	3-2	110
100	Marlow	v	Merstham	3-0	215
101	Tooting & Mitcham United	v	Horsham	0-0	180
	Horsham	v	Tooting & Mitcham United	1-2	368
102	Littlehampton Town	v	Dulwich Hamlet	2-0	264
103	Tonbridge	v	Hythe Town	3-1	429
104	Whyteleafe	v	Slade Green	2-1	139
105	Peacehaven & Telscombe	v	Southwick	4-1	338
106	Folkestone	v	Bognor Regis Town	1-2	260
107	Margate	v	Gravesend & Northfleet	2-2	651
	Gravesend & Northfleet	v	Margate	1-4	465
108	Redhill	v	Whitehawk	2-3	114
109	Pagham	v	Oakwood	4-0	103
110	Cove	v	Windsor & Eton	1-3	210
111	Sittingbourne	v	Whitstable Town	1-1	385
	Whitstable Town	v	Sittingbourne	1-4	435
112	Dover Athletic	v	Ashford Town	1-0	1210
113	Wick	v	Dorking	0-3	111
114	Carshalton Athletic	v	Erith & Belvedere	3-0	204
115	Eastbourne United	v	Crawley Town	0-2	180
116	Worthing	v	Chatham Town	3-0	206
117	Havant Town	v	Langney Sports	4-0	167
118	Kingstonian	v	Staines Town	2-1	571
119	Hampton	v	Hailsham Town	0-1	195
120	Herne Bay	v	Lewes	0-1	121
121	Salisbury	v	Hungerford Town	2-0	264
122	Bournemouth	v	Abingdon Town	2-1	50
123	Abingdon United	v	Farnborough Town	0-1	214
124	Slough Town	v	Feltham	8-0	436
125	Trowbridge Town	v	Newbury Town	3-0	398
126	Wycombe Wanderers	v	Maidenhead United	3-0	1910
127	Warminster Town	v	Wokingham Town	0-1	233
128	Chippenham Town	v	Lymington AFC	1-1	126
	Lymington AFC	v	Chippenham Town	1-0	100
129	Melksham Town	v	Calne Town	2-1	110
130	Waterlooville	v	Newport IOW	1-1	323
	Newport IOW	v	Waterlooville	3-0	758
131	Stroud	v	Gosport Borough	4-1	117
132	Chard Town	v	Romsey Town	4-4	107
	Romsey Town	v	Chard Town	3-0	117
133	Barry Town	v	Clevedon Town	0-0	263
	Clevedon Town	v	Barry Town	0-3	142
134	Mangotsfield United	v	Bashley	2-2	304
	Bashley	v	Mangotsfield United	6-3 (aet)	323
135	St Blazey	v	Weymouth	0-2	249
136	Taunton Town	v	Swanage Town & Herston	1-2	302
137	Weston-Super-Mare	v	Maesteg Park	2-2	189
	Maesteg Park	v	Weston-Super-Mare	0-4	78
138	Cheltenham Town	v	Exmouth Town	2-2	736
	Exmouth Town	v	Cheltenham Town	3-3	288
	Cheltenham Town	v	Exmouth Town	3-0	653
139	Yate Town	v	Worcester City	1-3	464
140	Bristol Manor Farm	v	Bridgend Town	1-1	47
	Bridgend Town	v	Bristol Manor Farm	3-0	82
141	Tiverton Town	v	Ilfracombe Town	5-1	266
142	Saltash United	v	Poole Town	1-1	215
	Poole Town	v	Saltash United	2-2	234
	Saltash United	v	Poole Town	3-1	243
143	Falmouth Town	v	Dorchester Town	2-4	362
144	Liskeard Athletic	v	Wimborne Town	5-2	92

FACTS

F.A. CUP 1990/1

	SECOND ROUND QUALIFYING - 29 SEPTEMBER 1990			RESULT	ATT
1	Shildon	v	Fleetwood Town	0-4	182
2	Prudhoe East End	v	North Shields	0-1	203
3	Accrington Stanley	v	Blyth Spartans	2-1	805
4	Gretna	v	Guisborough Town	2-2	176
	Guisborough Town	v	Gretna	1-3	413
5	Harrogate Railway	v	South Bank	1-0	135
6	Easington Collieries	v	Langley Park	1-1	38
	Langley Park	v	Easington Collieries	0-1	56
7	Esh Winning	v	Spennymoor United	1-3	100
8	Horden CW	v	Northallerton Town	0-3	77
9	Lancaster City	v	Newcastle Blue Star	0-2	245
10	Seaham Red Star	v	Consett	1-1	140
	Consett	v	Seaham Red Star	2-0	190
11	Irlam Town	v	Horwich RMI	1-3	91
12	Caernarfon Town	v	Colwyn Bay	2-6	273
13	Maine Road	v	Altrincham	0-1	875
14	Atherton LR	v	Bangor City	0-0	300
	Bangor City	v	Atherton LR	4-0	240
15	Emley	v	Chorley	0-1	502
16	Bootle	v	Southport	2-0	400
17	Hednesford Town	v	Hyde United	2-2	447
	Hyde United	v	Hednesford Town	5-2 (aet)	621
18	South Liverpool	v	Curzon Ashton *(28-9-90 7,30)*	1-0	192
19	Leicester United	v	Droylsden	0-0	244
	Droylsden	v	Leicester United	2-2	410
	Leicester United	v	Droylsden	4-3	375
20	Worksop Town	v	Marine	1-3	142
21	Princes End United	v	Frickley Athletic	0-4	102
22	Blakenall	v	Nuneaton Borough	3-3	402
	Nuneaton Borough	v	Blakenall	3-0	1021
23	Alvechurch	v	Witton Albion	2-7	229
24	Bilston Town	v	Buxton	2-1	160
25	Corby Town	v	Matlock Town	2-0	324
26	Burton Albion	v	Hinckley Athletic	4-0	823
27	Buckingham Town	v	Shepshed Charterhouse	2-4	183
28	Evesham United	v	Atherstone United	1-2	397
29	Stourbridge	v	Sutton Coldfield Town	1-2	258
30	Sandwell Borough	v	Bromsgrove Rovers	0-2	253
31	Malvern Town	v	Tamworth	3-3	429
	Tamworth	v	Malvern Town	5-1	1525
32	Histon	v	Redditch United	1-1	142
	Redditch United	v	Histon	1-0	265
33	Boreham Wood	v	Rushden Town	1-0	172
34	Boston United	v	VS Rugby	3-1	1245
35	Wembley	v	Heybridge Swifts	2-2	118
	Heybridge Swifts	v	Wembley	3-1 (aet)	280
36	Great Yarmouth Town	v	Cambridge City	0-4	223
37	Harlow Town	v	Ford United	1-0	147
38	Braintree Town	v	Barnet	0-2	1411
39	Ruislip Manor	v	Hendon	2-1	301
40	Wivenhoe Town	v	Wealdstone	0-0	403
	Wealdstone	v	Wivenhoe Town	2-1	539
41	Chesham United	v	Enfield	0-3	588
42	Hornchurch	v	Chelmsford City	1-2	354
43	Hounslow	v	Bishops Stortford	1-5	179
44	Harwich & Parkeston	v	Redbridge Forest	1-3	573
45	Molesey	v	Dagenham	1-2	
46	Flackwell Heath	v	Grays Athletic	2-2	155
	Grays Athletic	v	Flackwell Heath	2-0	336
47	Egham Town	v	Witney Town	1-0	119
48	Billericay Town	v	Edgware Town	1-0	433
49	Andover	v	Bromley	2-0	377
50	Marlow	v	Royston Town	2-2	280
	Royston Town	v	Marlow	0-2 (aet)	251
51	Tooting & Mitcham United	v	Littlehampton Town	1-2	220
52	Whyteleafe	v	Tonbridge	0-2	261
53	Peacehaven & Telscombe	v	Bognor Regis Town	3-1	397
54	Whitehawk	v	Margate	0-1	216
55	Pagham	v	Windsor & Eton	0-3	210
56	Dover Athletic	v	Sittingbourne	2-0	1121
57	Dorking	v	Carshalton Athletic	2-0	438
58	Worthing	v	Crawley Town	3-2	372
59	Havant Town	v	Kingstonian	0-4	367
60	Lewes	v	Hailsham Town	0-3	152
61	Salisbury	v	Bournemouth	4-0	501
62	Slough Town	v	Farnborough Town	2-3	925
63	Trowbridge Town	v	Wycombe Wanderers	0-0	839
	Wycombe Wanderers	v	Trowbridge Town	2-1 (aet)	1850
64	Lymington AFC	v	Wokingham Town	1-1	223
	Wokingham Town *(at Reading FC)*	v	Lymington AFC	2-1	266
65	Melksham Town	v	Newport (IOW)	0-2	150
66	Romsey Town	v	Stroud	1-0	176
67	Barry Town	v	Bashley	0-2	309
68	Swanage Town & Herston	v	Weymouth	1-1	295
	Weymouth	v	Swanage & Herston	2-1	746
69	Weston-Super-Mare	v	Cheltenham Town	0-2	454
70	Bridgend Town	v	Worcester City	1-7	150
71	Tiverton Town	v	Saltash United	4-2	189
72	Liskeard Athletic	v	Dorchester Town	5-1	181

THIRD ROUND QUALIFYING - 13 OCTOBER 1990

				RESULT	ATT
1	Fleetwood Town	v	North Shields	2-0	371
2	Accrington Stanley	v	Gretna	2-1	1121
3	Harrogate Railway	v	Easington Colliery	2-0	355
4	Spennymoor United	v	Northallerton Town	2-0	241
5	Newcastle Blue Star	v	Consett	3-0	180
6	Horwich RMI	v	Colwyn Bay	1-3	288
7	Altrincham	v	Bangor City	3-0	1033
8	Chorley	v	Bootle	6-2	452
9	Hyde United	v	South Liverpool	1-1	688
	South Liverpool	v	Hyde United	3-1	325
10	Leicester United	v	Marine	0-2	410
11	Frickley Athletic	v	Nuneaton Borough	1-0	654
12	Witton Albion	v	Bilston Town	4-0	841
13	Corby Town	v	Burton Albion	0-1	736
14	Shepshed Charterhouse	v	Atherstone United	2-3	664
15	Sutton Coldfield Town	v	Bromsgrove Rovers	0-0	512
	Bromsgrove Rovers	v	Sutton Coldfield Town	4-2 (aet)	1081
16	Tamworth	v	Redditch United	2-0	1682
17	Boreham Wood	v	Boston United	1-1	564
	Boston United	v	Boreham Wood	4-0	1456
18	Heybridge Swifts	v	Cambridge City	1-0	369
19	Harlow Town	v	Barnet	1-3	1937
20	Ruislip Manor	v	Wealdstone	1-0	854
21	Enfield	v	Chelmsford City	1-1	879
	Chelmsford City	v	Enfield	1-0	1442
22	Bishops Stortford	v	Redbridge Forest	2-1	485
23	Dagenham	v	Grays Athletic	3-1	1114
24	Egham Town	v	Billericay Town	1-1	318
	Billericay Town	v	Egham Town	1-2	771
25	Andover	v	Marlow	0-1	701
26	Littlehampton Town	v	Tonbridge	0-0	525
	Tonbridge	v	Littlehampton Town	2-3	778
27	Peacehaven & Telscombe	v	Margate	1-0	612
28	Windsor & Eton	v	Dover Athletic	1-1	710
	Dover Athletic	v	Windsor & Eton	3-0	1415
29	Dorking	v	Worthing	1-1	460
	Worthing	v	Dorking	2-4	560
30	Kingstonian	v	Hailsham Town	4-0	1032
31	Salisbury	v	Farnborough Town	0-3	937
32	Wycombe Wanderers	v	Wokingham Town	4-1	2319
33	Newport (IOW)	v	Romsey Town	0-1	919
34	Bashley	v	Weymouth	2-2	884
	Weymouth	v	Bashley	2-3	1043
35	Cheltenham Town	v	Worcester City	4-2	2007
36	Tiverton Town	v	Liskeard Athletic	1-0	306

FOURTH ROUND QUALIFYING - 27 OCTOBER 1990

				RESULT	ATT
1	Accrington Stanley	v	Fleetwood Town	0-2	2096
2	Marine	v	Stafford Rangers	1-1	620
	Stafford Rangers	v	Marine	2-1	1217
3	Frickley Athletic	v	Witton Albion	0-2	636
4	Macclesfield Town	v	Altrincham	2-2	1843
	Altrincham	v	Macclesfield Town	3-0	2306
5	Chorley	v	Harrogate Railway	3-1	530
6	Northwich Victoria	v	Spennymoor United	1-1	740
	Spennymoor United	v	Northwich Victoria	2-1 (aet)	769
7	Bishop Auckland	v	South Liverpool	1-0	496
8	Colwyn Bay	v	Whitley Bay	1-4	742
9	Runcorn	v	Newcastle Blue Star	1-0	693
10	Dagenham	v	Aylesbury United	0-2	805
11	Burton Albion	v	Tamworth	0-0	2913
	Tamworth	v	Burton Albion	3-2 (aet)	2545
12	Telford United	v	Egham Town	2-0	1137
13	Barnet	v	Heybridge Swifts	3-1	1813
14	Halesowen Town	v	Ruislip Manor	5-2	1406
15	Bishops Stortford	v	Atherstone United	0-1	626
16	Chelmsford City	v	Kettering Town	0-0	2265
	Kettering Town	v	Chelmsford City	1-2	3292
17	Bromsgrove Rovers	v	Kidderminster Harriers	1-2	2372
18	Dartford	v	Boston United	1-1	805
	Boston United	v	Dartford	2-1 (aet)	1774
19	Yeovil Town	v	Marlow	3-1	2560
20	Farnborough Town	v	Gloucester City	4-1	838
21	Romsey Town	v	Littlehampton Town	1-2	586
22	Tiverton Town	v	Peacehaven & Telscombe	3-2	802
23	Woking	v	Bath City	2-1	2029
24	Wycombe Wanderers	v	Basingstoke Town	6-0	2203
25	Hayes	v	Kingstonian	2-0	759
26	Welling United	v	Bashley	1-0	1177
27	Dover Athletic	v	Merthyr Tydfil	0-0	1801
	Merthyr Tydfil	v	Dover Athletic	2-0	1050
28	Dorking	v	Cheltenham Town	2-3	903

FACTS

F.A. CUP 1990/1

FIRST ROUND PROPER - 17 NOVEMBER 1990				RESULT	ATT
1	Lincoln City	v	Crewe Alexandra	1-4	3596
2	Preston North End	v	Mansfield Town	0-1	5230
3	Chorley	v	Bury	2-1	2834
4	Witton Albion	v	Bolton Wanderers	1-2	3790
5	Bishop Auckland	v	Barrow	0-1	1645
6	Stafford Rangers	v	Burnley	1-3	4117
7	Halesowen Town	v	Tranmere Rovers	1-2	3699
8	Atherstone United	v	Fleetwood Town	3-1	1422
9	Darlington	v	York City	1-1	4638
	York City	v	Darlington	1-0	4035
10	Rochdale	v	Scunthorpe United	1-1	3259
	Scunthorpe United	v	Rochdale	2-1	3761
11	Runcorn	v	Hartlepool United	0-3	1675
12	Bradford City	v	Shrewsbury Town	0-0	6629
	Shrewsbury Town	v	Bradford City	2-1	3708
13	Chester City	v	Doncaster Rovers	2-2	1749
	Doncaster Rovers	v	Chester City	1-2 (aet)	3543
14	Tamworth	v	Whitley Bay	4-6	2600
15	Scarborough	v	Leek Town	0-2	1589
16	Halifax Town	v	Wrexham	3-2	2002
17	Blackpool	v	Grimsby Town	2-0	4175
18	Telford United	v	Stoke City	0-0	3709
	Stoke City	v	Telford United	1-0	11985
19	Chesterfield	v	Spennymoor United	3-2	4142
20	Altrincham	v	Huddersfield Town	1-2	3000
21	Rotherham United	v	Stockport County	1-0	4471
22	Wigan Athletic	v	Carlisle United	5-0	3947
23	AFC Bournemouth	v	Gillingham	2-1	6113
24	Birmingham City	v	Cheltenham Town	1-0	7942
25	Fulham	v	Farnborough Town	2-1	4990
26	Swansea City	v	Welling United	5-2	3156
27	Barnet	v	Chelmsford City	2-2	3217
	Chelmsford City	v	Barnet	0-2	2612
28	Brentford	v	Yeovil Town	5-0	4893
29	Colchester United	v	Reading	2-1	3761
30	Littlehampton Town	v	Northampton Town	0-4	3540
31	Hereford United	v	Peterborough United	1-1	4209
	Peterborough United	v	Hereford United	2-1	4179
32	Aldershot	v	Tiverton Town	6-2	2706
33	Aylesbury United	v	Walsall	0-1	3366
34	Maidstone United	v	Torquay United	4-1	2303
35	Leyton Orient	v	Southend United	3-2	6095
36	Boston United	v	Wycombe Wanderers	1-1	2755
	Wycombe Wanderers	v	Boston United	4-0	4954
37	Merthyr Tydfil	v	Sutton United	1-1	1279
	Sutton United	v	Merthyr Tydfil	0-1	1934
38	Exeter City	v	Cambridge United	1-2	4714
39	Woking	v	Kidderminster Harriers	0-0	3249
	Kidderminster Harriers	v	Woking	1-1	2827
	Kidderminster Harriers	v	Woking	1-2	3015
40	Cardiff City	v	Hayes	0-0	1844
	Hayes	v	Cardiff City	1-0	4312
	(at Brentford FC)				

SECOND ROUND PROPER - 8 DECEMBER 1990

				MATCH DATE	ATT
1	Shrewsbury Town	v	Chorley	1-0	3380
2	Rotherham United	v	Halifax Town	1-1	2986
	Halifax Town	v	Rotherham United	1-2	2132
3	Mansfield Town	v	York City	2-1	3800
4	Scunthorpe United	v	Tranmere Rovers	3-2	3576
5	Burnley	v	Stoke City	2-0	12954
6	Leek Town	v	Chester City	1-1	3048
	Chester City	v	Leek Town	4-0	2420
7	Wigan Athletic	v	Hartlepool United	2-0	2492
8	Chesterfield	v	Bolton Wanderers	3-4	4836
9	Crewe Alexandra	v	Atherstone United	1-0	4113
10	Huddersfield Town	v	Blackpool	0-2	6329
11	Whitley Bay	v	Barrow	0-1	2522
12	Woking	v	Merthyr Tydfil	5-1	4188
13	Birmingham City	v	Brentford	1-3	5072
14	Wycombe Wanderers	v	Peterborough United	1-1	5695
	Peterborough United	v	Wycombe Wanderers	2-0	5692
15	Aldershot	v	Maidstone United	2-1	3404
16	Swansea City	v	Walsall	2-1	3744
17	Colchester United	v	Leyton Orient	0-0	6150
	Leyton Orient	v	Colchester United	4-1	4623
18	Barnet	v	Northampton Town	0-0	5022
	Northampton Town	v	Barnet	0-1	5837
19	AFC Bournemouth	v	Hayes	1-0	6510
20	Fulham	v	Cambridge United	0-0	5929
	Cambridge United	v	Fulham	2-1	4996

FACTS

F.A. CUP 1990/1

THIRD ROUND PROPER - 5 JANUARY 1991				RESULT	ATT
1	Oldham Athletic	v	Brentford	3-1	12588
2	Wolverhampton Wanderers	v	Cambridge United	0-1	15100
3	Chelsea	v	Oxford United	1-3	14586
4	Sheffield United	v	Luton Town	1-3	13958
5	Shrewsbury Town	v	Watford	4-1	5327
6	Bristol Rovers	v	Crewe Alexandra	0-2	6242
7	Charlton Athletic	v	Everton	1-2	12234
8	Crystal Palace	v	Nottingham Forest	0-0	15396
	Nottingham Forest	v	Crystal Palace	2-2	23201
	Nottingham Forest	v	Crystal Palace	3-0	22164
9	Aston Villa	v	Wimbledon	1-1	19305
	Wimbledon	v	Aston Villa	1-0 (aet)	7496
10	Mansfield Town	v	Sheffield Wednesday	0-2	9076
11	Brighton & Hove Albion	v	Scunthorpe United	3-2	7785
12	Manchester United	v	Queens Park Rangers	2-1	35065
13	Port Vale	v	Peterborough United	2-1	7490
14	Aldershot	v	West Ham United	0-0	22929
	(at West Ham United FC)				
	West Ham United	v	Aldershot	6-1	21484
15	Blackpool	v	Tottenham Hotspur	0-1	9151
16	Chester City	v	AFC Bournemouth	2-3	1833
17	Blackburn Rovers	v	Liverpool	1-1	18584
	Liverpool	v	Blackburn Rovers	3-0	34175
18	Arsenal	v	Sunderland	2-1	35128
19	Millwall	v	Leicester City	2-1	10766
20	Barnet	v	Portsmouth	0-5	6209
21	Southampton	v	Ipswich Town	3-2	15101
22	Barnsley	v	Leeds United	1-1	22424
	Leeds United	v	Barnsley	4-0	21377
23	Leyton Orient	v	Swindon Town	1-1	6697
	Swindon Town	v	Leyton Orient	1-0	7395
	(after abandoned tie, 1-1 56 mins, 8579 frozen pitch)				
24	West Bromwich Albion	v	Woking	2-4	14516
25	Hull City	v	Notts County	2-5	6655
26	Middlesbrough	v	Plymouth Argyle	0-0	13042
	Plymouth Argyle	v	Middlesbrough	1-2	6956
27	Norwich City	v	Bristol City	2-1	12630
28	Coventry City	v	Wigan Athletic	1-1	10777
	Wigan Athletic	v	Coventry City	0-1	7429
29	Bolton Wanderers	v	Barrow	1-0	11475
30	Burnley	v	Manchester City	0-1	20331
31	Newcastle United	v	Derby County	2-0	19714
32	Swansea City	v	Rotherham United	0-0	6478
	Rotherham United	v	Swansea City	4-0	4233

FOURTH ROUND PROPER - 26 JANUARY 1991

				RESULT	ATT
1	Woking *(at Everton FC)*	v	Everton	0-1	34705
2	Newcastle United	v	Nottingham Forest	2-2	29231
	Nottingham Forest	v	Newcastle United	3-0	28962
3	Luton Town	v	West Ham United	1-1	16283*
	West Ham United	v	Luton Town	5-0	25659
4	Shrewsbury Town	v	Wimbledon	1-0	8269
5	Arsenal	v	Leeds United	0-0	30900
	Leeds United	v	Arsenal	1-1	27753
	Arsenal	v	Leeds United	0-0	30433
	Leeds United	v	Arsenal	1-2	27170
6	Liverpool	v	Brighton & Hove Albion	2-2	32670
	Brighton & Hove Albion	v	Liverpool	2-3 (aet)	14440
7	Norwich City	v	Swindon Town	3-1	14408
8	Cambridge United	v	Middlesbrough	2-0	9531
9	Notts County	v	Oldham Athletic	2-0	14002
10	Tottenham Hotspur	v	Oxford United	4-2	31665
11	Manchester United	v	Bolton Wanderers	1-0	43293
12	Port Vale	v	Manchester City	1-2	19132
13	Millwall	v	Sheffield Wednesday	4-4	13663
	Sheffield Wednesday	v	Millwall	2-0	25140
14	Portsmouth	v	AFC Bournemouth	5-1	15800
15	Crewe Alexandra	v	Rotherham United	1-0	6057
16	Coventry City	v	Southampton	1-1	14112
	Southampton	v	Coventry City	2-0	17001

(* inc 4169 on CCTV at West Ham)

F.A. TROPHY 1990/1

FIRST ROUND QUALIFYING - 22 SEPTEMBER 1990				RESULT	ATT
1	Easington Colliery	v	Durham City	4-1	40
2	Accrington Stanley	v	Whitley Bay	3-2	402
3	Ferryhill Athletic	v	North Shields	0-0	91
	North Shields	v	Ferryhill Athletic	0-2	125
4	Stockton	v	Fleetwood Town	1-4	73
5	Emley	v	Southport	2-1	302
6	Consett	v	Whitby Town	2-1	105
7	South Liverpool	v	Brandon United	3-1	109
8	Whickham	v	Alnwick Town	0-1	58
9	Morecambe	v	Workington	3-0	236
10	Horwich RMI	v	Alfreton Town	1-0	136
11	Congleton Town	v	Newtown	3-1	98
12	Moor Green	v	Hednesford Town	1-0	304
13	Winsford United	v	Droylsden	1-4	150
14	Alvechurch	v	Mossley	0-1	140
15	Halesowen Town	v	Colwyn Bay	1-3	1157
16	Gainsborough Trinity	v	Worksop Town	2-0	453
17	Rhyl	v	Goole Town	1-0	249
18	Stalybridge Celtic	v	Shepshed Charterhouse	1-0	308
19	Grantham Town	v	Atherstone United	0-1	325
20	Redditch United	v	Eastwood Town	1-0	163
21	Bedworth United	v	Willenhall Town	4-0	141
22	Matlock Town	v	Buxton	3-2	458
23	Caernarfon Town	v	Leicester United	0-1	150
24	Cambridge City	v	Chalfont St Peter	3-0	283
25	Sutton Coldfield Town	v	Boreham Wood	2-2	170
	Boreham Wood	v	Sutton Coldfield Town	1-1	175
	Boreham Wood	v	Sutton Coldfield Town	1-1	217
	Sutton Coldfield Town	v	Boreham Wood	1-0	192
26	Burnham	v	Wembley	2-2	134
	Wembley	v	Burnham	3-1 (aet)	76
27	Bishops Stortford	v	Rushden Town	2-1	414
28	Chelmsford City	v	Tamworth	0-1	724
29	Uxbridge	v	Stourbridge	1-1	139
	Stourbridge	v	Uxbridge	0-2	403
30	Marlow	v	Aveley	2-1	175
31	Yeading	v	Bury Town	3-1	140
32	Barking	v	Witney Town	4-1	67
33	St Albans City	v	Chesham United	0-4	304
34	Banbury United	v	VS Rugby	1-5	343
35	Grays Athletic	v	Heybridge Swifts	1-0	339
36	Staines Town	v	Harlow Town	0-3	204
37	Corby Town	v	Hayes	0-1	243
38	Whyteleafe	v	Tooting & Mitcham United	0-1	209
39	Fareham Town	v	Worthing	3-0	157
40	Basingstoke Town	v	Molesey	1-1	271
	Molesey	v	Basingstoke Town	1-0	120
41	Crawley Town	v	Hampton	0-0	343
	Hampton	v	Crawley Town	2-2	208
	Crawley Town	v	Hampton	4-2	402
42	Walton & Hersham	v	Lewes	2-0	140
43	Andover	v	Canterbury City	1-1	196
	Canterbury City	v	Andover	2-3 (aet)	166
44	Dulwich Hamlet	v	Bromley	0-0	348
	Bromley	v	Dulwich Hamlet	4-1	581
45	Gosport Borough	v	Bashley	2-1	312
46	Bognor Regis Town	v	Erith & Belvedere	5-2	255
47	Dorking	v	Waterlooville	2-1	257
48	Ashford Town	v	Southwick	1-1	287
	Southwick	v	Ashford Town	1-0	193
49	Croydon	v	Folkestone	5-3	86
50	Bridgend Town	v	Bideford	2-2	25
	Bideford	v	Bridgend Town	0-2	185
51	Dorchester Town	v	Taunton Town	3-0	663
52	Barry Town	v	Saltash United	5-0	224
53	Cwmbran Town	v	Maesteg Park	1-0	66
54	Weston-Super-Mare	v	Newport AFC	0-0	494
	Newport AFC	v	Weston-Super-Mare	3-1	1011
55	Gloucester City	v	Ton Pentre	2-2	551
	Ton Pentre	v	Gloucester City	0-2	381
56	Stroud	v	Poole Town	3-0	124

F.A. TROPHY 1990/1

FACTS

SECOND ROUND QUALIFYING - 20 OCTOBER 1990			RESULT	ATT
1 Accrington Stanley	v	Easington Colliery	2-1	602
2 Consett	v	Alnwick Town	1-1	97
Alnwick Town	v	Consett	1-0 (aet)	121
3 Shildon	v	Morecambe	0-3	159
4 Ferryhill Athletic	v	Emley	0-0	145
Emley	v	Ferryhill Athletic	4-1	438
5 South Liverpool *(at Marine)*	v	Fleetwood Town	0-1	175
6 Congleton Town	v	Radcliffe Borough	1-0	157
7 Redditch United	v	Bedworth United	1-2	142
8 Stalybridge Celtic	v	Colwyn Bay	0-1	321
9 Droylsden	v	Matlock Town	3-3	210
Matlock Town	v	Droylsden	0-2	555
10 Gainsborough Trinity	v	Moor Green	1-3	319
11 Horwich RMI	v	Rhyl	3-2	136
12 Leicester United	v	Dudley Town	5-2	254
13 Mossley	v	Atherstone United	1-3	272
14 Sutton Coldfield Town	v	Baldock Town	2-1	217
15 VS Rugby	v	Grays Athletic	1-1	588
Grays Athletic	v	VS Rugby	0-2	407
16 Barking	v	Uxbridge	1-2	95
17 Bishops Stortford	v	Harlow Town	2-3	585
18 Marlow	v	Wembley	5-0	309
19 Cambridge City	v	Yeading	1-1	277
Yeading	v	Cambridge City	2-1	180
20 Hayes	v	Hitchin Town	1-1	304
Hitchin Town	v	Hayes	1-2	482
21 Tamworth	v	Chesham United	1-2	1188
22 Gosport Borough	v	Crawley Town	1-1	234
Crawley Town	v	Gosport Borough	0-1 (aet)	449
23 Andover	v	Salisbury	1-2	593
24 Dorking	v	Tooting & Mitcham United	2-2	306
Tooting & Mitcham United	v	Dorking	0-1	324
25 Fareham Town	v	Bognor Regis Town	0-2	254
26 Walton & Hersham	v	Croydon	6-0	172
27 Margate	v	Bromley	2-1	462
28 Southwick	v	Molesey	0-3	150
29 Gloucester City	v	Llanelli	3-0	638
30 Cwmbran Town	v	Dorchester Town	1-1	125
Dorchester Town	v	Cwmbran Town	4-1	616
31 Barry Town	v	Bridgend Town	4-0	294
32 Newport AFC	v	Stroud	0-3	886

F.A. TROPHY 1990/1

THIRD ROUND QUALIFYING - 1 DECEMBER 1990				RESULT	ATT
1	Emley	v	Morecambe	2-1	367
2	Spennymoor United	v	Chorley	0-0	239
	Chorley	v	Spennymoor United	1-0	343
3	Frickley Athletic	v	Seaham Red Star	2-0	230
4	South Bank	v	Blyth Spartans	2-2	103
	Blyth Spartans	v	South Bank	1-1	420
	South Bank	v	Blyth Spartans	2-0	175
5	Bishop Auckland	v	Newcastle Blue Star	3-1	281
6	Tow Law Town	v	Alnwick Town	2-1	119
7	Fleetwood Town	v	Marine	2-0	339
8	Guisborough Town	v	Accrington Stanley	4-1	245
9	Colwyn Bay	v	Witton Albion	1-3	603
10	Boston United	v	Leicester United	3-2	1054
11	Droylsden	v	Bromsgrove Rovers	3-3	390
	Bromsgrove Rovers	v	Droylsden	1-3 (aet)	762
12	Nuneaton Borough	v	Burton Albion	1-2	1261
13	Sutton Coldfield Town	v	Horwich RMI	1-3	154
14	Congleton Town	v	Moor Green	0-3	210
15	Bedworth United	v	Bangor City	1-1	139
	Bangor City	v	Bedworth United	1-2	275
16	Dagenham	v	Enfield	0-1	556
17	Margate	v	VS Rugby	1-1	483
	VS Rugby	v	Margate	5-0	543
18	Leyton-Wingate	v	Wealdstone	0-1	363
19	Harrow Borough	v	Fisher Athletic	0-2	211
20	Hayes	v	Kingstonian	3-2	401
21	Metropolitan Police	v	Harlow Town	3-2	82
22	Yeading	v	Molesey	0-1	125
23	Atherstone United	v	Wivenhoe Town	0-2	577
24	Gravesend & Northfleet	v	Hendon	3-0	311
25	Marlow	v	Chesham United	1-2	475
26	Bognor Regis Town	v	Worcester City	3-0	280
27	Stroud	v	Uxbridge	3-1	122
28	Walton & Hersham	v	Windsor & Eton	0-1	326
29	Weymouth	v	Gloucester City	1-1	684
	Gloucester City	v	Weymouth	3-0	682
30	Dorking	v	Gosport Borough	2-1	219
31	Carshalton Athletic	v	Dorchester Town	5-0	335
32	Barry Town	v	Salisbury	0-0	337
	Salisbury	v	Barry Town	1-0	342

F.A. TROPHY 1990/1 **FACTS**

FIRST ROUND PROPER - 12 JANUARY 1991				RESULT	ATT
1	Northwich Victoria	v	Tow Law Town	2-1	561
2	South Bank	v	Bishop Auckland	1-0	300
3	Horwich RMI	v	Bedworth United	2-0	164
4	Guisborough Town	v	Witton Albion	2-2	414
	Witton Albion	v	Guisborough Town	2-1	965
5	Runcorn	v	Boston United	2-0	853
6	Droylsden	v	Fleetwood Town	2-1	384
7	Hyde United	v	Stafford Rangers	1-2	680
	(tie awarded to Hyde United as Stafford Rangers played an ineligible player)				
8	Burton Albion	v	Moor Green	3-0	1300
9	Barrow	v	Chorley	2-0	1523
10	Macclesfield Town	v	Gretna	0-2	1060
11	Gateshead	v	Billingham Synthonia	2-2	487
	Billingham Synthonia	v	Gateshead	0-3	585
12	Leek Town	v	Altrincham	0-4	1054
13	Telford United	v	Emley	0-0	1240
	Emley	v	Telford United	1-0	1331
14	Barnet	v	Farnborough Town	2-3	1016
15	Slough Town	v	Bath City	2-4	860
16	Wokingham Town	v	Wivenhoe Town	1-2	542
17	Kidderminster Harriers	v	Sutton United	4-2	1201
18	Carshalton Athletic	v	Dartford	0-0	552
	Dartford	v	Carshalton Athletic	1-1	572
	Carshalton Athletic	v	Dartford	2-3 (aet)	411
19	Enfield	v	Chesham United	1-0	618
20	Dover Athletic	v	Dorking	1-0	1125
21	Gloucester City	v	Yeovil Town	1-0	1368
22	Gravesend & Northfleet	v	Cheltenham Town	2-2	523
	Cheltenham Town	v	Gravesend & Northfleet	5-1	610
23	Fisher Athletic	v	Redbridge Forest	1-2	420
24	Salisbury	v	VS Rugby	1-4	542
25	Wycombe Wanderers	v	Wealdstone	1-0	2692
26	Windsor & Eton	v	Colchester United	0-1	727
27	Bognor Regis Town	v	Aylesbury United	2-4	503
28	Molesey	v	Merthyr Tydfil	1-1	378
	Merthyr Tydfil	v	Molesey	1-0	684
29	Welling United	v	Hayes	3-1	1004
30	Kettering Town	v	Woking	2-0	4021
31	Stroud	v	Metropolitan Police	2-2	113
	Metropolitan Police	v	Stroud	0-2	183

Bye for Frickley Athletic

SECOND ROUND PROPER - 2 FEBRUARY 1991				RESULT	ATT
1	Dartford	v	Cheltenham Town	0-2	559
2	Colchester United	v	Runcorn	2-0	2348
3	Kidderminster Harriers	v	Dover Athletic	1-0	1455
4	Merthyr Tydfil	v	Gloucester City	1-3	752
5	Hyde United	v	Emley	0-0	1041
	Emley	v	Hyde United	3-2	1348
6	Welling United	v	Aylesbury United	2-1	1117
7	Farnborough Town	v	Bath City	1-3	621
8	Barrow	v	Kettering Town	0-0	3033
	Kettering Town	v	Barrow	2-1 (aet)	2522
9	VS Rugby	v	Wycombe Wanderers	0-1	1835
10	Northwich Victoria	v	Droylsden	4-1	737
11	Horwich RMI	v	Gretna	2-1	313
12	Enfield	v	Wivenhoe Town	0-2	608
13	Witton Albion	v	South Bank	3-2	843
14	Redbridge Forest	v	Frickley Athletic	2-1	326
15	Altrincham	v	Gateshead	3-1	1191
16	Stroud	v	Burton Albion	3-2	680

FACTS

F.A. TROPHY 1990/1

THIRD ROUND PROPER - 23 FEBRUARY 1991

				RESULT	ATT
1	Horwich RMI	v	Redbridge Forest	2-1	409
2	Witton Albion	v	Gloucester City	3-0	1162
3	Welling United	v	Altrincham	1-2	1344
4	Colchester United	v	Wivenhoe Town	3-0	4923
5	Emley	v	Kettering Town	3-2	2726
6	Kidderminster Harriers	v	Bath City	3-1	1412
7	Northwich Victoria	v	Stroud	2-0	683
8	Wycombe Wanderers	v	Cheltenham Town	2-1	3143

FOURTH ROUND PROPER - 16 MARCH 1991

				RESULT	ATT
1	Colchester United	v	Witton Albion	0-2	3079
2	Kidderminster Harriers	v	Emley	3-0	2408
3	Altrincham	v	Horwich RMI	5-0	1486
4	Northwich Victoria	v	Wycombe Wanderers	2-3	1968

FA CHALLENGE TROPHY COMPETITION
SEMI-FINAL TIES

First Leg - 6 April 1991				RESULT	ATT
1	Kidderminster Harriers Whitehouse 86	v	Witton Albion	1-0	2865
2	Wycombe Wanderers Carroll 12 Scott 72	v	Altrincham Rowlands 5	2-1	5248

Second Leg - 13 April 1991

1	Witton Albion Thomas 22, 73 (pen) Grimshaw 91 McClusky 120	v	Kidderminster Harriers Weir 36 Howell 105 Hadly 111	4-3 (aet)	3800
2	Altrincham	v	Wycombe Wanderers West 65 Scott 90 (pen)	0-2	3500

Wycombe Wanderers beat Altrincham 4-1 on aggregate

Witton Albion drew with Kidderminster Harriers 4-4 on aggregate

Replay

Kidderminster Harriers Hadley 50 Forsyth 89	v	Witton Albion Thomas 24	2-1	3277

Tuesday 16 April 1991, at Stafford Rangers FC, kick-off 7,45

FINAL Saturday 11th May 1991 at Wembley

WYCOMBE WANDERERS Scott 16, West 64	v.	KIDDERMINSTER HARRIERS Hadley 60	2-1	34,842

NORTH WEST COUNTIES LEAGUE

First Division

	P	W	D	L	F	A	Pts.
KNOWSLEY UNITED	36	25	8	3	95	37	83
COLWYN BAY	36	22	10	4	85	32	76
ASHTON UNITED	36	20	7	9	80	45	67
EASTWOOD HANLEY	36	16	12	8	42	29	60
VAUXHALL G.M.	36	15	10	11	42	36	55
PRESCOT	36	13	12	11	57	55	51
FLIXTON	36	14	7	15	48	72	49
ST. HELENS TOWN	36	13	9	14	52	47	48
MAINE ROAD	36	13	9	14	58	61	48
SKELMERSDALE UNITED	36	12	11	13	56	49	47
NANTWICH TOWN	36	13	8	15	43	56	47
LEYLAND DAF	36	12	10	14	51	53	46
BOOTLE	36	10	9	17	55	64	39
BACUP BOROUGH	36	9	12	15	38	47	39
CLITHEROE	36	10	8	18	50	63	38
DARWEN	36	9	11	16	44	62	38
PENRITH	36	10	8	18	41	65	38
ATHERTON L.R.	36	9	11	16	42	68	38
SALFORD CITY	36	6	10	20	30	68	28

Second Division

	P	W	D	L	F	A	Pts.
GREAT HARWOOD TOWN	34	27	5	2	81	22	86
BLACKPOOL ROVERS	34	25	4	5	84	33	76
BRADFORD PARK AVENUE	34	20	9	5	72	41	69
BAMBER BRIDGE	34	20	6	8	78	46	66
BLACKPOOL MECHANICS	34	18	7	9	51	30	61
NEWCASTLE TOWN	34	16	12	6	48	30	60
CHEADLE TOWN	34	17	3	14	55	54	54
GLOSSOP	34	12	10	12	47	42	46
BURSCOUGH	34	12	8	14	39	51	44
WESTHOUGHTON TOWN	34	11	10	13	50	64	43
CASTLETON GABRIELS	34	11	9	14	42	47	42
CHADDERTON	34	10	6	18	51	61	36
MAGHULL	34	9	8	17	37	54	35
KIDSGROVE ATHLETIC	34	7	10	17	37	65	31
ASHTON TOWN	34	9	2	23	43	86	29
OLDHAM TOWN	34	8	4	22	35	66	25
FORMBY	34	5	9	20	46	63	24
ATHERTON COLLIERIES	34	6	4	24	37	78	22

NORTHERN COUNTIES EAST LEAGUE

Premier Division

	P	W	D	L	F	A	Pts.
GUISELEY	30	24	4	2	78	25	76
NORTH SHIELDS	30	23	2	5	75	29	71
SPENNYMOOR UNITED	30	19	4	7	55	29	61
NORTH FERRIBY UNITED	30	14	8	8	55	42	50
BRIGG TOWN	30	13	8	9	40	40	47
MALTBY M.W.	30	13	7	10	44	46	46
HARROGATE RAILWAY	30	12	9	9	49	40	45
OSSETT TOWN	30	10	10	10	42	38	40
ARMTHORPE WELFARE	30	10	6	14	52	55	36
WINTERTON RANGERS	30	9	9	12	49	65	36
THACKLEY	30	9	7	14	43	46	34
SUTTON TOWN	30	9	6	15	53	60	33
BELPER TOWN	30	7	10	13	37	52	31
OSSETT ALBION	30	3	12	15	34	51	21
DENABY UNITED	30	5	6	19	33	81	21
PONTEFRACT COLLIERIES	30	4	4	22	34	74	16

Division One

	P	W	D	L	F	A	Pts.
SHEFFIELD	24	21	1	2	60	16	64
HALLAM	24	18	1	5	61	27	55
LIVERSEDGE	24	15	2	7	61	35	47
PICKERING TOWN	24	15	2	7	54	41	47
ECCLESHILL UNITED	24	14	2	8	58	36	44
GARFORTH TOWN	24	11	7	6	45	33	40
SELBY TOWN	24	10	3	11	60	41	33
HATFIELD MAIN	24	9	5	10	38	42	32
R.E.S. PARKGATE	24	7	6	11	40	49	27
YORK RAILWAY INSTITUTE	24	7	3	14	32	47	24
GLASSHOUGHTON WELFARE	24	4	5	15	18	50	17
YORKSHIRE MAIN	24	3	0	21	16	81	9
MEXBOROUGH TOWN	24	3	0	21	16	81	9

NORTHERN LEAGUE

First Division

	P	W	D	L	F	A	Pts.
GRETNA	38	30	5	3	86	23	95
GUISBOROUGH TOWN	38	21	12	5	79	43	75
BLYTH SPARTANS	38	20	8	10	80	50	68
BILLINGHAM SYNTHONIA	38	20	8	10	72	43	68
CONSETT	38	19	11	8	67	43	68
WHITBY TOWN	38	16	13	9	66	49	61
TOW LAW TOWN	38	16	10	12	65	64	58
FERRYHILL ATHLETIC	38	16	9	13	55	50	54
NORTHALLERTON TOWN	38	14	11	13	50	46	53
NEWCASTLE BLUE STAR	38	13	13	12	59	48	52
SEAHAM RED STAR	38	12	12	14	44	46	48
SOUTH BANK	38	9	16	13	40	43	43
MURTON	38	10	11	17	47	59	41
SHILDON	38	10	9	19	49	75	39
WHICKAM	38	10	9	19	44	71	39
PETERLEE	38	7	17	14	57	65	38
BRANDON UNITED	38	9	11	18	44	70	38
STOCKTON	38	10	6	22	40	79	36
ALNWICK TOWN	38	7	10	21	40	78	31
DURHAM CITY	38	6	9	23	47	86	27

Second Division

	P	W	D	L	F	A	Pts.
WEST AUCKLAND TOWN	36	24	7	5	72	39	79
LANGLEY PARK	36	24	4	8	83	40	76
EASINGTON COLLIERY	36	20	8	8	80	42	68
HEBBURN	36	22	5	9	89	56	68
BILLINGHAM TOWN	36	21	5	10	69	39	68
EVENWOOD TOWN	36	20	8	8	69	40	65
ESH WINNING	36	19	6	11	77	57	63
PRUDHOE EAST END	36	16	10	10	71	46	58
NORTON & STOCKTON ANCIENTS	36	16	3	17	60	67	51
DARLINGTON CLEVELAND BDGE'	36	14	7	15	53	60	49
BEDLINGTON TERRIERS	36	14	6	16	60	73	48
ASHINGTON	36	14	6	16	47	68	48
CROOK TOWN	36	13	8	15	57	64	47
RYHOPE C.A.	36	13	4	19	54	57	43
SHOTTON COMRADES	36	7	9	20	43	73	30
CHESTER LE STREET TOWN	36	6	11	19	45	68	29
WASHINGTON	36	7	6	23	44	79	27
WILLINGTON	36	4	9	23	34	77	21
HORDEN C.W.	36	2	10	24	37	99	16

LEAGUE TABLES - FEEDERS TO ISTHMIAN LEAGUE

COMBINED COUNTIES LEAGUE

	P	W	D	L	F	A	Pts.
FARNHAM TOWN	32	24	4	4	88	29	76
CHIPSTEAD	32	24	2	6	87	27	74
MALDEN TOWN	32	22	6	4	74	33	72
MERSTHAM	32	19	6	7	67	41	63
ASHFORD TOWN (MIDDX.)	32	15	9	8	57	38	54
FARLEIGH ROVERS	32	15	7	10	65	50	52
BEDFONT	32	15	4	13	46	44	49
ASH UNITED	32	13	8	11	45	43	47
FRIMLEY GREEN	32	12	5	15	53	64	41
COBHAM	32	11	6	15	46	51	39
WESTFIELD	32	11	5	16	60	63	38
STEYNING TOWN	32	10	6	16	47	56	36
GODALMING TOWN	32	9	7	16	35	47	34
HARTLEY WINTNEY	32	8	5	19	29	64	29
CRANLEIGH	32	7	6	19	36	69	27
HORLEY TOWN	32	7	4	21	37	85	25
SANDHURST TOWN	32	1	8	23	22	90	11

ESSEX SENIOR LEAGUE

	P	W	D	L	F	A	Pts.
SOUTHEND MANOR	28	20	4	4	52	20	64
BRENTWOOD	28	18	6	4	66	30	60
BURNHAM RAMBLERS	28	17	8	3	57	30	59
SAWBRIDGEWORTH TOWN	28	15	5	8	47	26	50
BOWERS UNITED	28	14	7	7	50	32	49
STAMBRIDGE	28	13	5	10	50	38	44
FORD UNITED	28	13	4	11	47	33	43
EAST THURROCK UNITED	28	11	9	8	46	38	42
CANVEY ISLAND	28	9	7	13	34	47	34
STANSTED	28	7	8	13	40	42	29
ETON MANOR	28	6	9	13	35	45	27
HULLBRIDGE SPORTS	28	5	8	15	16	38	23
MALDON TOWN	28	6	5	17	27	57	23
EAST HAM UNITED	28	5	4	19	35	95	19
WOODFORD TOWN	28	5	3	20	33	64	18

LONDON SPARTAN LEAGUE Premier Division

	P	W	D	L	F	A	Pts.
WALTHAMSTOW PENNANT	36	24	9	3	77	30	81
BARKINGSIDE	36	24	8	4	77	32	80
NORTHWOOD	36	23	9	4	85	33	78
CHESHUNT	36	20	7	9	56	38	67
CORINTHIAN CASUALS	36	22	3	11	78	40	66
HARRINGEY BOROUGH	36	18	8	10	67	44	62
BRIMSDOWN ROVERS	36	18	6	12	54	47	60
HANWELL TOWN	36	15	7	14	58	56	52
WALTHAM ABBEY	36	14	8	14	49	47	47
AMERSHAM TOWN	36	13	6	17	62	67	45
SOUTHGATE ATHLETIC	36	13	6	17	55	67	45
BROOK HOUSE	36	12	8	16	52	60	44
BEACONSFIELD UNITED	36	12	6	18	48	65	42
BECKTON UNITED	36	12	5	19	61	71	41
CROYDON ATHLETIC	36	12	3	21	60	76	39
HILLINGDON BOROUGH	36	8	7	21	47	73	31
NORTH GREENFORD UNITED	36	7	7	22	44	76	28
ELTHAM TOWN	36	7	5	24	39	93	26
THAMESMEAD TOWN	36	6	6	24	43	97	24

SOUTH MIDLANDS LEAGUE Premier Division

	P	W	D	L	F	A	Pts.
THAME UNITED	38	25	5	8	76	28	80
WOLVERTON AFC	38	24	8	6	98	51	80
BIGGLESWADE TOWN	38	22	9	7	77	43	75
LEIGHTON TOWN	38	22	8	8	77	38	74
SHILLINGTON	38	21	10	7	77	40	73
LETCHWORTH GARDEN CITY	38	19	10	9	65	45	67
HARPENDEN TOWN	38	19	8	11	64	53	65
WINGATE	38	18	8	12	71	62	62
HODDESDON TOWN	38	16	8	14	74	60	56
ELECTROLUX	38	13	16	9	50	38	55
TOTTERNHOE	38	13	12	13	74	64	51
WELWYN GARDEN CITY	38	13	9	16	51	57	48
LANGFORD	38	13	8	17	45	54	47
PIRTON	38	12	9	17	56	54	45
THE 61 F.C.	38	11	5	22	54	84	38
PITSTONE & IVINGHOE	38	10	3	25	43	77	33
NEW BRADWELL	38	9	6	23	42	87	33
BRACHE SPARTA	38	8	7	23	37	84	31
MILTON KEYNES BOROUGH	38	7	7	24	40	84	28
WINSLOW UNITED	38	3	8	27	27	95	17

MIDLAND COMBINATION Premier Division

	P	W	D	L	F	A	Pts.
West Midlands Police	40	22	14	4	84	41	80
Solihull Borough	40	24	6	10	74	35	78
Evesham United	40	21	11	8	83	46	74
Sandwell Borough	40	20	14	6	63	31	74
Stratford Town	40	19	12	9	81	43	69
Northfield Town	40	18	13	9	63	37	67
Stapenhill	40	18	12	10	61	50	66
Coleshill Town	40	18	11	11	57	42	65
Highgate United	40	18	11	11	48	35	65
Hinckley	40	18	9	13	56	47	63
Wallsall Wood	40	17	8	15	53	48	59
Boldmere St. Michaels	40	14	11	15	51	56	53
Kings Heath	40	12	14	14	65	62	50
Knowle	40	14	7	19	47	66	49
Bloxwich Town	40	11	11	18	64	73	44
Bolehall Swifts	40	12	5	23	41	79	41
Mile Oak Rovers	40	9	10	21	40	73	37
Chelmsley Town	40	9	9	22	43	77	36
Princes End United	40	10	6	24	34	71	36
Polesworth North Warwick	40	5	12	23	39	86	27
Kings Norton Ex-Service	40	4	8	28	32	80	20

WESTERN LEAGUE Premier Division

	P	W	D	L	F	A	Pts.
MANGOTSFIELD UNITED	40	28	8	4	113	39	92
TORRINGTON	40	25	7	8	91	41	82
PLYMOUTH ARGYLE RES.	40	25	8	7	100	28	79
TIVERTON TOWN	40	22	11	7	85	45	77
WESTON SUPER MARE	40	20	10	10	74	57	70
SALTASH UNITED	40	20	6	14	67	46	66
TAUNTON TOWN	40	18	9	13	62	49	63
LISKEARD ATHLETIC	40	18	7	15	85	69	61
DAWLISH TOWN	40	15	16	9	58	49	61
PAULTON ROVERS	40	16	11	13	74	60	59
CLEVEDON TOWN	40	16	10	14	52	55	58
BIDEFORD	40	13	10	17	61	76	49
FROME TOWN	40	14	6	20	56	78	48
BRISTOL MANOR FARM	40	12	9	19	52	66	45
WELTON ROVERS	40	11	11	18	40	61	44
CHARD TOWN	40	11	10	19	48	86	43
CHIPPENHAM TOWN	40	10	12	19	42	64	42
OTTERY ST. MARY	40	11	4	25	43	88	37
EXMOUTH TOWN	40	9	8	23	59	93	35
BARNSTAPLE TOWN	40	8	10	22	44	86	34
RADSTOCK TOWN	40	4	5	31	46	116	17

EASTERN LEAGUE Premier Division

	P	W	D	L	F	A	Pts.
WISBECH TOWN	40	27	10	3	97	39	91
BRAINTREE TOWN	40	25	10	5	85	38	85
HALSTEAD TOWN	40	26	4	10	105	52	82
HAVERHILL ROVERS	40	24	8	8	82	45	80
HARWICH & PARKESTON	40	23	4	13	85	51	73
WATTON UNITED	40	20	10	10	62	50	70
WROXHAM	40	17	13	10	63	64	64
CORNARD UNITED	40	16	12	12	73	59	60
LOWESTOFT TOWN	40	16	12	12	56	51	60
HISTON	40	17	7	16	55	53	58
STOWMARKET TOWN	40	15	11	14	51	52	56
CLACTON TOWN	40	15	9	16	64	56	54
FELIXSTOWE TOWN	40	14	11	15	59	58	53
THETFORD TOWN	40	14	10	16	65	81	52
MARCH TOWN UNITED	40	12	9	19	48	62	45
TIPTREE UNITED	40	12	6	22	45	65	42
GORLESTON	40	11	5	24	53	74	38
GREAT YARMOUTH TOWN	40	9	6	25	43	90	32
BRANTHAM ATHLETIC	40	6	9	25	41	74	27
NEWMARKET TOWN	40	6	8	26	32	87	26
CHATTERIS TOWN	40	5	6	29	29	92	21

HELLENIC LEAGUE Premier Division

	P	W	D	L	F	A	Pts.
MILTON UNITED	34	20	11	3	66	26	71
FAIRFORD TOWN	34	22	5	7	69	38	71
BICESTER TOWN	34	19	6	9	70	37	63
DIDCOT TOWN	34	18	8	8	65	30	62
HEADINGTON AMATEURS	34	18	8	8	54	34	62
SHORTWOOD UNITED	34	18	5	11	77	60	59
ABINGDON UNITED	34	17	6	11	57	37	57
BANBURY UNITED	34	17	4	13	58	51	55
HOUNSLOW	34	16	5	13	63	47	53
ALMONDSBURY PICKSONS	34	13	9	12	57	58	48
KINTBURY RANGERS	34	12	8	14	54	57	44
CARTERTON TOWN	34	10	7	17	49	62	37
RAYNERS LANE	34	10	6	18	34	63	36
BISHOPS CLEEVE	34	9	8	17	43	79	35
PEGASUS JUNIORS	34	8	7	19	46	68	31
SWINDON ATHLETIC	34	6	10	18	31	64	28
MORETON TOWN	34	5	7	22	30	73	22
WANTAGE TOWN	34	4	8	22	31	70	20

UNITED COUNTIES LEAGUE Premier Division

	P	W	D	L	F	A	Pts.
BOURNE TOWN	42	29	6	7	83	45	93
ROTHWELL TOWN	42	25	10	7	75	37	85
EYNESBURY ROVERS	42	24	9	9	68	42	81
POTTON UNITED	42	23	7	12	64	46	76
NORTHAMPTON SPENCER	42	22	8	12	84	59	74
RAUNDS TOWN	42	21	8	13	72	43	71
DESBOROUGH TOWN	42	19	13	10	62	40	70
COGENHOE UNITED	42	17	12	13	68	58	63
LONG BUCKBY	42	18	8	16	60	64	62
STOTFOLD	42	18	5	19	71	59	59
BAKER PERKINS	42	17	8	17	56	59	59
MIRRLEES BLACKSTONE	42	16	10	16	61	59	58
HOLBEACH UNITED	42	17	6	19	75	77	57
IRTHLINGBOROUGH DIAMONDS	42	13	10	19	80	81	49
KEMPSTON ROVERS	42	11	16	15	56	61	49
WELLINGBOROUGH TOWN	42	11	16	15	54	65	49
HAMLET STEWART & LLOYDS	42	11	14	17	49	54	47
ARLESEY TOWN	42	11	13	18	57	75	46
WOOTTON BLUE CROSS	42	14	7	24	42	81	40
BRACKLEY TOWN	42	9	10	23	51	83	37
STAMFORD	42	9	6	27	54	106	33
BURTON PARK WANDERERS	42	5	8	29	38	86	23

WESSEX LEAGUE

	P	W	D	L	F	A	Pts.
HAVANT TOWN	38	24	8	6	76	30	80
SWANAGE & HERSTON	38	24	6	8	88	41	78
BOURNEMOUTH	38	24	4	10	69	33	76
ROMSEY TOWN	38	20	11	7	59	35	71
WIMBORNE TOWN	38	22	4	12	80	45	70
THATCHAM TOWN	38	19	11	8	68	32	68
BROCKENHURST	38	17	8	13	56	51	59
B.A.T. SPORTS	38	16	10	12	54	48	58
AFC LYMINGTON	38	16	9	13	60	50	57
FLEET TOWN	38	17	6	15	64	57	57
RYDE SPORTS	38	17	6	15	62	55	57
EASTLEIGH	38	13	8	17	40	62	47
EAST COWES VICS	38	12	10	16	45	52	46
AFC TOTTON	38	13	6	19	54	70	45
CHRISTCHURCH	38	11	10	17	37	55	43
AEROSTRUCTURES	38	11	6	21	32	62	39
PORTSMOUTH R.N.	38	10	5	23	51	102	35
BEMERTON HEATH HARRIERS	38	7	11	20	42	59	32
SHOLING SPORTS	38	6	8	24	39	84	26
HORNDEAN	38	5	5	28	39	92	20

LEAGUE TABLES - FEEDERS TO SOUTHERN LEAGUE

SUSSEX LEAGUE Division One

	P	W	D	L	F	A	Pts.
LITTLEHAMPTON TOWN	34	24	5	5	89	30	77
PEACEHAVEN & TELSCOMBE	34	24	5	5	70	31	77
LANGNEY SPORTS	34	23	5	6	89	42	74
PAGHAM	34	20	7	7	85	44	67
WICK	34	18	5	11	61	49	59
BURGESS HILL TOWN	34	17	7	10	66	43	58
THREE BRIDGES	34	15	9	10	65	47	54
ARUNDEL	34	14	12	8	54	46	54
OAKWOOD	34	14	5	15	53	60	47
WHITEHAWK	34	12	9	13	39	36	45
SHOREHAM	34	11	7	16	53	77	40
RINGMER	34	9	10	15	51	66	37
HAILSHAM TOWN	34	10	6	18	55	75	36
HAYWARDS HEATH TOWN	34	9	8	17	52	61	35
BEXHILL TOWN	34	8	8	18	46	77	32
EASTBOURNE TOWN	34	7	7	20	32	54	28
SEAFORD TOWN	34	5	8	21	34	79	23
SELSEY	34	3	3	28	28	105	12

KENT LEAGUE Division One

	P	W	D	L	F	A	Pts.
SITTINGBOURNE	40	32	8	0	87	19	104
CRAY WANDERERS	40	27	11	2	91	33	92
HERNE BAY	40	24	11	5	83	28	83
TONBRIDGE	40	24	8	8	72	34	79
DEAL TOWN	40	23	8	9	88	43	77
FAVERSHAM TOWN	40	20	10	10	62	33	70
WHITSTABLE TOWN	40	20	8	12	67	44	68
ALMA SWANLEY	40	18	9	13	59	53	63
SLADE GREEN	40	16	10	14	65	49	58
RAMSGATE	40	16	9	15	60	63	57
TUNBRIDGE WELLS	40	16	6	18	71	79	54
CHATHAM TOWN	40	13	9	18	61	71	48
DARENTH HEATHSIDE	40	12	9	19	44	68	45
BECKENHAM TOWN	40	12	7	21	37	54	43
CROCKENHILL	40	10	11	19	47	89	40
THAMES POLY	40	10	7	23	49	76	37
GREENWICH BOROUGH	40	10	5	25	49	77	35
DANSON	40	7	13	20	41	80	34
KENT POLICE	40	8	9	23	51	77	33
METROPOLITAN POLICE (Hayes)	40	5	10	25	37	89	25
SHEPPEY UNITED	40	6	4	30	39	105	22

WEST MIDLANDS LEAGUE Premier Division

	P	W	D	L	F	A	Pts.
GRESLEY ROVERS	42	32	5	5	104	36	101
CHASETOWN	42	24	13	5	79	32	85
OLDBURY UNITED	42	23	14	5	75	37	83
DARLASTON	42	20	11	11	89	67	71
HINCKLEY ATHLETIC	42	20	10	12	75	51	70
WEDNESFIELD	42	21	7	14	76	59	70
ILKESTON TOWN	42	19	12	11	75	49	69
WEST BROMWICH TOWN	42	19	11	12	76	51	68
LYE TOWN	42	19	19	13	53	41	67
HALESOWEN HARRIERS	42	19	9	14	84	54	66
ROCESTER	42	18	12	12	72	44	66
RUSHALL OLYMPIC	42	17	12	13	67	51	63
STOURPORT SWIFTS	42	15	13	14	74	56	58
BLAKENALL	42	14	16	12	56	59	58
PELSALL VILLA	42	10	14	18	49	64	44
WOLVERHAMPTON CASUALS	42	11	10	21	50	98	43
PAGET RANGERS	42	10	8	24	50	94	38
OLDSWINFORD	42	9	10	23	60	89	37
TIVIDALE	42	9	15	28	45	100	32
WESTFIELDS	42	9	11	22	49	87	32
MALVERN TOWN	42	6	7	29	36	106	25
TIPTON TOWN	42	4	8	30	27	97	20

CENTRAL MIDLANDS LEAGUE Supreme Division

	P	W	D	L	F	A	Pts.
HUCKNALL TOWN	32	23	6	3	79	30	75
HEANOR TOWN	32	21	4	7	70	33	67
LINCOLN UNITED	32	20	6	6	70	25	66
ARNOLD TOWN	32	18	11	3	59	22	64
NETTLEHAM	32	15	6	11	43	40	51
HARWORTH COLLIERY INST.	32	13	9	10	47	36	48
SHEFFIELD AURORA	32	13	8	11	71	47	47
ROSSINGTON MAIN	32	11	9	12	43	45	42
BOSTON	32	12	6	14	50	65	42
LOUTH UNITED	32	11	8	13	47	53	41
OAKHAM UNITED	32	9	10	13	40	46	37
BORROWASH VICTORIA	32	11	1	20	46	66	34
GAINSBOROUGH TOWN	32	8	6	18	36	66	30
PRIORY (EASTWOOD)	32	6	11	15	37	58	29
MELTON TOWN	32	7	8	17	49	81	29
WOMBWELL TOWN	32	7	6	19	37	75	27
BLIDWORTH	32	6	7	19	40	76	25

SOUTH WESTERN LEAGUE

	P	W	D	L	F	A	Pts.
BODMIN TOWN	32	25	5	2	87	31	55
ST. BLAZEY	32	22	8	2	105	29	52
FALMOUTH TOWN	32	18	9	5	82	39	45
NEWQUAY	32	20	5	7	73	40	45
ST. AUSTELL	32	17	7	8	83	46	41
TORPOINT ATHLETIC	32	16	8	8	66	37	40
TRURO CITY	32	16	6	10	67	44	38
BUGLE	32	16	6	10	57	37	38
APPLEDORE & BAAC	32	13	5	14	66	59	31
WADEBRIDGE TOWN	32	10	8	14	47	52	28
MILLBROOK	32	12	3	17	70	79	27
TAVISTOCK	32	8	9	15	46	67	25
PORTHLEVEN	32	11	2	19	52	72	24
CLYST ROVERS	32	10	1	21	43	100	21
LAUNCESTON	32	6	8	18	46	75	20
HOLSWORTHY	32	3	4	25	32	110	10
PENZANCE	32	1	2	29	31	136	4

TERRACE TALK

DOVER ATHLETIC

"Where do you come from?"
"Dover."
"Oh, Dover. I passed through there on my way to France a couple of years back."

If I was given a strip of sheet-metal for every time I've taken part in the above exchange I would surely have enough on my hands to build a new grandstand on the open side of "Crabble". For the benefit of the majority who have yet to stay in Dover for any longer than a tedious two hours in the Eastern Docks departure lounge, "Crabble" is South East Kent's very own venue of legends, and also the home of Dover Athletic Football Club of the Beazer Homes League Premier Division.

Dover is probably one of Britain's most famous yet most transient towns and would probably hold no immediate connections with football to your average cockney booze-cruisers on their daily stumble to Boulogne hypermarket than say Woking has with the ferry industry. Julius Caesar was the first to sneak through Dover's passport control in 55 B.C. to give Dovorians heads their first taste of Italian football; it is home to a humungous Norman castle which could surely have Edinburgh Castle in a one-to-one fist fight; it once had 365 pubs which seems to be the claim of most towns but in Dover's case was probably true; it is the hometown of Topper Headon, the drummer of The Clash who first plied his trade in the "Louis Armstrong" pub; it is the world's busiest ferry port at least until the channel tunnel opens but moreover a shabby yet big-hearted town which nestles uncomfortably between Vera Lynn's enormous White Cliffs. However, on the far side of town away from those greyish rocky promontories that stirred the nation in the 1940s is the said Crabble, a corrugated cauldron of a football ground where the boys in white and black have weaved their spell for exactly one hundred years.

As mid-twenties senility sets in, my own early memories of watching Dover are by now more vague than a David Icke weather forecast. I must have been about three or four when I was first taken up to Crabble to watch my eldest brother playing for the Dover youth team, although my parental chaperones prevented me from assuming my now customary place on the River End. Then there was an occasion where I recall a police motorcycle display team jumping through rings of fire on the pitch, which was either an attempt at a revolutionary new formation copied from Don Revie's Leeds United or not a football match at all. My first unescorted visit to see the Dover first team was circa 1976 to watch Geoff Hurst playing for Telford in the Southern Premier in the days before the league acquired the ludicrous "Beazer" epithet. I remember checking out his face against a bubblegum card representation of him as he took a throw-in, just to prove to myself that I'd seen a famous footballer. However, Geoff was stuttering through the last bars of his swansong, the ageing ex-Hammer's performance meriting no Wolstenholmian superlatives on that occasion. To say this first encounter fuelled my love-fires for Dover Athletic would be a downright untruth, but subsequently my visits became more frequent and by 1978-79, the year that we won the Southern League Division 1 championship by 15 clear points (with the magnificent Alf Bentley, a man-mountain of a local publican as manager), a regular occurence.

In the bleak days of the early '80s when the club hurtled towards bankruptcy and was cursed by a stream of gifted mismanagers, crowds dwindled and the club languished in the nowhere-land of the Southern Division. The large crowds and immense interest in the club which Dover people have always provided was temporarily on hold. Memories of Dover's 4-1 F.A. Cup annihilation of then 3rd Division Colchester in 1975 and the days of competing with the likes of Hereford, Yeovil and Wimbledon for that elusive "good cup run"/League place were shut firmly in the nostalgia drawer. In the summer of 1983 dear-old Dover F.C. folded, a move which paradoxically heralded the resurgence of Dover football. In the same summer the club was reformed, joining the same league with the same ground, kit, playing staff, supporters, nickname and programme editor who modelled for the Shroud of Turin, the only tangible difference being the addition of the word "Athletic", a pointless and at times highly ironic suffix which no-one likes.

But other plans were afoot in the clubhut. A new board of directors took over who *were* and *are* actual supporters of the club, although recent signs suggest that some of them may be getting a bit big for their Gucci loafers. Dover fans do though consider themselves lucky that our board are on the whole sound local blokes with the benefit of the club at heart, when "being a fan" in football is so often the claim of aspirant property speculators and intransigent councils, as clubs like Wealdstone and Folkestone can surely vouch. Much of our recent rise however is attributable to the appointment of ex-Maidstone player Chris "Godhead" Kinnear as player-manager in 1985, whose astute leadership and often dirt-cheap dealings in the transfer market culminated in our record-breaking and well-documented Championship season of 1989-90.

Two views of the 1990 championship celebrations proceeding in and around the dismantled old main stand at the Crabble.

If all this infers that Dover Athletic are a rich club then it must be stated categorically that we are not, not even in Beazer Homes League circles. There is no great private benefactor keeping the club afloat; the £300,000 spent on the ultimately thwarted GMVC ground improvements last summer came from Dover District Council, the owners of Crabble, in a moment of uncharacteristic generosity and sense of community. Despite being home and away (honestly!) one of the best supported teams in non-league football we find it difficult to compete in the current climate of inflated transfer fees which are ravaging the upper echelons of the Pyramid; last season for example we could not afford to fork out an alleged

£15,000+ fee for the much needed strike-power of Trevor Booker from Welling, merely the price of a good curry to the likes of Barnet and Kettering. Such constraints make Dover's success in re-establishing ourselves as a "name" in non-league football more remarkable, and these achievements are starting to have a positive spin-off effect as more quality players consider coming to Dover, when in the past many have curiously been put off by the town's geographical location (which is not as remote as a cursory glance at the map suggests.)

One potential problem is perhaps an over reliance on the large attendances which success has ensured. The real test will come when things are not going quite so well. The "good old boys" would still travel to Moor Green on a wet November Wednesday, but there is a whole generation of shell suited 16 year old Dovorians only accustomed to seeing the Whites tonk the opposition. Their loyalty to the hometown club is commendable, but in order to stop Dover people succumbing to the dubious lure of Priestfield or Highbury instead of Crabble, youth team players will have to be nurtured for the first team instead of poached by others, and, alas, money in amounts of the large kind may have to be spent. Unfortunately some of the current squad are coming to the end of their shelf life - others have quite simply gone off.

However, with steady and dedicated manager Chris Kinnear at the helm the future does look bright for Dover Athletic, and the role of established title challengers in the Conference, rather like Wycombe, is something which we Dover fans can realistically look forward to in the future. But as you know, we should have been there anyway. It's enough to set Vera Lynn spinning in her bathchair.

So next time you're stranded at the docks surrounded by your crates of Kronenbourg, hijack the Sealink bus and come to Crabble to watch the Beazer's greatest exponents of the Kick and Hope game. I assure you - you won't leave before the end of the match.

Andy Stevens

POSTSCRIPT TO A SUCCESSFUL SEASON

A creditable fourth place in the Beazer Premier, a memorable 3-2 victory in the Premier Inter-League Cup final over Southport and a magnificent 1-0 win with only ten men against Gravesend in the Kent Senior Cup Final at Gillingham are the hard products of a long and difficult 1990-91 season.

Dover's sustained challenge to retain the league title realistically ended in mid-March, when goalkeeper Maurice Munden (widely considered to be one of the best in non-league football) and ageing-but-still-dangerous striker Lennie Lee both incurred broken legs, leaving us without two players who could ultimately have made a difference. These injuries cannot totally excuse some of the non-performances, chiefly at home, which Dover fans have had to endure this season, but these and the seemingly perennial problem of fixture-backlog (caused by the welcome encumbrance of cup runs) certainly contributed to the jaded play of some of the team. We're left to build again for next season as the popular cliche goes, but despite the disappointment of missing out on Conference football this time round there have been many positive aspects to the last season. Farnborough's promotion is the Beazer's loss and the Conference's gain, as they have proved to be an exciting side and one of the most hospitable clubs around. What's more, Dover beat them on three occasions last season. Aside from the acquisition of pewter jugs, another positive sign is the form of Joe Jackson, who looks like being a tremendous asset to the club. Dover's record signing from Yeovil Town, Joe is proving to be a worthy investment, showing a class of play against the grain of Beazer Premier midfielders. Going 3-0 up in the Kent Senior Cup semis against a full-strength Gillingham side; the 2-1 win at Bromsgrove despite losing the keeper after only 20 minutes; the "Spirit of the Blitz" performance of Dover fans when 4-0 down at deeply-inhospitable Gloucester City; the stirring performance in the

Dover's new main stand.

2-2 draw at Halesowen in mid-April by the Dover team and supporters when hopes of the league title had all but faded are abiding memories.

And there's one other good thing. Despite the ignominy of losing at home to bitter rivals Wealdstone in our final game it seems that the acrimony between supporters of the two clubs has diminished. Rifts were to a great extent healed when a large group of Dover and Wealdstone fans joined together on a pub crawl round Dover, both sets putting previous antipathy behind us. They have a good bunch of dedicated, loyal supporters, just like Dover, and what's more we actually got on well with each other. Many beers were consumed, tearful farewells and warm handshakes exchanged. We can now concentrate on stuffing each other on the pitch rather than on threats of pitched battles on the terraces. A Dover v. Wealdstone supporters match is planned for next season. It's what being a Beazer boy is all about.

AWAYDAY IN DOVER

Dover has a wealth of pubs to ensure an enjoyable alcoholic frenzy for the undiscerning beer-monster. Most pubs are owned by either Fremlins or Shepherd Neame (both Kentish brewers) and allow yourself a few hours before the match to drink in the delights of this noble old port. Assuming that you arrive by train, let us suggest the following itinerary.
Arriving at Dover Priory Station, your first stop will inevitably be the Priory Inn, which is unfortunately a full 30 seconds walk away. Whistles wet, go down Folkestone Road towards the town centre, and after about 50 yards you will see the Alma on your right. OK for a swift one, this was a strikers' pub during the 1987 Seamen's Strike so avoid if you've ever worked for P&O or are a strong advocate of Mrs. Thatcher's trade union legislation. Turning left at the roundabout, pop into the Golden Lion, then The Prince Albert on the corner of the High Street, where Dover Football Club was formed in a rash moment in 1891. Continue past the monolithic 16th Century Town Hall into Ladywell where you'll find The Falstaff (Whitbread) and The Park Inn. The latter is a deceptively large free house which serves a massive array of real ales and draught beers. Moving along into Maison Dieu Road you'll pass The Louis Armstrong, also a free house whose landlord (the hairy ginger chain smoker in the corner) is, surprisingly, a jazz buff. Some good beers with live music and an atmosphere as evening constituents.

Back on the High Street, edging ever closer to the venue of Legends is The Eagle, a Courage pub frequented by colourful local characters prepared to exchange inarticulate theories on Dover football and the state of the Beazer Homes League. From here its pubs-a-plenty on your way to Crabble - The Cherry Tree (Fremlins), the Old Endeavour (Shepherd Neame - sample the local loony-juice Hurlimanns in moderation), The Bull (Fremlins), up Crabble Hill to The Three Cups (including the historic oche of former world darts pro Tony Brown), The Gate (Shepherd Neame), then down Crabble Lane to The Cricketers - the mecca of Dover supporters right outside the ground, due mainly to the ropey state of the beer in the social club.

If you plan to make a weekend of it (like many fans of Midlands sides do) try some of the places near the seafront and around the Market Square in the evening. The Elephant and Hind, Roman Quay and Bluffs wine bar (where you may be lucky enough to meet some Dover players) should help you plummet to new depths of stupor; The Castle and The Britannia - Dover's liveliest pubs in the town centre - are also worth stumbling into on a Saturday night. The hideously mistitled Nu-Age opposite The Mogul in Chapel Place becomes a night club/youth club after closing time, and The White Horse (across the car-park from The Castle) is a spit and sawdust 14th Century watering-hole with 15th Century clientele serving a good selection of ales. An ideal place to savour that 20th pint.

If you've still managed to avoid the stomach pump and fancy a boogie or a curry, try Images Night Club (just off the Market Square), the Champion Chinese restaurant or The Curry Garden (both in the High Street) for cheap, perfectly edible stomach liners. If you're here for a couple of days, then Tontine Street in Folkestone is awash with nightclubs, pubs and restaurants assuring a lively night out. It's only seven miles up the road - if you get a taxi use Invicta Cabs - the cheapest by far.

Then of course there are the inevitable "day-trips", a concept at the very nub of every Dovorian's existence and an integral part of weekends in Dover to Moor Green and Halesowen fans. Stock up with crates of necessaries for the return to your provincial backwater, and for a clear conscience travel by Sealink or Hoverspeed. Calais is obviously the best known day-trippers' paradise, but is really little more than a glorified hypermarket. For a better day out go to Boulogne which has a superb beach (except in mid-winter), and enough bars, duty-free supermarkets and cheap Stella to sate even the most demanding gullet.

COMPILED BY THE D.A.F.C. CHILLIBURGERS

TERRACE TALK

WITTON ALBION

AN EX-FANZINE EDITOR WRITES

During the heady days of "Bishop, 3-1"'s existence I used to travel everywhere watching Witton. But the particularly close-knit nature of the fans got to me in the end, in particular the lack of contributions to the fanzine. It seemed as if the entire Witton following, with a few exceptions, closed ranks against the intrusion of a publication that dared to criticise their club. Faced with a wall of mounting indifference, I gave up the fanzine, then stopped watching the team. To be perfectly honest, although I still get a buzz when Witton are doing well (especially when Northwich get beat), I'm not missing attending the games (fanzine editors beware: becoming too involved can seriously damage your football). The six years I spent following Witton have, however, given me a good insight into the club, seeing things as an outsider that Albion fans wouldn't notice, and have enabled me to pen the following lines.

THE GROUNDS

Until recently, Witton played at the Central Ground. Words cannot adequately describe the atmosphere that existed there, suffice to say it had that indefinable something - character. It had warmth, homeliness, and at times a certain (friendly) intimidatory atmosphere (experienced by more than a few "blind" refs and linesmen). Reaction to the sale of the ground was mixed, most sad to see the old place go but realistic enough to appreciate the financial security to be gained. The last game on the hallowed turf, a 1-1 draw with Frickley Athletic, was something of an ati-climax, seemingly over in the blinking of an eyelid.

The sale of the Central Ground, now covered by a new Sainsbury's superstore, enabled the club to move to a new purpose built stadium at Wincham Park, about a mile away. Opinion is divided about the worth of the new ground, which is very similar to Aylesbury's. Having seen Wycombe's new ground on TV, Wincham Park pales into insignificance by comparison, and for me highlights the lack of genuine ambition shown by the club. While much has been spent on playing staff, nothing was spent on improving the basic main stand, open ends and terrace with bus shelter cover that was built by the developers, save for providing a hard, loose surface for car parking. After one year both ends were covered, with a little help from the Supporters Association, posing the question why didn't they do it when the ground was being built?

But the main complaint about the stadium is the terracing - it is very, very shallow, so much so that it becomes difficult to see at big games (and there have been several this season) if you're not at the front. The reason for the shallowness is 'It was the minimum that complied with F.A. requirements - any more would have required crush barriers'. Or, put another way, it would have cost too much money. Even worse, to change to steeper terracing 'would not be cost effective as we would have to tear down the existing foundations'. Or in other words, it seems that Wincham Park was built to house a good Conference team, nothing better. Of course, if Witton manage to consolidate in the Conference, as they surely will, Wincham Park will be an entirely adequate stadium for most games. Still, it is interesting to speculate what will happen should they seek to progress further.

THE FANS

The mix of fans watching Witton has undergone a noticeable change in recent seasons. Three or four years ago it was still a typically Northern crowd, i.e. mainly men in their later years. Since then more and more young people are turning up, and in the last couple of years a noisy away support has been following the team regularly. Attendances have virtually doubled since the move to Wincham Park, although there are still disappointingly few prepared to get actively involved in the club. The large majority of the crowd are trouble-free, although will cheerfully voice their doubts over the parentage of the ref/centre forward/centre half in a loud voice. There are one or two idiots, but hopefully the club will manage to keep them under control.

THE RIVALRY

Despite the efforts of certain people, Northwich remains a town with two senior non-league teams. Witton and Northwich Victoria have been battling for supremacy since the last century, with things generally being even until the formation of the NPL. Then, because of the selection criteria which took into account the finishing order of the teams in the season two years prior to the formation of the NPL, Witton found themselves remaining in the Cheshire County League whilst rivals Vics managed to gain entry into the NPL. This was seen as a good thing in the Northwich camp: to quote one director "The town isn't big enough for two teams".

Northwich stayed one leap ahead when the APL was formed, Witton moving into the NPL. This artificial elevation of Vics' status in the town became a source of constant annoyance to Witton fans, who were heartily sick of smug Vics supporters' superior attitudes. Unfortunately the few chances that arose to put one over on the Vics usually were spoilt by poor Witton performances. Such is the feeling between the two clubs that when Vics were threatened with eviction from the

OLD & NEW: The Central Ground in the process of demolition, and below, aerial view of Wincham Park. Inset: Paul Lodge receives the HFS Loans League trophy from league chairman Ken Marsden. (Northwich Chronicle).

Drill Field an offer from Witton's board to share the Central Ground caused a massive outcry from Witton's fans.

This season the rivalry with the Vics will become even keener now that they are in the same league. Witton at last have a chance to slug it out over a complete season for the title of Top Team in Northwich. Vics fans, of course, give us little chance. The remarkable success of last year has caused resentment among a handful, with letters appearing in the local papers stating how Witton will struggle in the stronger league, even one hoping Witton 'would get stuffed' by Kidderminster in the Trophy. The next few years should prove interesting!

THE PLAYERS

Witton have had their famous players in the past. Peter Mellor (Fulham's F.A. Cup Final v. West Ham) and Chris Nicholl both spent part of their formative years at the Central Ground. Bert Trautmann was there for a while, and Brendan Batson spent his last playing days wearing the red and white stripes before finally admitting defeat in his battle against a crippling knee Problem. The last player to make the grade into League football was Mike Whitlow, currently doing the business for Leeds in the first division, who went for £30,000 along with Neil Parsley.

As for the current squad, everyone will know they strolled the HFS Loans League this year. Mind you, with half of Colne Dynamoes title winning team, anything less would have been a dismal failure. They wrapped the championship up fairly early before an intensive period, when they were playing virtually every other day, exposed some tired legs and resulted in a few defeats. They proved their Conference worth in the F.A. Trophy run, inflicting a rare home defeat on Colchester, and only losing out to Kidderminster in the semi-final to a last minute goal in a third game at Stafford. Local rivals Northwich Victoria were another Conference club to succumb, in the County Cup.

THE FUTURE

Having managed to climb out of the HFS Loans League, Witton's playing future is entirely in their own hands. Despite some rumblings about certain players not wanting to play Conference football they should have a large enough squad to cope with any wimp-outs. Whether Stan Allan remains in charge is also in doubt at this moment, Football League clubs are known to be interested in him.

After the non-stop success of last season attendances will almost certainly fall unless another very successful season ensues. It will be interesting to see how the team rise to the challenge of Conference soccer, but whatever happens - as long as they finish higher than the Vics you won't find many Witton fans complaining.

Laurie Alder

TERRACE TALK

DAGENHAM

Over the last few years Dagenham haven't been the nearly men, or even the nearly nearly men, more the never got started men. Since the club was formed in 1949 the progress it has made has been excellent. The club reached Wembley in 1970, 1971, 1977 and 1980, finally winning at the fourth attempt. In 1981 the club was promoted to the Alliance Premier League. The Daggers made national headlines in 1984/85, reaching the third round of the F.A. Cup before losing 1-0 at second division Carlisle. However, since beating Cambridge 2-1 the following season the lack of success has been, to say the least, positively frightening. Nobody can even remember where the key to the trophy cabinet is any more.

1987/88 is best forgotten. 21 points from 42 matches, bottom of the Conference, a mid-season walkout of players (better off without 'em actually) and a game of managerial musical chairs, including a 24 hour stay for Terry Harris, don't make for good memories. Worst of all, the club missed out on a potential windfall when Brighton signed ex-Daggers Nicky Bissett and Robert Codner from Barnet for a combined fee of over £200,000. Bissett had joined Barnet from Dagenham four months earlier for just £20,000, and Dagenham got bugger all from Brighton because they hadn't negotiated anything with Barnet. If you think we missed out there, Dagenham had let Codner go on a free transfer!

Our first season back in the relative obscurity of the Isthmian League was nothing to write home about, finishing 18th, but the following season Dagenham broke with recent tradition by keeping most of the squad. With probably the most reluctant manager in history, Joe Dunwell, Dagenham at last achieved some stability and finished 6th. The success continued into 1990/91, until injuries to key players highlighted the need for a reserve team, and the side plummeted back into the bottom half of the table. Long-standing supporters are beginning to wonder exactly what went wrong – the achievements of the first forty years and the facilities that exist at Victoria Road give the club a pedigree that unfortunately it's not living up to at present.

A very disappointing aspect of the club is the nature of its support. With West Ham, Arsenal and Spurs within easy reach on public transport attendances can suffer badly. Even when we were in the Conference attendances rarely topped 1000. Of course, we have a hardcore of about 350 and a regular away support which, although it has been better of late, has always been small for a club of Dagenham's stature. Back in the late 1960s when the club was approaching the forefront of amateur soccer there would always be two or three coaches to away games. Nowadays the away support varies between five (when there's an AC/DC concert on) and seventy (when the social club runs a coach). The average is about twenty, but if some of the occasionals went more often we could regularly top fifty, which for our league is pretty good.

Of the home support, a lot just come when West Ham are playing outside London. There is rarely a large 'behind-the-goal' contingent: most stand in the Shed along the touchline. Our star supporters are the Dagger Seals, who are often imitated at away matches when we go and do our seal impressions. This started as an in-joke in the 1987/88 season (too complicated to explain here) and it has stuck. People

Dagger seals at Bognor

think we're stupid, and they may have a point, but we don't care, we usually have a good time at away matches and we never resort to abusive chanting like has been heard from Woking or Aylesbury fans for instance.

Since Redbridge Forest F.C. moved in to share our patch the future of Dagenham has been in doubt. Part of the groundshare agreement was that they pay for all the necessary improvements to bring Victoria Road back up to Conference standards, which have obviously increased considerably in our absence. Unfortunately, the so-called improvements make the ground look worse than before. What used to be the Clock End (though it is rumoured the clock is to return) was landscaped so there is a second access point for emergency vehicles, and it does look marginally better because there is now tidy wooden fencing rather than tatty netting behind the goal. Our beloved grass bank behind the other goal was also excavated and replaced with another identical fence which has the undesirable effect of reducing the ground's capacity slightly and making it look like a sauna.

That's not the only way Redbridge Forest have been spoiling things for us. Their behaviour in the last two years suggests they want to take us over. When plans for their third merger in just over ten years were announced last July, the supporters were kept completely in the dark by both clubs until December, when it was called off, supposedly for tax reasons. While negotiations were taking place the book was closed to full members, so nobody who wasn't already a full member could join and have a vote on the merger. The club had every right to do this, but it made it look like the vote was being fixed. Redbridge Forest F.C. consists of the undead remains of Ilford F.C., Leytonstone F.C. and Walthamstow Avenue F.C., living off the proceeds of the sale of their grounds. They're bound to try it again, simply because the only other option open to Redbridge is a long-term groundshare. They have bob hope of developing a new ground because they don't have enough money to do it themselves and the council just don't want to know - and personally I don't blame them.

Dagenham F.C. is in financial difficulties, but what is more worrying is the apathy of the club towards the situation. It appears that no effort is being made to put the club back on the right tracks, and as long as Redbridge Forest are around Dagenham's future is in grave doubt. All we require of the club is more than the minimum effort in all departments - e.g. start a reserve team again, give us a better programme, start communicating with the supporters a bit more, at least that will be a start back on the right road.

Derek Robinson

TERRACE TALK

GATESHEAD

"No atmosphere" was the description of Gateshead Stadium in the first edition of 'Where's The Bar?' Ouch! Although Gateshead may be short on both supporters and atmosphere fans of the club have not been short of controversy, excitement and suspense during its eventful history.

Younger readers have probably never heard of Gateshead's 30 year stay in the Football League so the bitterness and resentment at their loss of League status, which still survives in the town to this day, may mean little to them. Nevertheless, the facts are that, after finishing in the top eight of the 3rd Division (North) for the first five seasons of the 1950s and reaching the sixth round of the F.A. Cup in 1953, going out to then-mighty Bolton Wanderers, Gateshead fell on hard times towards the end of the decade, and faced the indignity of applying for re-election in 1960 for the first time in 23 years. Re-election was viewed, fatally, as a formality. Gateshead had finished third from bottom and were making only their second ever application for re-election. Hartlepool, on the bottom, were making their fourth, and Southport, one point above Gateshead, their third in a row. "Ashen-faced" has become a football joke courtesy of 'Private Eye', but on this occasion it would be true to say that Gateshead's representatives exited the Cafe Royal ashen faced after gaining only 18 votes, compared to newly-elected Peterborough's 35. Gateshead's geographical position was all that could be blamed for their loss of League status and their unwarranted dismissal, coupled with their snubbing by League clubs in later attempts to regain League status (1971 saw them denied even a single vote), produced a lasting bitterness in the town that in my view partly accounts for their paltry support in recent years. In addition, like so many teams with a great past behind them, the present Gateshead team face constant comparisons with the greats of the 50s by older supporters; compared to the heady thrill of Cup success over the likes of Liverpool, HFS Loans League football or even GMVC football seems small beer indeed.

The Gateshead team who lost their place in the League are no more, liquidated in 1972, their Redheugh Park ground redeveloped and obliterated from the map. A new club, Gateshead Town, was formed in 1973, playing at what was then known as the Gateshead Youth Stadium, close to the banks of the Tyne. But they lasted only a season before being replaced by South Shields of the Northern Premier League who, having lost their ground, moved lock, stock and barrel to Gateshead, retitling themselves Gateshead United. Gateshead United's second season in the League, 1974/5 marked my first visit, for a match against Wigan Athletic, lost 1-0. A Newcastle supporter in those days, I was not exactly captivated, but I went back again later that season to see Gateshead win 4-1 (I forget the opposition) and from then on I was hooked, an interest encouraged by my father, a Gateshead fan in their League days, who was no doubt also happier to see me at Gateshead than Newcastle, for the mid-seventies was very much the peak era for soccer hooliganism in Britain. Ironically the next season saw the only hooliganism I have ever witnessed with Gateshead during a second round F.A. Cup tie with Rochdale, which saw Gateshead go out in a replay after a notable scalp in the previous round when they disposed of Grimsby, inflicting their first defeat at Blundell Park in a year. But despite their cup successes and some attractive football Gateshead United always struggled for support and I vividly remember the day in the summer of 1977 when I came home from school to be told by my mother that Gateshead United had folded - indeed I still have a copy of the local paper carrying the story.

Football clubs in Gateshead had a high mortality rate it seemed. But not everyone had given up on the idea: a group of local businessmen led by Bill Gibson rallied round to create a new club. Barely weeks before the start of the 1977/8 season the new club, Gateshead F.C., began business with a hastily purchased set of strips and footballs and a manager, Ray Wilkie, who had won the Amateur Cup with Crook and had been manager of Gateshead United before their demise. Wilkie had his critics, some of them fierce, and I remember having one blazing argument with him outside the ground following a disappointing result in a night match with Gateshead's bogey team, Workington, but his passion for Gateshead was obvious, his skill at publicising the club impressive and his eventual achievements undeniable.

Gateshead's first four seasons in the Northern Premier League followed an identical pattern of struggle in the first half of the season and a miraculous recovery from the threat of relegation in the second half. My memories of those years

Gateshead personalities: from top - Manager Ray Wilkie holds aloft the 1982/3 NPL trophy with skipper Terry Hibbitt alongside; Dave Parnaby, who played in the 1982/3 and 1985/6 championship sides and managed the promotion team of 1989/90; Jim Pearson, leading scorer in the 1982/3 side and assistant manager in 1989/90.

are bitter-sweet. There were days of agony, most notably the December day in 1978 when a talented but wilful Gateshead side crashed out of the F.A. Trophy 6-1 at Accrington Stanley. There was behind the scenes conflict too, encapsulated a year later when the players mutinied against an elderly bus bought by the directors for away games, refused to travel on it and were transfer listed as a result. Gateshead's "Bust-up" brought some hilarity to the local press but triggered a much-needed shake-up and the young reserves unexpectedly given a first team place rose to the opportunity, albeit suffering some heavy defeats at first, including an 8-0 drubbing at Burton that served as the club's record defeat until a certain infamous encounter with Sutton last season.

Season 1980/1 was a typically eccentric one as Gateshead failed to win in the League until Boxing Day, yet reached the first round of the F.A. Cup, courtesy of an ineligible player fielded by the 4th Qualifying round conquerors, Marine. The season saw the arrival of former Newcastle favourite John Tudor at the Stadium, the first of a number of ex-Newcastle players who were to arrive at the club and help transform its fortunes. The following season saw the arrival of Terry Hibbitt and Jim Pearson and for once pre-season expectations were high that Gateshead would not face their annual relegation struggle. And so it proved. Gateshead went top early on in 1981/2 and might have won the League but for an injury which robbed them of leading scorer Bob Topping for most of the campaign. The following season, with Topping fit again and partnered by Jim Pearson in attack, Gateshead enjoyed the sort of season you only dream of, winning 32 of their 42 games, scoring 114 goals, amassing 100 points. For the popular and long-serving Topping it must have been a dream come true. Soldiering on his own up front in previous seasons he had done a heroic job, but now chances fell like confetti. As target man he still took most of the knocks and most of the marking, leaving Pearson, Kevin Pugh and young winger Martin Henderson to come through and pick up the pieces. My abiding memory of that season is of being thoroughly spoiled. A 3-0 victory was average, a 1-0 victory disappointing, defeat unthinkable. The midfield lacked a ball winner and the defence lacked pace, but it didn't matter.

Gateshead's seasons in the Conference have been ones of struggle. 1983/4 is best remembered as the last hurrah of the veteran Topping, who had joined in the club's first season. Work commitments kept him away from the side early on as they struggled to cope with the higher class of football. Recalled in November, his goals (including three hat-tricks) kept them afloat, one hat-trick coming in an amazing 5-5 draw against Boston. Sadly attendances still hovered around the 300 mark and the following season the task of running the side on a shoestring proved too much and Gateshead tumbled to relegation, their usual late rally proving just too late this once.

1985/6 saw the departure of Wilkie for Barrow but not before he had taken a reshaped side to the brink of promotion. I was at Oswestry the night they clinched the championship, where a disillusioned home supporter commented sadly that their appeal for funds to build a new stand (their old one had fallen foul of fire regulations following the Bradford fire) had barely raised enough for a new tea-bar. In football success and sadness are often intermingled, something I was to remember the next time I saw Gateshead clinch promotion, in 1989/90. In the intervening years Gateshead's return to the Conference lasted but a season, following which the managerial hotseat, briefly inhabited by Terry Hibbitt and George Smith, had been given to popular club captain Dave Parnaby, who had joined the club in 1980. Parnaby's first season as player-manager, 1987/8, was an extraordinary one in which more behind-the-scenes turmoil resulted in the departure around Christmas of Parnaby himself, chairman Bill Gibson (in his second spell in charge), plus the coach, assistant manager and virtually the whole first team squad. A new manager and chairman were appointed but before the end of the season they had gone too. A staggering 37 players were used that season, which ended with Gateshead 5th from bottom. It was a bizarre campaign but then Gateshead supporters have grown accustomed to such things.

The following season saw Parnaby and Gibson back at the helm and the council represented on the board as the club's new major shareholder. Their share purchase had helped rectify the club's dire financial position; they were now broke but at least they didn't owe so much. Resources for the manager were non-existent and the team for that season was probably the weakest in the club's history. Relegation seemed a formality, but for once fortune smiled on Gateshead as the knock-on effect of Newport's demise meant that only the bottom club went down. So Worksop, who must have been bad - even Gateshead beat them twice - went down and Gateshead fortuitously survived and began to build a stronger side. Several popular ex-Gateshead players, including Peter Harrison, Derek Bell and Keith McNall, were lured back and the aim for 1989/90 was a comfortable place in the top half of the table. But things did not work out quite that way. The 1989/90 campaign started tamely but ended with possibly the most nailbiting finish I have ever known - and I've seen quite a few. Early on it was apparent that Gateshead would not go down but nor did they look good enough to win the league - especially as Colne Dynamoes, with their full time squad, looked set to win tit by a mile despite losing an early season match 3-2 at Gateshead - their first defeat, our first win. At Christmas Gateshead were tucked into seventh place, 28 points behind Colne and 16 behind second placed Witton Albion. By now I was quite enjoying the unique experience of a season with no great drama or suspense about it, having endured almost constant promotion challenges or relegation battles since Gateshead's formation. Winter turned to spring and Gateshead put together a solid run of results which took them to the final of the HFS Loans League Cup, where they lost 1-0 to Hyde at Maine Road. Disappointment was tempered by excitement two days later when the local press revealed that a bigger prize was a possibility, when the first doubts were expressed that Colne's promotion to the GMVC might not happen. When Frickley came to the Stadium in mid-April Gateshead were still 5th and although they won 1-0 they were left with an injury crisis for the crucial midweek trip to Witton Albion. Without six first team regulars and with manager Parnaby forced to turn out for the first time since the previous September, Gateshead won 1-0 with a late Derek Bell goal and it was that result which really proved the promotion clincher. Promotion was finally sealed by the last match of the season, away to South Liverpool. I have always considered myself something of a jinx in Gateshead's away games but with Colne now definitely not entering the Conference this was a game I could not miss.The game was played at Bootle, and an old non-league football book told me that the nearest railway station to the ground was Bootle Oriel Road. I set out on a glorious May morning and my travel went remarkably smoothly until I disembarked at the station. The ticket collector could not tell me where Bootle's ground was but an old lady overheard my question and told me to get such and such a bus. The bus duly arrived, I paid my fare, sat down and was whisked by a cheerful Scouse driver along an apparently endless road. The journey seemed surprisingly long, but she had been very sure... Finally I was deposited at a bus stop with no football ground in sight. But there were some football supporters nearby so I went to ask them only to be told that, yes, I was at the right stop for the football ground.... Everton's! By now it was 2.15 and panic was beginning to set in. Bootle's ground, I learned, was in the opposite direction. The first two buses going back the way I had come didn't touch the ground. Eventually (it was now 2.25) I was told to get the first bus and change at a particular stop. Plenty buses there, I was told. On arrival there (2.35) I rushed to the new stop and raced frantically between buses. "Do you pass Bootle's football ground?" No, came the unanimous answer, you want... and each driver told me a different bus I needed to catch. 2.45 and panic had very definitely set in. I was on the point of ringing the ground and asking them not to start without me when a taxi hove into sight... and miraculously it was driven by an ex-South Liverpool player who knew exactly where the ground was! I arrived at 3.02, just in time to see Gateshead go one down. The jinx was working again, it seemed. But one of the hallmarks of that season was the way that Gateshead would start poorly and get stronger as the match unfolded, and so it proved. Mick Fagan hit a daisycutting half volley from outside the box to equalise just before the interval, Perry Briggs put Gateshead ahead just after the break and they left us biting our nails by squandering chance after chance to make the game safe. Finally, with almost the last kick of the game, a clearance reached Steve Baxter in acres of space on the halfway line and he motored down the left wing before crossing for Derek Bell to sweep home the decisive goal and send the Gateshead support (both of us) wild with delight. By a strange coincidence it was the first league match I had seen Gateshead win away from home since 1986 at Oswestry - the last time they had been promoted. Perhaps I save my luck for the games that matter!

There was also time to think of the other side of football among the clebrations. Of South Liverpool, driven from their Holly Park ground by persistent vandalism, exiled to Bootle and uncertain where their future home would be. The hospitality and friendship of the club and their supporters helped make an already memorable day a golden one and I would like to pay tribute to them here.

And so Gateshead once again ventured into the Conference, by their own admission a year ahead of schedule. An injury to Keith McNall, the move of his striking partner Joe Olabode to Whitley Bay and the failure to persuade targeted front-runners to join Gateshead in the close-season saw the club desperately weak up front. The first two months of the new season brought Gateshead a meagre two goals and cup elimination at the hands of local rivals North Shields saw manager Dave Parnaby tender his resignation. When his partner Jim Pearson stepped down too a week later the last connection with Gateshead's championship team of 1982/3 was gone. I will remember them both as gentle-

Action at Gateshead (v. Southport) in front of a typically less-than-packed main stand!

men - which in the dog-eat-dog world of football is all that need be said.

Parnaby and Pearson's departure coincided with the worst week most Gateshead fans have experienced in the club's history. It began reasonably enough with the 1-1 F.A. Cup draw at North Shields earned through a late goal by Keith McNall. The Monday after saw a side which, embarassingly, looked less fit than Shields, go down 1-0 in the replay thanks to a last minute winner. After the match Parnaby resigned. The Parnaby/Pearson tenure had brought some much needed stability after the turmoil of the 1986-88 period. Now things were up in the air again but fans hoped that the popular and respected Pearson could steady the ship as caretaker manager and pick up some much-needed league points at home to Sutton. Instead the match produced the worst defeat in Gateshead's history.

To those who ask what it's like watching your team lose 9-0, I can answer that on this occasion it was a bizarre, surreal experience. Midfielder Derek Bell received some derision in the local press for saying after the match that he didn't think Sutton were a particularly good side, but it was true. They weren't a good side, and even after we fell two behind I felt we could recover. But enter the referee, Mr. Coddington from Sheffield who booked McNall after he had clearly been impeded by a visiting defender, sent off captain Peter Harrison for protesting about the incident and followed this up in the second half by dismissing McNall for an admittedly foolish challenge, but one borne out of frustration, together with caretaker manager Pearson. Sutton's players seemed as bemused as Gateshead's by the refereeing and with the score 5-0 manager Keith Blunt took off his two strikers, presumably as an act of mercy, only to see the substitute score twice with his first two touches. Gateshead played as if in a dream (or a nightmare) as virtually every shot Sutton hit flew in, and at the end the referee waited an hour before emerging from his room, no doubt anticipating a lynch mob. But all Gateshead's followers had long since gone home, heads reeling, deprived even of the dubious consolation of having set a new league record. It seems someone else had managed to lose 9-0 previously. What a week! Things could surely only get better.

And things did get better. Billingham manager Tony Lee pipped ex-Newcastle favourite Tommy Cassidy for the manager's job, boldly declaring on arrival that Gateshead would not be relegated. The team was totally reshaped and by the end of the season only goalkeeper Simon Smith and captain Derek Bell were still first team regulars. In came a slew of ex-Billingham players, including forwards Charlie Butler and Richie Allen whose contributions of 12 goals apiece were crucial in Gateshead's survival. Defensive jitters continued and the team ended the season with the worst goals-against record in the league. If we were biting our nails towards the end of the season as a series of long away trips took their toll on the team, nevertheless survival (at the expense of Sutton, of all teams!) must be considered a triumph for Tony Lee. There were magic moments: A 1-1 draw at Barnet, coming from behind with a superb Keith McNall header to match and at times outplay the Londoners; our 5-1 demolition of high-flying Telford, when Charlie Butler turned ex-Stoke centre-half Paul Dyson inside out, scoring a hat-trick; our crucial late season home win over Kidderminster, won by a superb Richie Allen volley 5 minutes from time, a tense and ultimately jubilant night.

And so we look forward to next season. Defensive improvements are obviously needed and Tony Lee apparently has two men in mind to plug the gaps. Money is in short supply, the bank overdraft is daunting and commercial manager Tommy Cassidy will have his work cut out to raise the necessary funds. But then football in Gateshead has always had to struggle to survive against the odds. A few Conference clubs (and their supporters) might, I suspect, like to see the back of us in order to cut down on their travelling expenses, but we hope to go on frustrating them - and anyway, surely long trips are the price you pay if you want to be part of a national league? If Gateshead do go out of the Conference I want it to be in the right direction - upwards. It may still be a dream, but at the time of writing not, I think, an impossible one any longer.

John Bourn

TERRACE TALK

FARNBOROUGH TOWN

The finale to Farnborough Town's first ever season in the Beazer Homes League was almost too incredible for words. Submitted as a script for "Roy of the Rovers" it would probably have been rejected as too preposterous. But there we were - five minutes to go, 1-0 down to mid-table Atherstone and needing a victory to ensure a return to Conference football. The swirling wind and bumpy pitch, allied to a below par performance, meant the large contingent of Boro fans who had travelled to Warwickshire were relying on Bromsgrove to hold Gloucester. Then BANG! Ex Aldershot striker Paul Coombs heads home a Keith Rowlands cross to level the scores in the 85th minute. CRASH! Just ninety seconds later Boro skipper Colin Fielder buries a 25 yard screamer beyond the Adders keeper to spark amazing scenes of jubilation on the terraces. As the Farnborough fans swarmed onto the pitch - after what seemed the longest three minutes in their lives - news filtered through that Gloucester had scored an 87th minute winner at Bromsgrove. It was that close - a draw or defeat for Boro and their West Country rivals would have snatched the title in the dying seconds of the season.

So now Farnborough belong to that select band of clubs that have returned to the Conference just one season after they left it, and are one of the few to have played in three different leagues in three years. Most of the credit must go to manager Ted Pearce, a man who has become virtually a legend in non-league football. Whilst some clubs in the league seem to have money to burn, Ted managed on a shoestring. Beg, steal or borrow, Ted papered over the cracks when Boro were hit by injuries or suspension. In fact the only money Boro spent last season was a modest club record fee of £6000 on much travelled Runcorn striker Mick Doherty. The final piece in the Boro 'jigsaw', Doherty's move was entirely financed by the directors - straight from their pockets. If nothing else, the season proved that clever management, a real fighting team spirit, and a belief in playing the game properly (i.e. on the ground and to players' feet) is worth more than the colour of anyone's money.

Ted Pearce is far and away the longest serving manager in senior non-league football, after over 1100 games in charge. The club was only formed in 1967 (and indeed celebrated its 'coming of age' by clinching promotion to the Conference from the Vauxhall League), with Ted taking the helm in 1970/1. In his first season Boro won promotion to the Premier Division of the Surrey Senior League. But that was just the start. Two seasons later they joined the Spartan League, where they won the championship for four consecutive years. A new ground at Cherrywood Road was developed and Boro were accepted into the Athenian League. They immediately won the Division Two championship in 1976/7 and entered Division Two of the Isthmian League. They narrowly missed out on promotion in their first year, but made amends the following season, securing the title by a clear ten points. After six years in Division One they finally captured the title in 1984/5. Three seasons in the Premier followed until 1988/9 when they finished runners-up to Leytonstone/Ilford. But because of the apalling state of the champions' ground - and their failure to secure a ground-sharing deal - Farnborough took their place in the Conference.

After a bright start Boro began to struggle, hampered by a relatively small squad and perhaps restricted by their belief in playing football instead of 'hoof and chase'. They basically 'bottled it' against the more physical sides willing to scrap to the final whistle, while playing their best against those who liked to play it about a bit. Four points were secured off champions Darlington, yet only three out of a possible 24 from their fellow strugglers Enfield, Chorley, Fisher and Stafford. On the last day of the season they travelled to Stafford knowing a win would keep them up and send their hosts down, but after taking an early two goal lead Boro lost their heads and eventually went down 3-2. Boro were relegated for the first time in their history. Their lowest position before then was NINTH!

But the same supporters who sat disconsolately on the ter-

SON
PARKWOOD

FACING PAGE: Top - Paul Coombes, who scored a vital equaliser at Atherstone on the last day of the season. Bottom - Jamie Horton in action at Craven Cottage where Boro were robbed of a replay by a dubious penalty award two minutes from time. (Neil Jackson)

races at Stafford were the ones that almost a year later celebrated at Atherstone. My own involvement with Boro goes right back to 1975/6, in many ways among the most disappointing times in the club's history. Twice, that season and in 1976/7, Farnborough reached the semi-finals of the F.A. Vase, and twice they lost to eventual winners Billericay. Their record in the cups is also quite phenomenal. They have a recent record second to none in the Hampshire Cup, reaching ten finals and fourteen semi-finals in the last 17 years, lifting the trophy in 1975, 1982, 1984, 1986 - and two days after clinching the BHL championship they travelled to Fratton Park, Portsmouth to complete the double by beating Waterlooville 1-0. In the F.A. Cup they have reached the first round eight times, including seven of the last eight seasons. But as yet they haven't progressed further, losing to Barking, Hereford (twice), Bath, Swindon and Cambridge United. This season only a highly dubious penalty two minutes from time deprived them of a replay at Cherrywood Road against Third Division Fulham - but the memory of how Farnborough completely outplayed and out-footballed the Craven Cottage side will live on for a long time.

Next season the aim for Farnborough must be to 'survive'. This time we did it properly - people often accused us of 'sneaking in through the back door' although we were the victims of circumstance when Leytonstone/Ilford failed to get promoted - and hopes are high that a better, more experienced squad will be enough to live with the cream of non-league football.

Whatever happens, you can be assured of two things. We always go out to play football and we'll always give you a warm welcome at Cherrywood Road. Crowd trouble (fingers crossed) is unheard of in this part of Hampshire, and although our ground is modest in size, it is well kept and well serviced. We have excellent facilities, including a superb bar and refreshments, and our programme is one of the best in non-league football.

Of course, at present we don't get the crowds we deserve. All season we averaged around 600, until the last few vital games when the figures were 949, 1202, 807 and 900. Local football supporters though have proved before that they do have the appetite for Conference football. Crowds virtually doubled when we first went up.

"Justice has been done". said Ted after that final game at Atherstone. "We're back where we belong" - and if you believe that the Conference is the home of the best non-league sides in the country, you can't deny Farnborough their place.

Adrian Creek

TERRACE TALK

MARGATE

I don't think it would be too presumptuous of me to suggest that many people regard Margate F.C. to be a bit of a sleeping giant on the Kent non-league scene. Best known for our glorious F.A. Cup adventures of seasons past, from Q.P.R. and Crystal Palace in 35/36 through Bournemouth in 60/61 to Swansea and the third round home tie with Spurs in 72/73. However, in recent years you could be forgiven for thinking that the 'giant' had slipped into a coma.

A gradual decline in our fortunes through the 70s meant things had hit rock bottom by the time I started attending matches at Hartsdown in the 80/81 season as a fresh faced, innocent nine year old. Now a hardened, cynical (but still fresh faced) nineteen year old I can look back on the last ten years of devotion with a feeling of sadness and occasional despair.

I certainly didn't pick a good time to start supporting the club. Indeed after the first couple of seasons I almost felt I was some kind of unlucky mascot! In my first season I witnessed this once proud old side struggling at the foot of the Southern League with huge debts and an inexperienced team. Things were so desperate that the club took the drastic step of changing its name in an attempt to revive fortunes. Thus for 81/82 Thanet United was born.

Thanet Utd. squad of 1981/2 which finished bottom of the Southern League.

There followed eight monumentally mediocre years under the new moniker. Any hopes that a change of name would bring a change in luck were soon dashed as we promptly finished bottom of the Southern League in an appalling campaign. The memory of that awful side still haunts us all.

In terms of league 'success' the 1980s became one long relegation struggle with only 5th place finishes in 84/85 and 87/88 to lift the gloom. Thanet United's brief moments of glory came in the shape of an Eastern Floodlit Cup runners-up place in 84/85 and a stunning victory over Ramsgate in the highly prestigious and earth shattering Isle of Thanet Gazette Cup in 86/87.

Towards the end of 88/89 (another relegation struggle) a light emerged at the end of our tunnel. A new board took over with big ideas and stacks of cash. More importantly, perhaps, they wanted to revert to our old name.

Among older supporters the change to Thanet United was always unpopular and the club certainly lacked identity under the new name. For a start nobody knew where the bloody hell Thanet was. Mention Margate however and everyone thinks immediately of a tacky seaside resort forever blighted by a particularly crap Chas'n'Dave song. Thanet is in fact the name given to the landlocked 'isle' which houses the three towns of Margate, Broadstairs and Ramsgate. Many older supporters refused to watch the club under its new name and it's interesting to note that even in Thanet's most successful seasons crowds rarely averaged much above 200, while in the last couple of mediocre seasons back under the old title gates have been a healthier 300-ish.

The last two seasons have not seen the boardroom hyperbole matched by on-field performances. The new Margate have been stuck in the lower half of the BHL Southern Division nearly all this time. Instead the Hartsdown patrons have seen a succession of managers come and go, each new Messiah finding the Southern Division rather

Isle of Thanet Gazette Cup - not to be sneezed at when it's the only thing you've won in living memory! (Thanet Gazette - not surprisingly!)

harder than he first thought.

Trevor Ford, hijacked from Bromley, said at the start of 89/90 "I'll be happy with a place in the top six". The highest place we reached that season was 12th (we finished 16th) and Ford resigned in March leaving his assistant Colin Powell (no, not he of 'Desert Storm' fame) at the helm.

Powell seemed equally confident. In the summer of 1990 he proclaimed "I am confident we will have a good season" and suggested Bury Town were our only threat. Bury spent most of 90/91 fighting relegation and a quick look at the final table will show us not to have had a 'good season'. Powell resigned in October after the embarassing F.A. Cup defeat at that glorified old people's home on the Sussex coast, Peacehaven.

Ex-Dover boss Steve McRaye was then brought in but he only lasted a couple of months and will be best remembered for threatening to beat up some Margate fans on the coach home from VS Rugby. Chairman Gordon Wallis, in his weekly newspaper column, said of him "He was more of a coach than a manager". More of a boxer than a manager if you ask me!!

So Margate fans, a little wearily, welcomed the ex-West Ham and Orient fave Tommy Taylor to Hartsdown. The first signs are good and Taylor gives the impression that he knows what he's doing. He has to succeed. How much longer can the club afford to pump out large amounts of cash on wages and transfer fees for no real success on the field? With a number of wealthy sides in East Kent (Hythe, Dover and Sittingbourne) it is only going to get harder to attract decent players to Hartsdown Park. 91/92 could really be a make or break season for Margate.

Neil Wyatt

TERRACE TALK

CHORLEY

I suppose it must be difficult for Liverpool and Arsenal fans to understand the attractions which people like me find in non-league football. Watching averagely skilled (at best) players on grounds which in many cases make bombsites look well ordered seems a strange way of spending a winter Saturday. Nevertheless we do it in our thousands, week in, week out. The reasons, I guess, are as diverse as the standards of play available in non-league from the Conference downwards. Tradition, identifying with your home town team, lack of hassle and hooligans (generally), relative cheapness etc. etc. are probably all contributory factors in why idiots like me travel to godforsaken places like Goole on a freezing December day.

I often wonder whether Liverpool fans ever get sick of winning pots. As someone once said rather perceptively, "If you don't have bad days, you can't enjoy the good ones." In Liverpool's case you can substitute the word 'seasons' for 'days'. Indeed, Liverpool fans of my acquaintance say that the atmosphere at Anfield has diminished over recent years as the fans have come to regard winning as a virtual formality. The type of dominance Liverpool enjoyed through the 80's is rare in the non-league world and even when it does happen (e.g. Colne Dynamos) the club keeps moving up so any league is only a one-horse race for a single season.

The fortunes of Chorley F.C. in the 80s show the topsy-turvy way that you feel football really should be - they have certainly put their fans through the emotional mangle.

Victory Park, Chorley

Early in the decade Chorley regained their Northern Premier League place after finishing runners-up to Hyde in the Cheshire League. In addition they sensationally toppled Alliance Premier League Barrow in the Lancashire Junior Cup final thanks to a goal from 'The King' - Terry O'Connor. Their first season back saw Chorley finish a highly creditable fourth as Gateshead ran up 100 points to take the title. Centre-half Geoff Twentyman (now of Bristol Rovers) more than lived up to his name by scoring a remarkable 25 goals. Once again the Junior Cup ended up on the Victory Park mantelpiece.

The season though was not to end in joy. The departure of highly rated manager Peter Wragg to Hyde plunged the fans into despair. They were right to be gloomy. New manager Tom Howarth, a former Chorley full back, proved he had been a better player than he ever was a manager and the Magpies plummeted into the nether reaches of the NPL. Howarth's inevitable dismissal led to the arrival of Ken Wright - now this was to be a different story! The first couple of chapters though seemed pretty much the same. Having inherited a bunch of incompetents Wright struggled initially as anyone would have done. Gradually though he got rid of the dead wood replacing it with a series of good signings like Mark Edwards, Paul Moss and Craig Wardle. Nevertheless in his first season only a point from the last match at Mossley spared Chorley the indignity of having to apply for re-election.

Slowly the 'Wright approach' paid off. The side was completely rebuilt and as it improved so did the league positions. A truly marvellous F.A. Cup run which saw the Magpies beat Wolves 3-0 after two draws made a tremendous difference to the club's finances. We started inviting the bank manager to matches! Chorley's reward for beating Wolves could hardly have been greater - a second round clash with neighbours Preston. An aggregate gate of over 30,000 watched the 0-0 draw at Blackburn Rovers which Chorley used for their 'home' venue and the replay at Deepdale which Preston won 5-0. The bank manager was now beside himself with joy!

The following season, 1987/8 capped Wright's achievements. Chorley won promotion to the Conference for the first time ever, clinching their place on the last day of a memorable campaign by getting the point they needed in a 1-1 draw at Matlock. The match was played on a bank holiday and while Matlock is a beautiful town and their football ground one of the prettiest you could find, the place is a nightmare to get to on public holidays. A majority of the 700 or so Chorley fans who made the trip only arrived at half-time due to the traffic. By then Paul Moss had put the Magpies ahead and although Matlock equalised after the interval we held on. So began an all too brief stay at the pinnacle of non-league football. Two seasons were all Chorley could manage at the highest level before being relegated back to the HFS Loans League, as it is now.

The first season was moderately successful with a final spot just below midway fair enough for a first attempt. Chorley took the Conference by storm rocketing to the top after winning six of their opening seven games. Nobody expected it to last and it didn't. The second season was much more traumatic with boardroom wrangles not helping as a power-struggle developed within the club. One upshot of the squabble was the resignation of Ken Wright with a third of the season to go and the appointment of former Forest star John McGovern in his place. Wright, in truth, had outstayed his welcome and a managerial change should have been made at least six months earlier. Basically an extremely nice guy, he remained far too loyal to some players whose limitations at the higher level were there for all to see. Relegation, as promotion two years earlier, came on the last day. The really sickening thing was that it was the first time all season the Magpies had occupied one of the relegation spots. With Enfield doomed the other two to drop came from the trio of Farnborough, Chorley and those bastards Fisher!

Chorley's final game was at home to Barnet so it didn't appear there was much chance of any joy from that one and there wasn't - Barnet won 4-1. But for Chorley to go down either Farnborough or Fisher had to win. All afternoon rumours flew around the terraces as Barnet clinically took us apart. Farnborough looked as though they might do it as they led at Stafford but eventually lost 3-2 and were down. Surely Fisher couldn't win at Merthyr - could they?! I don't know what they were on that day but it bloody worked - incredibly they won 4-1! Shit!

So what of the future for this great old club? The 1990/91 campaign, a brilliant F.A. Cup run apart, was crap. Another new manager, John Williams, was appointed in the summer of 1990 and he has been a huge disappointment thus far. Hopefully some decent close season signings will prove me wrong but at the time of writing it looks like we are going to be in the doldrums for a little while yet. But you never know. And that's the beauty of it. I can virtually guarantee that Liverpool and Arsenal will be up at the top of the first division again next season. But who will win the HFS? Altogether a more interesting question I reckon. Anyway, I'll see you at Goole!

Dave Hindle

TERRACE TALK

NEWPORT

Ticker tape reception for Newport at Abingdon United.

TO HELL(ENIC) AND BACK

For two or three months following the formation of Newport A.F.C. in June 1989 it was difficult to pick up a soccer magazine without reading about how this club, formed by the supporters of Newport County, had to travel 85 miles to play its home games. Indeed, the novelty value was so great that even Sky Television and Saint & Greavsie featured us. Once all the publicity had died down though, the club were left alone to concentrate on bringing League football back to Newport. The foothill of this huge mountain was to be the Hellenic League. Road maps were bought in order to find out where teams such as Kintbury and Shortwood played, and it became apparent most journeys would have to be made along the M4 or M50, surely the two most boring motorways in Britain. It wasn't long before we had our first anecdote to tell, when our first away game at Ruislip was postponed because they had forgotten to plant any grass for the new season.

In a league which normally saw 'crowds' of between 20 and 50, word got around that Newport AFC would provide a big payday with over 200 fans travelling. This had its advantages, such as arriving at Didcot Town to find their smartly dressed officials on their hands and knees extending the covered accomodation by ten feet specially for the visiting fans. There were disadvantages too: in order to guarantee yourself a programme at away games it became necessary to camp outside the secretary's front door, follow him to the printers and then plead with him to sell you one as he carried the entire print run of 30 to his car. Some clubs had limited parking facilities and so kindly borrowed neighbouring fields for the day. Wantage Town, however, forgot to warn anyone that their field was usually the residence of a large number of cows, and so more than 200 Newport fans spent most of the match cleaning cow pats off their trainers.

Those of you who have read "Never Say Dai" will no doubt be aware that Kintbury Rangers are to Newport AFC what a mistimed fart was to Neil Armstrong. Their record attendance before our visit had been 16, when a minibus full of Morris dancers had converged on the village after taking the wrong turning off the M4. No doubt Kintbury officials had sat in their marquee the week before rubbing their hands at the prospect of making some money from our visit. They decided to have a barbecue. After all, when the sun's beating down on you and you're wearing just a pair of shorts, topping up your suntan, what can be better? Unfortunately it was about -10%C and the burgers and 'hot' dogs had come straight out of the freezer and bypassed the smoking charcoal. On top of this, all alcoholic beverages had risen in price and were served at a temperature hotter than the language of those who had just bitten into their burgers. Oh yes, and we lost 3-0. On visiting the City of Oxford most travelling fans are used to being treated badly. Usually this is the result of a trip to the Manor Ground. On a cold, wet, February day about 200 members of the travelling Amber army were thrown out of the bar at another Oxford ground - that of Headington Amateurs. This wasn't due to any hooliganism or other acts of misbehaviour, but because it was closing time, one hour before kick-off!

For players and spectators it took a while to get used to this level of soccer, but once it became apparent that the suppor-

Neglect at Somerton Park after being empty for a year.

ters could have a good day out and that the players could concentrate on playing their natural passing game without being kicked off the park, Newport AFC stormed up the table until in May, when what seemed like half of Newport converged on Abingdon for the League Championship decider. A ticker-tape reception unlike any since Argentina 1978, and which did not amuse the 'Keep Abingdon Tidy' committee, greeted the team, and in the end the party atmosphere proved too much for the home team. Newport AFC had won the Hellenic League and (after much nailbiting) promotion to the Beazer Midland Division.

Steve James

TERRACE TALK

HALESOWEN TOWN

Hands up everybody who's heard of a little known poet called Brett Young. Nobody? Alright then, how about an obscure late 70s/early 80s band called The Bloomsbury Set?? Still no takers? Okay, what about Lee Sharpe? Ah, now we're getting somewhere. The fact that this group of people are probably the most famous things ever to come out of Halesowen (and the vast majority of the population seem to think that Lee Sharpe is from Manchester) goes some way to explaining why the footy team has probably done more to spread the name of the town than anything else.

The club was formed in 1873 and spent the next 110 years without winning anything much of note and usually languished somewhere near the foot of the Birmingham Combination or West Midlands League. Apart from a brief aberration in the 60s the cupboard wasn't so much bare as a completely unneccessary piece of furniture. Then along came Paddy Page and things have never been the same since. Gone are the days when a win at home was celebrated as if we'd won the league.

During the 1980s, with Paddy in charge (after being mysteriously overlooked in favour of Bobby Robson for the England job), we tasted the delights of three visits to Wembley in the F.A. Vase, losing to V.S. Rugby in '83 (after beating them three times that season - sickening!!) but thrashing Fleetwood and Southall in '85 and '86. With the old boys club known as the Beazer Homes League doing its best to keep us out, despite winning the West Midlands League four years on the trot by a massive margin, we eventually gained access to this shrine of semi-professional football for the 1986/7 season. We spent three seasons threatening to win the Midland Division, finishing 5th, 6th and 4th, then won it in style in 1989/90, scoring 100 league goals along the way.

For this season it's been the Beazer Premier, the highest level we've ever played. It's been a nice change to visit some different grounds, even if some of them are a bit of a distance (especially when living in Plymouth!). We finished a highly creditable 8th and are looking forward to being there or thereabouts next season. Other ambitions? To win a match in the Trophy - I'll settle for that for a start!

A BRIEF PUB GUIDE TO HALESOWEN

For all you travelling supporters and groundhoppers the clubhouse sells Banks's but is a bit on the small side. There are three pubs on the Stourbridge Road within two minutes of the ground, including the Samson & Lion (M&B) and the Edward (free house). The main pub for a pre-match pint is the Waggon and Horses which has a mighty fine selection of real ales at reasonable rates, but it doesn't open until seven in the week so for evening matches the Edward is the popular choice beforehand (and a swifty at half time!).

Action from Halesowen's last home game of 1990/1, versus Dorchester Town.

TERRACE TALK

CHELTENHAM TOWN

The recent fortunes of Cheltenham Town have invoked a complex mixture of emotions. From joy and hope to disappointment, despair and at times total confusion. The club is 100 years old next year and whilst it is probably in as good a shape as it has ever been, watching them is still an utterly frustrating experience.

Between the late 1960s and mid 1980s there was very little to get excited about at Whaddon Road. A succession of managers, some good players but indifferent teams; plummeting gates; financial crises and mid-table mediocrity led to the belief among the townsfolk that their local team was really a bit of a duffer. In fact this apathy is a lingering phenomenon. The town has a population of over 80,000 and no nearby Football League clubs but home crowds hover around the 1000 mark. These hardy souls exist as something of an encapsulated community, viewed with scorn, pity and envy (we like to think) by the majority of the "do the garden on a saturday and go to Villa once a season" mob who call themselves football supporters.

On the pitch fortunes began to look up in 1982/3, when, after previously having failed to qualify for both the Alliance Premier League and the reformed Southern League Premier Division (two dazzling feats of incompetence), the club began to climb back up the pyramid by winning the Southern League Midland Division. Midfield supremo Paul Tester was offloaded to Shrewsbury for £10,000 and with a healthy mixture of youth and experience in the squad a renewed optimism arrived. The following season, after an indifferent start, Alan Wood, the championship winning manager, was sacked and replaced by 28 year old defender John Murphy. At the time it seemed that the board had finally flipped their lids and were developing a strategy aimed at tactical relegation (crap team, save money), but before long it had proved an inspired choice.

Murphy gathered round him a team of young, eager and talented players for 1984/5 and, inspired by the midfield play of Brian Hughes and freescoring genius of Mark Boyland, the Southern League Championship Shield was lifted (or rather winched up on a block and tackle due to its size). The memories of that season are so rich and varied that propping up the bar conversation in the club still returns to Hughes's clinching penalty in the final game; Jordie's goal against RS Southampton; the army of supporters that travelled to such cosmopolitan cathedrals of football as Alvechurch and Witney (sarcastic, me?) and Boylo's magnificent hat-trick at Glaarrstrrr. Promotion was confirmed before a crowd of 1999 (did someone really count them all and was honest enough not to add the extra one?) and the Robins got ready for the big time. Rather like sparking a dormant Frankenstein back to life with a car battery, the championship and promotion finally brought some urgency and local interest to a club that was in danger of becoming a mausoleum.

Watching our six seasons of Alliance football to date has provided a good insight into the way the game has changed at non-league level since promotion to Division 4 was introduced. Greater professionalism, better grounds, more competitiveness and more money have not, in my humble opinion, made the football much better. Even so, the Robins cannot claim to have set the football world alight during this period. In the first three seasons with Murphy in charge we threatened to finish in the top ten or so but indifferent form and an admirable but at times naive commitment to attack led to placings of 11th, twice, and 13th. There were some good runs in the F.A. Trophy and disasters in the F.A. Cup, until a memorable visit to

Wolves in 1987 when 2000 fans cheered the Robins to a 5-1 defeat at the hands of Steve Bull. That season also witnessed the emergence of Brett Angell, who is now knocking them in for Southend.

Things began to go wrong the season after, however. It became clear that the manager had lost the ability to motivate the players, who in turn had lost faith in him. The team was disrupted by some ill-judged signings and, despite possessing the talented Peter Shearer, now of Bournemouth (and subject of a £500,000 bid from Wimbledon which would have netted us 20% if the prat hadn't gone and broken his leg), they showed some poor form. After a despicable cup defeat at Gloucester City Murphy resigned and an era was over.

The bold decision was then taken to appoint a full time manager, and the choice was Jim Barron, former first division goalie, coach of Neville Southall and mate of Ron Atkinson. After avoiding relegation that season the club geared itself up for its most serious tilt so far at league and cup honours. The wage bill expanded as the better players signed extended contracts and then, on the eve of the season, amid much hype and speculation, Andy Gray of Scotland and Sporting Triangles arrived to lead the forward line. Gray took some stick during his 27 appearances for not scoring enough goals, but he was so obviously class that it was a privilege to watch him.

Chris Burton nods the winner against Yeovil Town.

Despite having a team of good players such as Gray, Mardenborough, Willetts and Buckland, indifferent form around Christmas put paid to any outside title hopes after a good run of results had created some excitement around the place. A poor defeat at Dorchester in the Cup and a disgraceful performance against Kingstonian in the Trophy led to the forming of a school of thought among the directors that the club was not getting a good return on its investment and with the back balance dipping into the red cost cutting measures were planned. In October of last season Jim Barron was told he would not be offered another contract although the chairman, a man with genuine ambition and first and foremost a supporter of the club, disagreed and resigned. In their wisdom, the board decided to offer the manager's job to John Murphy, then, as now, manager of Trowbridge Town. Murphy jumped at the chance but nobody could have foreseen the hornets nest about to be stirred up. Supporters were immediately critical of the appointment and, sensing that Murphy had suddenly become a student of the long ball game, began barracking from the moment he nestled back into the hotseat. Murphy also began to receive hate mail. God knows who from or what for, but it obviously shook him up. More significantly however, the players, acting in a manner akin to an infants school class, decided they didn't want to play for the new manager. The air was hot with flying transfer requests, tantrums were thrown and the whole thing got rather silly. John Murphy's first match back in charge had been the superb F.A. Cup performance at Birmingham City when, after matching the third division side for most of the game, we were narrowly beaten and applauded off the field by the home support. Within three weeks however, he had gone back to Trowbridge; his assistant manager (I didn't know he had one) had already left; the football secretary resigned and the youth development officer was released. The fanzine editor and travel club organiser were blamed for stirring up trouble and banned from the club (only to be re-admitted a week later) whilst the team fell to the bottom of the league. Drama? We could have taught Shakespeare a few tricks.

Faced with this gathering maelstrom the board opted to allow Dave 'Notcher' Lewis, club record goalscorer and North Gloucestershire folk hero, the chance to keep the club in the Conference by giving him the managers job until the end of the season. Alarmingly it also appeared that the whole team was up for sale, and whilst Simon Brain (the pint-sized poacher) was gifted to Hereford for £10,000, Mick Nuttell and Chris Burns were transfered to Wycombe and Portsmouth respectively for surprisingly high fees. Eventually, with a combination of positive motivation, a few short term signings, games in hand and some dreadful opposition in the closing weeks, relegation was quite safely avoided.

What effect such a traumatic season will have on the club is hard to tell. In the past two seasons a good spirit had existed between players and supporters, away support was healthy and terrace moaners were shouted down as a positive atmosphere was created. This was in evidence when Simon Brain dived into the crowd of delirious supporters behind the goal after scoring his second at Dorking in the F.A. Cup; it would be a shame if the development of the club was hampered by the torrid time of last season.

Nothing at Cheltenham Town can ever be taken for granted and, while rumours abounded that Lewis would be given a contract or taken on as assistant to coach, Ian Bowyer, more surprises were in store. As I write, Ally Robertson, the former West Brom. and Wolves defender has just been appointed manager in a full time capacity by the same board that got rid of the last one saying we didn't need/couldn't afford a full time boss. Cheltenham produced some good sides in the 50s and 60s under Scottish managers so, ever hopeful, it would appear the club is once more going in a positive direction.

I'll end with a quote from one of the players: "Cheltenham Town is a lovely club: the people are friendly, the supporters are great, the facilities are good, it's when you start to talk about football that the problems start".

Paul Godfrey

TERRACE TALK

BANGOR CITY

"Which team do you support?"
"Bangor City."
"Yes, but which *first division* team do you support?"

As followers of non-league football I suppose we've all heard that one; it does not seem to penetrate the heads of Liverpool or United supporters that there is life beyond the Football League. Here in North Wales these supporters are of an even higher percentage, thus only between three and four hundred will venture to Farrar Road, the home of Bangor City Football Club. Mind you, there's been a couple of times when the turnstiles have turned endlessly, with the visit of A.C. Napoli in '62 and more recently Atletico Madrid in the European Cup Winners Cup. These days may be fresh in the memory of a City fan, but even fresher are the memories of bankruptcy, scandal and managerial calamities!

1990/1 was hoped to be our season for promotion back to the Conference, laughable when you think back. We started the season in the charge of Kevin Mooney, who was appointed from the ranks during the previous season following John Aspinall's deserved dismissal. Kevin was a good enough lad but he did nothing apart from signing all his mates from Scouseland to play for City, which did nothing to improve their footballing ability. This team was utterly crap and Mooney was promptly sacked.

This was seen by the majority of City fans as the re-opening of the once-bolted door for the return of the prodigal son, John Mahoney, the most successful manager of recent times. John was the person who steered Bangor to the Welsh Cup final and that memorable match in Madrid. Unfortunately this avenue was not chosen; instead the powers that be decided to upgrade reserve team manager Brian Owen. A proven North Wales football manager, his ability at Welsh League level was never questioned, but his right to this prestigious post was. His reign started amicably but deteriorated to sheer embarassment. Even after enlisting the help of the highly qualified and experienced former Watford manager Ernie Walley things didn't go to plan. There were a couple of interesting signings in Scot Healey and Bob Colville who gave the team a bit of a boost, but this was short-lived as Healey became another addition to the long term injury list and Colville was fighting a lone battle up front. Even with this mediocre team Bangor reached the Welsh Cup quarter final, losing to Hereford on a penalty shoot-out, as well as the semi-finals of both HFS League Cup and Presidents Cup, so it wasn't all gloom.

With only three weeks of the season remaining Brian Owen announced he would not continue as first team supremo next season, and is to terminate his involvement with City. In a complete U-turn the Board decided to re-employ John 'Josh' Mahoney in an attempt to save their own credibility and bring back the glory days. John left the City in '87 following the club's announcement that if they won the league they would not apply for promotion due to financial uncertainties. Hopefully things are about to change under the leadership of 56 times capped former Welsh international Mahoney, and I'll drink to that!

A BIT FOR THE WELSH TOURIST BOARD

Bangor is indeed known as the 'Gateway to Snowdonia and the beautiful isle of Anglesey'. What better reason to come and follow your team and make a wee bit of a holiday out of it? Bangor itself is a university City, acclaimed for its Victorian pier and shopping facilities, plus the magnificent football team and fantastic nightlife (?) Down the road are our poor neighbours Caernarfon Town F.C., the place with the big castle, least said about them the better. Also 10 miles inland stands the astounding Mount Snowdon, 'Y Wyddfa'. Which brings me to the subject of the language that you will hear spoken all around, including in the game. No, they are not talking about you; we're too busy slagging off the players! Before the match try the Waterloo Inn just off the High Street; the landlord's a City director. Closer to the ground are the Harp Inn and the Football Club, both fairly quiet and not very luxurious but at least all the talk is football. CROESO I GYMRU, welcome to Wales!

Gareth Jones

TERRACE TALK

HITCHIN TOWN

You either know Hitchin Town or you don't; for those of you who don't, it's a market town in North Hertfordshire with a 30,000 population and a keen interest in the national sport.

Despite being surrounded by three much larger towns with football clubs (Letchworth Garden City, Stevenage Borough and Luton Town), the Canaries usually attract 350 for home games, although when things are going well the interest proves phenomenal, underlining the potential if the club was to fulfil ambition and rise up to the GMVC.

Conference football, for the time being at least, is merely a dream - the club has just been taken over and for the first time since the successful late sixties it seems it is being run by someone whose head is screwed on correctly, although their first task is to cure the club's horrific debts, brought about by those people who gave the impression that they had their heads screwed on the correct way - but of course didn't. Adding to the problems of finance, Top Field's facilities would need upgrading for Conference football - lovely as it is, its limited space, wooden terracing and knackered perimeter fencing fails to meet approval with the ludicrous new ground grading systems being enforced, surely an enforcement which will split non-league football in two if not controlled sensibly - 99% of the clubs outside the Football League don't wish to play at that level.

1990/1 was another 'nearly' season for the Canaries. 5th in Division One, again failing to return to the Premier although they led for a lengthy period and looked likely to go up until March. Nevertheless, the club won its first senior silverware for ten years, the Herts. Charity Cup final against our old friends, Borehamwood, Martin Maguire's drive into the top corner sending the Town End wild and forcing skipper Mark Burke to lift the cup - and promptly drop it! The Southern Combination Senior Floodlit Cup was also won, with a 2-1 win over Berkhamsted Town at the rural setting of Stotfold.

Much sought after striker Mark Smith shields the ball in the 2-0 home win over Lewes.

Such was the success as a club, Hitchin Town are currently having a trophy cabinet constructed following the reserves' treble winning season - including the Essex & Herts. Border Combination championship - seeing off the challenges of teams such as Cambridge City, Leyton-Wingate and Redbridge Forest with ease. It was also commonly suggested, and rightly so, that the young reserves played better football than the first team - which is probably why they averaged 180 gates while Hitchin's first team were often plaing away in front of crowds half that size. There is no doubt that this reserve side is the nucleus of the club's future. The youth team also won the East Anglian Cup, Eastern Junior Plate and Chiltern League, and as of 1991/2 the Hitchin Town club will be fielding a first team, reserve team and 10 youth sides.

1990/1 did have its high spots for the loyal locals. The 3-1 win over Stevenage Borough and 3-0 triumph over Baldock Town at home in cup games were almost embarassing, such was the ease with which victory was attained! Borough revenged against a depleted Town in the Herts. Senior, while Hayes kicked every moving object over 180 minutes of football to end our F.A. Trophy hopes, this after Town tore the Premierites apart away from home. In the F.A. Cup Braintree Town's shock 1-0 win at Top Field was none too pleasing while a questionably weal Canaries side crashed out of the AC Delco Cup at Uxbridge. In the Loctite Cup, a superb 4-2 away win at Marlow thanks to four second half crackers probably wins the award as best display of the season, although Wivenhoe ended our hopes in the last sixteen.

In years gone by Town fans have been heavily critical about the lack of goals, and although the trend continues, it must have been satisfying to see them playing open attacking football at Top Field against sides content not to attack. Croydon were hit for six on the opening day of the season, Southwick's punishment for beating us 3-0 four weeks earlier was a 6-1 drubbing whilst Uxbridge were beaten 4-0. Poor old Worthing lost 9-1 at Top Field; the once great side of the 1980s were frankly awful.

The club's record signing, Ray Seekings, was eventually stamped a duff and sent back to Potton while manager Steve Norris was left to reflect on the success of two close season "free" signings. Jason Reed scored 19 following his arrival from Kempston Rovers. Big Jason is undoubtedly lazy, and if he'd played all season like he did early on, winning every aerial duel and breaking every centre-back's nose he'd have been the division's top scorer. The other plus was Gavin Covington. I'd probably be a sensible lad if I placed £10 on him being the fastest player in the entire Isthmian League and his bullet runs and pinpoint crosses from left back were so often the highlight of saturday afternoon. And the best thing about Gav is he's pledged to remain at Top Field, turning down a £25,000 move to Wycombe Wanderers.

Looking forward to 1991/2, with the club on its feet, under the right people, there has to be some optimism, even though the wage bill has been cut to grass roots level. The club owes thanks to the loyal playing staff, not to mention the faithful following both home and away - which keeps clubs like Hitchin alive - but it's not thanks they want. It's entertaining football, goals and most importantly, one thing rarely seen at Top Field in recent years but something I'm sure the club deserves - success!

Barry Swain

TERRACE TALK

BARROW

BARROW 3 LEEK TOWN 0. That result from the 1990 F.A. Trophy final is one that should give all fans of struggling non-league clubs heart and hope for the future. It is a result that says it is possible to rise from the depths of despair in the harsh world of non-league football, to shrug off disappointment, poor teams, no crowds and reach the pinnacle.

Until our failure to get re-elected in 1972 Barrow's record in the Football League can be summed up in one word, crap. Barrow did nothing apart from one promotion to Division 3 in 1966/7 and relegation three years later. Mind you, we did get re-elected ten times before being kicked out. Long time fans still dispute the decision on the grounds that we'd been in the third only two seasons previously and weren't even bottom that year, good points, but off set by our geographical isolation which led the Southern mafia to remove another long journey. See Workington for more evidence.

It's only recently that league clubs have had to find their feet in non-league on a regular basis, so when Barrow went down it was a rare event and , not surprisingly, a disaster. Crowds collapsed, decent players went, the ground rotted slowly away, crowds fell to the very low hundreds, the ground rotted some more and managers came and went. One lasted only 24 hours and the rest were the usual collection of incompetents, rip-off artists and the occasional half-decent one. But they were all linked by not really giving a damn.

After years of absolute mediocrity in the Northern Premier League Barrow became founder members of the Alliance in 1979 but we couldn't afford to build a team on mediocre crowds and went down to the NPL in 1983. Under Vic Halom, one of the better managers, we were back up next season as NPL champions and Charity Shield winners but it was yet another false dawn as we came back down to earth and into the wilderness of the NPL again. Geordie bookie Ray Wilkie arrived from Gateshead to replace Halom, but too late to save the team from relegation.

His arrival may have passed unnoticed, but in his five years in charge he has proved to be the longest serving and most successful manager in the club's history. The key to his success is a strong belief in the traditional values of the game. Knocking the ball around, strong defence and, best of all, two wingers. It may be a bit inconsistent but when it works no-one can live with us.

Wilkie inherited a club with crippling debts, little support and a ground which threatened to turn to dust at any moment. Worst of all there was no money for players. No problem to Wilkie as he doesn't like parting with cash anyway. He just got out his contacts book, and Barrow started to feature the best of the North-East combined with the best local talent.

Barrow have never been a cup side but the 1987/8 season saw them through to the NPL cup, which we lost on penalties to Goole Town, and a romantic run in the F.A. Trophy. Barrow knocked out Runcorn and old enemies Altrincham to reach the semi-finals for the first time against Enfield. Barrow lost the home leg 2-1 before 6000 fans and it looked all over. But they had developed a fierce team spirit as well as class and a 1-0 win at Enfield forced a replay, then a second replay at Stafford before bowing out 1-0. Barrow had had its first taste of cup fever for decades and it wasn't to be the last.

League success had to come and it did. Based on a nucleus of outstanding players like veteran striker Colin Cowperthwaite, defenders Kenny Gordon and Glenn Skivington, former Liverpool keeper Peter McDonnell and the brilliant Kenny Lowe Barrow walked the HFS League in 1988/9 with 26 wins out of 42. It was the prize we all wanted. Back in the top flight, we now had a team which could last in the Conference and rapidly growing crowds to sustain it.

Some would argue that the real aim that season was to stay in the Vauxhall Conference, and true as that is it is difficult to beat a day in the sun at the national stadium. A dull victory over Bangor gave no hint of glory. Beating the Neanderthals from the Metropolitan Police 1-0 was a victory over thuggery but it was the 2-0 replay victory over difficult Yeovil in a hurricane that got the bandwagon rolling. After throwing away a 2-0 lead against Kingstonian in the quarter final Barrow won the replay 1-0 at home to meet one man's vanity team Colne in the semis. Barrow won 1-0 away and a 35 yard classic from Kenny Lowe at

FACING PAGE, from top: Colin Cowperthwaite on the way to 300 goals for Barrow; and one at Wembley; the F.A. Trophy being displayed to the people of Barrow. (North West Evening Mail)

TEL. 32032
HARRISON & Co.
BUILDERS MERCHANTS
NOBODY
DOES IT
BETTER

PUMA
DUNGEON

Holker Street sent Barrow to Wembley. Tears all round. The final was like a bizarre Roy of the Rovers script as Barrow turned on the style in front of 13000 Barrovians. Kenny Gordon scored twice in his last game for the club before emigrating and after 600 appearances and 250 goals Colin 'God' Cowperthwaite got the other. Barrow returned home to 20000 people on the streets and at long last we had become the premier sporting club in the town, as the pathetic rugby league club lost all but one of their matches and conceded over 1000 points! Oh, happy days!

This season Barrow continued their success. We went out of the Trophy early to league leaders Kettering, but the Trophy was old hat anyway. This year it was the big one, the F.A. Cup. We were long overdue a run, 25 years since we were last in the third round. Wins against

Colin Cowperthwaite: after years of struggle, the smile says it all. (N.W. Evening Mail)

Chorley and Whitley Bay gave us a trip to Bolton Wanderers, top of the third. Another 6000 travelled to Bolton and there was only one goal in it as Bolton were made to work for their win. If aliens had come to the match they wouldn't have been able to tell who was thw non-league side. Barrow also stayed in the Conference with a record number of points and reached the Bob Lord final, only to give in to relegated Sutton 5-0. A measure of Barrow's success is that the Bob Lord final passed off as a non-event, whereas a few years ago it would have been a major event. Times have certainly changed.

Fans of Barrow A.F.C. have a lot to be optimistic about these days. Our erratic board have managed to clear the club's debts with the sale of Kenny Lowe to Barnet for 4o grand and the cup runs, even if they did ban our fanzine, "Give 'Em Beans".

Crowds have been well over 1000 in every match this season with plenty of young kids paving the way for the future. It only needs a bit of success to get the crowds back. The team needs some new blood, but we're confident a couple of midfielders will see us keeping up the high standards of success we're becoming used to. Barrow may never win the league because they lose to poor teams while thrashing the likes of Barnet in epic matches. But who cares as long as they remain committed to open football?

Glenn Skivington, Barrow & England (N.W. Eve. Mail)

Barrow A.F.C. has known hard times and the town itself is in the midst of chronic economic recession, but Barrow's recent history should give hope to all the thousands of non-league fans who week in, week out, watch their own mediocre teams. After all, who would have thought that unfashionable Barrow were candidates for a miracle?

Paul Clarke

TERRACE TALK

NORTHWICH VICTORIA

UPDATE

A quick glance at the final Conference table shows Vics as a safe mid-table side - 13 points clear of relegation. Why then were people selling clean underwear to Vics fans at the Moss Rose in April?

After a fairly indifferent start to the season things finally started to click in mid-September. Successive 2-0 home wins over Bath and Yeovil were followed by an amazing 5-4 victory at Welling and then probably the game of the season, at home to Macclesfield. Despite the handicap of losing Mark Hancock early on with a ruptured kidney and the even bigger handicap of replacing him with *the* Peter Barnes Macc were slaughtered 4-1, with Vics even scoring for the Silkmen. The Macc game saw the last appearance of Neil Morton in a green shirt. After a superb start to the season it was only a matter of time before a large cheque came our way; in the end it was Chester who paid a bargain £50,000. Less than a fortnight later Derrick Parker's Vics career was at an end. The most natural finisher the club has had for years and one of the most popular players, the Legend scored over 50 goals for the Vics in just 114

(+25) appearances before joining Frickley for regular first team football. Soon afterwards Mal O'Connor suffered actual bodily harm following a tackle from Telford's Martin Myers, a more than adequate replacement for Anton Joseph, which put him out of the game for over a month.

Vics went into the F.A. Cup qualifier with Spennymoor with what could be called a scratch side - three of the four strikers that started the season gone or injured, a goalkeeper making his debut and ex-Port Vale star wobbly Phil Sproson making his second appearance. Despite creating enough chances to win several games only one was converted and not surprisingly the Moors scored a late equaliser. The replay was a complete disaster - again Vics led and conceded an equaliser. Extra time came and in a crazy second half Mark Jones was sent off for a wild challenge and then Steve Johnson tried to kill a linesman and also took an early bath. Two minutes before the end loan signing Brian Mills hit the bar and with their next attack Spennymoor scored the winner. Steve Johnson was kicked out of the club a week later and the extremely talented Brian Mills headed back to Port Vale.

November and December saw Vics maintain a mid table position with even more loan players coming and going. The usual Xmas present of six points for Runcorn was delayed due to the bad weather, but they received it eventually. Only one game was lost in January and February, Runcorn, but no GMVC games were won. Progress was made in the F.A. Trophy thanks to 'easy' draws against Droylesden and Tow Law Town and wins were also recorded in the Cheshire and Staffordshire Senior Cups.

Finally things up front improved; Steve Buxton came on a free transfer from Telford and a man some people know as God joined the club - Andy Graham. Graham secured a point with a debut goal at Yeovil and a week later he created the goals that put Stroud out of the Trophy. On March 2nd Vics actually won a league game, first of the year, with Graham again scoring. Vics warmed up for the Trophy quarter final tie with Wycombe by being thrashed 5-2 at bottom club Fisher. The Wycombe game saw the highest Drill Field gate for two years and in a highly entertaining game the Wanderers ran out slightly undeserving 3-2 winners. With the Wembley dream shattered Vics were free to concentrate on improving their league position and lifting the Cheshire Senior Cup. Unfortunately arch rivals Colne Dynamoes - sorry, Witton Albion (can you tell the difference?) - put us out of the Senior Cup.

Finally some of the Morton money was spent and winger Tony Hemmings arrived from Rocester for around £8,000 but the league position continued to deteriorate. Following a charity match in aid of Merthyr Tydfil F.C. manager Cliff Roberts was sacked. Player-coach Paul Maguire took over and in his first game as boss a last minute penalty secured a 2-2 draw against Colchester. Unfortunately wins didn't materialise and with seven games left Vics were perilously close to the relegation spots. The position worsened when Bath put four past Trevor Ball and two days later an extremely nervous Vics lost at home to Welling. Then came Macclesfield.

Probably the most nervous set of Vics fans in history headed for sheep country and waited for a relegation-clinching thrashing but it didn't work out that way. Asuperb volley from the Boss, created brilliantly by Andy Graham, gave Vics a half time lead. Tony Hemmings made it 2-0 with twenty minutes left but almost immediately Macc pulled one back and went all out for the equaliser. Somehow Vics held on for three priceless points. That man Graham scored again to defeat Slough and Conference football was guaranteed following a 1-1 draw with Wycombe.

The nightmare of relegation banished it was fun time. Promotion chasing Altrincham were soundly beaten in front of over 2000 silent Alty fans and then Mal O'Connor scored four out of five against Cheltenham.

The season was closed by defeat in the two most important competitions known to man - the Mid-Cheshire Senior Cup and the Staffordshire Senior Cup.

Martin Dobson was appointed manager during the close season and hopefully he is the man to inject some discipline into the side and make the changes necessary to make Vics a major force once more.

Mark Edgeley

POSTSCRIPT: Martin Dobson walked out after just 39 days in the Vics hotseat to become manager of Bristol Rovers. After a week of total panic Sammy McIlroy took over, bringing in Gordon Clayton as his assistant. Despite his lack of experience and non-league knowledge the Board are confident they have made the right choice. Once more we wait and hope they are right.

TERRACE TALK

KIDDERMINSTER HARRIERS

The first Harriers game I attended was in 1981 and since then we've appeared at Wembley twice, won the F.A. Trophy, reached two Welsh Cup finals and won the Worcestershire Senior Cup six times. In fact, in the last ten years Kiddy have had more success than most of the West Midlands' Football League teams put together!

In the early 80s Harriers competed in the Southern League Premier, where matches were played in front of crowds of 4-500. For me the main attraction was being unofficial ballboy: I used to sit on the tarmac which surrounded the pitch and every time the ball went out of play I'd be up quick as a flash to give it back to my heroes in red and white.

It wasn't until the arrival of current manager Graham Allner, appointed in 1983/4, that the club began to take off. The previous season we won promotion by default when Allner's previous club, Leamington, won the Southern League only to be told that their ground wasn't up to scratch. Our first season in the Alliance Premier started disastrously and when Allner arrived we had yet to win a game. He set about completely restructuring the club, stressing the importance of growing your own talent by introducing an extremely successful youth policy. Within weeks the fortunes of the club changed and we have never looked back. In his first two years in charge Allner assembled a side which had the fans flocking to Aggborough from miles around, a team who knew only one way to play football and that was to attack. Unfortunately the defending bit was somewhat forgotten, which meant that watching the Harriers was never boring!

The 1985/6 season must go down as the most exciting in the club's history, mainly thanks to the most powerful attacking force ever seen in non-league football. The deadly trio of Kim Casey, Paul 'Ocker' Davies and Micky Tuohy scored a total of 139 between them that season. Casey, the hero of many a schoolboy, scored a remarkable 73 goals in 68 appearances. Davies' strength and power had defenders quaking in their boots and nearly every week he would hit one of his specials, cutting inside and curling the ball into the top corner from outside the area. Mick Tuohy completed the trio and set up many goals with his strength in the air. The team finished third in the league, scoring 99 times, a record beaten only this season by Barnet. But it was in the Welsh Cup where the greatest excitement came. We beat Shrewsbury and Newport before meeting Swansea City in the quarter final. After a last minute equaliser from Casey at the Vetch Field we won 4-0 in the replay at Aggborough, with Casey hitting a hat-trick. In the semi-final we faced Hereford, and after winning the home leg 4-1 looked to be on the way out as Hereford led 3-0 in the second leg. But then Micky Tuohy lobbed the keeper from thirty yards in the last minute to send the hundreds of Harriers fans behind the goal into dreamland and the team into the final. In the final we drew 1-1 with Wrexham at the Racecourse Ground in front of 5000, but narrowly lost the replay, 2-1 in front of over 4000 back at Aggborough.

1986/7 was in danger of turning into an anti-climax as the club dropped to a disappointing 12th in the league. But our chance of success came in the F.A. Trophy. During the weeks leading up to the final all anybody could talk about in Kiddy was Harriers going to Wembley. The week before the final I won a competition on local radio which was to make my day even more special. Me and my brother arrived at Wembley at midday and made our way to the Wembley restaurant where we met other fans of both Kiddy and Burton. We were then given a tour round Wembley, including the dressing rooms and out onto the famous Wembley turf, then we returned to the restaurant for lunch before taking our seats near to the Royal Box. The match didn't really live up to expectations with two hours of football failing to produce a goal. So, it was on to The Hawthorns on the tuesday. A crowd of over 15,000 (best of the season at The Hawthorns) watched a game that had everything. There was a disallowed goal from Burton in the first minute, then two from Davies gave Harriers a comfortable lead.Then with ten minutes left Burton pulled a goal back, and in the last minute came a moment that no Harrier will ever forget. Burton were awarded a penalty. Many couldn't bear to watch as Paul 'Ee-Aaw' Bancroft stepped up and saw his shot saved by Harriers' experienced keeper Jim Arnold. The Harriers fans got just slightly excited!

The following season saw many young players break into the first team from the reserves and youth team. In 1988/9 this mixture of youth and experience saw Harriers charge to the top of the league early on, where they stayed for fifteen weeks until February, when the team began to run out of steam and thoughts yet again turned to the Welsh Cup. We beat Cardiff and Hereford on the way to the final but were hammered 5-0 by Swansea City on a sweltering day at the Vetch Field.

Despite this defeat and a final league position of 5th, many Harriers were thinking in terms of the Championship as the beginning of 1989/90 rolled around. But they were in for a shock as by Christmas it was obvious that this successful side had run its course and was going nowhere fast. By the end of the season many of the old favourites had gone, including Kim Casey and Mick Tuohy, much to the annoyance of many fans who could not understand why Allner was breaking up the Trophy-winning side despite the fact that the club had just finished in their lowest ever league position.

As 1990/1 started the local papers were filled with letters predicting doom and gloom, but Allner did not let this worry him as he continued to rebuild. Delwyn Humphries, an extremely talented winger from Bridgnorth who has already forced his way into the England set-up, David Hadley, a strong, powerful striker, and Dave Barnett, signed from Wallsall on a free transfer and just what we've been missing in the centre of defence have all become firm favourites with the fans. This season they have combined with youngsters like Steve Lilwall and Richard Forsyth to produce an exciting team for the future. In the last month of the season they beat title challengers Barnet and Kettering and drew with Colchester. The reward for all their efforts was a place in the F.A. Trophy final at Wembley. Though we lost 2-1 to Wycombe (whose goals were both blatantly offside!) there were a lot of positive things to come out of the match and I believe we are only one or two players short of a team that could eventually fulfil their Football League ambitions.

Peter Lewis

TERRACE TALK

WEALDSTONE

UPDATE

Another season, another manager! 1990-91 started surprisingly well for Stones, with the team playing attractive football, winning a few games and actually reaching a flattering second place in the BHL at one point. However, their deficiencies at both ends of the pitch were exposed, and after a few defeats, including yet another F.A. Cup embarassment, this time at Ruislip Manor, Alan Gane was controversially sacked and replaced with Brian Hall, who took Wealdstone to the famous 'double' in 1984-85.

Hall managed at least to instil some discipline into the defence, but all too often they played as if you got points for catching your opponents offside twenty times even if you lost 1-0, tactics that won Wealdstone few friends. With continuing goalkeeping problems and a lightweight attack drastically unsuited to Hall's favoured long ball style there was no discernible improvement as the season progressed, and Stones stuttered to a third consecutive position of mid table anonymity. Disillusion set in among the fans as the famous Lower Mead atmosphere became a thing of the past, and even the traditionally large away following dwindled to almost nothing.

Ironically the highlight of the season was a defeat: 1-0 at Wycombe in the F.A. Trophy, where the team acquitted themselves well and created enough chances to have won, and the fans had an all-too-rare taste of big match atmosphere again. Victory at Dover on the last day of the season was sweet aswell, with the Kent club having assumed the mantle of bitterest rivals once held by Enfield.

All in all its almost a good thing events on the pitch took a back seat again. After Lower Mead was apparently granted a four year reprieve in 1990 the club did yet another about turn in announcing they would relocate at the end of 1990-91 after all. The Willesden Athletics Stadium which was to have been Wealdstone's temporary home during the last set of relocation machinations would now be our permanent home, with the club retaining only the main stand and building a brand new ground around it, groundsharing at Harrow Borough for a season while the work was carried out. It turned out that the club had rather foolishly been counting their chickens, because the plan was opposed by local residents and Brent Council promptly pulled out of the deal. Simultaneously it emerged that Stones were already committed to selling Lower Mead to Tesco for £6m (as opposed to £8m which we were told the ground would raise little over a year previously). To compound the problem if Wealdstone did not have a permanent home in the pipeline the Vauxhall League would be unlikely to sanction the Borough groundshare. Six weeks from the end of the season Stones had nowhere to play in 1991-92, and fears for the continued existence of the club were rife.

The deal with Watford came as a complete shock. A tie up with a more minor local club such as Wembley was seen by supporters as the only forseeable way forward, but all of a sudden Wealdstone were going to a first division (recently) ground. In simple terms Wealdstone were to pay £2½m for a half share in a new company which would own and operate the Vicarage Road stadium. Reaction was mixed. On the plus side it looked an excellent deal from the financial viewpoint. With land prices around Wealdstone sky-high even a modest new stadium would have cost far more than £2½m, and the club had been looking unsuccessfully for a site for years. It also showed foresight and ambition.

Celebrations as Tony Kelly scores Wealdstone's last ever Southern League goal at Lower Mead
(P. Fruin)

On paper the club not only had a ground equipped for the Football League, but the money to build a team which would get them there. The minus side concerned leaving Lower Mead. Ramshackle and neglected though it was by the time the final curtain fell, it was still a classic non-league ground with superb views and unique atmosphere. With Watford being so close all Wealdstone supporters have watched football at Vicarage Road from time to time, and all know that 10,000 at Watford don't begin to create the noise and passion of 1000 at Wealdstone. What crowds of 500 at Vicarage Road would be like doesn't bear thinking about. I'm convinced it is Lower Mead itself which sustained the loyalty of the Wealdstone fans during the remarkable ups and downs of the twenty years during which I've followed the club.

The last league match at Lower Mead, v. Cambridge City on April 27th, was an emotive occasion. A small crowd of 820 witnessed the event , disappointing but not entirely surprising in view of the local apathy which has long blighted the club. Predictably the Wealdstone fans turned it into a non-stop drunken party which continued long into the night, though many tears were shed too at the passing of what was an integral part of many of our lives.

The day was soured too by the first rumours that the Watford deal was actually anything but 'signed, sealed and delivered. Despite official denials it seemed clear the property deals were not as uncomplicated as they originally appeared, and rumours continued throughout the summer that Wealdstone were closer to the brink of extinction than the dawning of a glorious and wealthy new era. By midsummer the Supporters Club had expressed 'no confidence' in the board, who retaliated by disowning the Supporters Club. With the true facts surrounded by a secrecy worthy of MI5 the only thing you could say with certainty was that, with only days left to the first pre-season friendlies the club had signed no new players - and presumably not because Brian Hall doesn't think we need any! - while some of the better players in the squad (which admittedly isn't saying much!) had declined new terms and/or expressed a desire to leave. Even if the club manage to mount the massive PR effort which will be required to get fans through the turnstiles at Watford, something they've been notoriously bad at in the past, the prospects on the field are so bleak it's hard to see many potential new supporters coming back for more. The loyal supporters have grown good at being patient; we were sad to leave Lower Mead and disappointed not to be going to a custom-built ground; the compensating factor was the money which should have been adequate to virtually guarantee success on the field. Now even that will have to wait.

Martin Lacey

TERRACE TALK

NUNEATON BOROUGH

NOTHING BOROUGH HEARTACHE

So how does it feel when your football club is taken from you? When the creditors, debtors and grey things descend on the carcass? Increasingly, the threat of liquidation haunts the supporters of British football clubs. Initially there is talk of savings to be made; of economies. But when it really happens and your pride and joy are wound up, it hurts.

I was born in Coventry, and I follow the Sky Blues. But my father and grandfather hail from Nuneaton, just a few miles up the road. When City and Nuneaton Borough are both at home my loyalties are stretched to the limit. Those accustomed to the Football League might find that difficult to understand. Yet on a cold January Saturday this season, when Coventry City were beating Villa, the auld enemy, at Highfield Road for only the second time in history, I was jumping up and down with a few hundred loonies in blue and white scarves about eighteen miles away. The Borough had gone 3-0 up, away to Leicester United.

Each Borough game could, literally, be the last. Remarkably, with the sword of Damocles hanging over them, they maintained an assault on the Beazer Midland Division during 1991. Having missed out on promotion last season, finishing third, they looked poised to actually do it this year. Then they had four points deducted for fielding an ineligible player and the whole league table took on a different aspect. Tamworth, Stourbridge, Corby and Hednesford all scrambled with indecent haste above Borough. It's a familiar, if depressing, story.

That January Saturday was a fairly typical example of a normal, average sort of day in the life ot a Nuneaton Borough supporter. Les Green, a competent and popular manager, had been sacked, purely as an economy measure, during the week. Borough's regular goalkeeper, Linden Parslow, had signed for local rivals Atherstone United. Paul Sugrue, ex-Manchester City, Cardiff, Middlesbrough and Newport County, was appointed player-manager (probably on the grounds that, having suffered the death-throes with Newport, he could handle such an emotional trauma again.)

Hundreds of Borough fans made the trip and sang songs of defiance throughout. Despite having their top scorer suspended and midfield Gazza stereotype Adrian Waters sidelined with a broken leg, Boro' romped it. Defender Paul Carty then wrote his car off on the way back, injuring Sugrue, and putting him out of action for six weeks. This added meat to a saga that has more melodrama than 'Neighbours'.

Nuneaton Borough were officially wound up at County Court, Coventry, on December 18th 1990, and put into the hands of the Official Receiver. They were allowed to continue to fulfil fixtures at their decaying Manor Park ground, but morale was low. Collections were taken at home games, and sponsored events kept fans' hopes alive. Clubs like Kettering Town rallied round, offering their services for friendly matches. Still, there was a sense of impending doom. Lightning certainly does strike more than once, as supporters of nearby Coventry Sporting and A.P. Leamington can testify.

Whatever happens now, I have no doubt that the loyal band of players, some of who had turned out for nothing, will have to go. Even if they had won promotion the fear remains that League officials would concoct yet another form of punishment to ensure that some other nonentity supported by a handful of farm labourers in a bus shelter were elected in their place.

You may detect from this bitterness that Nuneaton

Borough had really got to me. Lured away from Highfield Road after thirty years! Enchanted by that smell of faggot and pea batches at the quaintly named Cock and Bear End. Besides, I had already siffered numerous drenchings and freezings at Highfield Road as "Dads Army", as they are locally known, creaked their way through various league and cup debacles. For £6 - £7 a game I shivered on the uncovered kop there, not able to buy anything to eat or drink. At Manor Park, for a third of the outlay, I could stand under cover, change ends at half time and watch a willing team who regularly beat, and quite often thrashed, the opposition.

The Boro' inspired me to buy my first football scarf since Wembley 1987, and to stick a "Don't Follow Me, Follow The Borough" sticker in the back window of my Y-reg Fiesta. I bought the lot. Funny hats. Keyrings, even Boro' Christmas cards. All memorabilia now, I suppose.

Some statistics may put the demise of Nuneaton Borough into perspective. In 1987 they were in the Vauxhall Conference. They finished six points and two places clear of the relegation zone, but were demoted anyway because their ground was deemed unsafe. It seems hard to believe that 22,114 crammed into it to watch Boro' draw with Rotherham in the F.A. Cup third round in January 1967.

Nuneaton Borough were founder members of the Alliance Premier League and finished runners-up in 1984 and 1985. They have arguably produced more Football League players (21) than any other non-league club post-war. Recent examples include Eddie McGoldrick (Crystal Palace), Trevor Morley (West Ham), Trevor Peake (Coventry City), Malcolm Shotton (Oxford United), Richard Hill (Oxford United), Paul Culpin (Peterborough), Dean Thomas (Northampton), Kirk Stephens (Coventry City/Luton), Timmy Smithers (Oxford) and Everton Carr (Peterborough).

Nuneaton is a fairly large town, with a population of 70,000 plus, making it larger than Bury, Crewe, Torquay, Aldershot, Wrexham, Shrewsbury and Mansfield. Even in the Beazer Midland, three tiers down from the Football League, they can pull in four figure crowds. The blueprint is there for success. All they have to do is survive. But that's not as easy as it sounds.

Whenever you get a bit down about the fortunes of your own team, think of the crushing blows fate has dealt out to Nuneaton Borough. Demoted from a league just before it became the feeder to Football League status. Playing Maidstone, Wimbledon and Scarborough one minute, Rushden Town and Spalding United the next. Victims of a vicious High Court battle between warring factions on the board ever since. Robbed of no less than five points over the last two seasons for fielding unregistered players. They pleaded innocence, unsuccessfully, over that. (It's hard to keep on top of the paperwork when you're only paid in fruit pastlles!)

Despite this defecit they clawed their way to the top of the league by February 1991. Hedley Brunt, the Receiver in charge, insidted that they must shed some more players and virtually double gates to survive. Some say his name is Cockney rhyming slang. With local rivals like Hinckley Town, Bedworth United and Atherstone United all a toilet roll's throw away from Manor Park, I suppose non-league fans won't have far to go for an alternative.

POSTSCRIPT 24/6/91

Throughout the summer rumour and counter-rumour have raged on. Never the most outgoing of clubs as far as its supporters are concerned, Borough successfully completed the season (although it was touch and go at the end). Despite their points deduction they finished fifth in the Beazer Midland and were finalists in two domestic cup competitions.

As the turnstiles closed, so did the ranks. An ominous silence descended over Manor Park. The "Borough Hotline" became unobtainable. The only thing which remained constant, as a sign the club were still functioning, was their monthly removal by direct debit of my £5 subscription to

Light at the end of the tunnel? Chairman Howard Kerry (right) greets new manager George Rooney. (Nuneaton Evening Tribune)

the "Borough 800 Club", ostensibly a lottery, but basically a monthly donation by concerned fans.

Early in June I had a telephone conversation with Keith Parker, the club secretary. He seemed genuinely to know as much as I did. The club were still in receivership and facing up to liquidation. A sale had been proposed to 'an interested party', but quite honestly this is the sort of gossip which has been flying round the town for months. There was, insisted Keith, no question of the club going out of existence.

On 21st June a local paper carried a story claiming that a 'consortium of businessmen' had bought the club. Apparently it ensures that football will go ahead at Manor Park next season. Noel Kelly, one of many ex-chairmen involved in a plot more tortuous than 'Howards Way' failed to regain control and will get back the £10,000 he claims to have invested in the club in February.

At a press conference the following day the former Altrincham and Bath City manager, George Rooney, was announced as new manager in place of caretaker Paul Sugrue. A 'fresh start' and a glorious future were promised.

The blokes with the blue and white scarves have heard it all before. Is this the happy ending? Has the blood letting finished? The potential is still there for Nuneaton Borough to take their rightful place in League football. Whether Graham Kelly will have dismantled the access apparatus by then remains to be seen.

Geoff Veasey

TERRACE TALK

SUTTON COLDFIELD TOWN

Context and perspective are crucial to an understanding of Sutton Coldfield Town. The context is the town itself, a large and dull middle-class suburb of Birmingham, which, with a population of around 100,000 is one of the country's largest towns without a Football League club. The perspective is that Sutton's average gate is a mere 200, so who cares much anyway?

The club's history is largely irrelevant before the mid 1960s, but there are a couple of interesting points surrounding the very first match, which took place on 1st February 1879 against a team called Birmingham F.C. The match was played on Meadow Plat in the vast Sutton Park, an area where I played as a schoolboy in the late 70s. The teams for that first game changed at the Station Hotel, which is my prefered watering hole these days and reputedly the biggest selling pub in the West Midlands. Not a great deal has changed about The Station in the last 112 years and this remarkable continuity never ceases to amaze me whatever the state of my consciousness.

Until the sixties the club's achievements were distinctly unremarkable (Wallsall Senior League Champions 1949) and Sutton Town, as they had been known since the war, persistently struggled in the harsh professional environment of the Birmingham League. 1964/65 saw the arrival at the club of several key figures such as Maurice Flint and Stan Sims, who were to leave an impression on the club for decades afterwards.

In 1965 the new regime took the rechristened Sutton Coldfield Town into amateur football in the Worcestershire Combination (now Midland Combination). Knowing that amateur clubs big on hospitality and 'footballing values' could pull in quality players and an awful lot of respect, Sutton's quality administration laid the foundations for steady advancement on and off the field. In 1972 the splendid clubhouse was opened and this has been the backbone of the club since; the council owned Coles Lane ground is home to several other sporting set-ups, not all of which are universally welcomed. Sutton had begun to taste success in the Amateur Cup when it was abolished in 1974, but the committee typically chose the F.A. Trophy against the Vase on the grounds of prestige.

There was no doubting Sutton's organisational credibility but it took a special man to transform playing fortunes. 1977 saw the appointment of the late Rhys Davies as manager, a near-legend who had put Alvechurch on the footballing map. Rhys put together a terifically entertaining side, way too good for the Midland Combination; the title was won in 1978 and 1979.

Star of the side was the abnormally talented Brian Kenning, a player with Platini-like skills in a frame less athletic than Gascoigne, and Sutton 'discovered' Barry Cowdrill (now at Bolton) and the brilliant Kim Casey. Davies moved back to Alvechurch in 1980, leaving Kenning to assume the glory of a West Midlands League title as player-manager. The following season, 1980-81, witnessed the greatest day in Sutton's history when Billy Bremner's Doncaster Rovers came to Coles Lane in the F.A. Cup first round. They won 2-0, but Kenning's early failure to convert an eight yard indirect free kick is the only blemish on my memory of a childhood hero.

Southern League status was finally granted in 1982 and a superb run-in took us into the 20 club Premier Division with a side too heavy on clogging to achieve much success - Kevin Richardson, Paul Knox and Andy Keeling blotted out the skills of the outstanding Graham Clegg. In contrast to the previous season, a disastrous finish led to our immediate relegation to the Midland Division in 1984, where the club has remained ever since.

Ron Timmings, a widely respected figure in Midlands non-league football who had overseen Sutton's rapid elevation in the early 1980s, managed to persuade Eddie Caulfield to desert newly promoted local rivals Paget Rangers for the distinctly more comfortable managerial surroundings of Coles Lane in 1987. The pick of the talented young Paget side came too and with the help of some astute signings Sutton came fifth in 1987-88, playing some attractive football. It seemed that the return to the Premier Division that the whole club yearned for would soon become a reality, but competition in a traditionally strong division proved too hot for an averagely-resourced club. Likewise, cup exits were suffered at frustrating moments with glory just around the corner.

In 1990 a putsch occured in the committee room which saw the trusty 'old guard' replaced by a 'nouveau riches' leadership headed by Charles Holt, owner of a small chemicals business within puking distance of St. Andrews. Bafflingly, more money was paid to the team without proportinately strengthening it, beginning the trend towards an unhealthy cash culture at Sutton. Fortunes on the pitch declined rapidly when the two best players suffered long-term injuries in October; the loyal Bob Whittingham's broken leg ended a run of 206 consecutive appearances and the complex muscle injury sustained by the talented Johnny Hunt has deprived supporters of the pleasure of his unbounded skills.

Eddie Caulfield's future was already looking bleak when he instigated one of football's more bizarre management arrangements in December 1990. The story goes that Eddie invited the hitherto obscure Phil Sharpe to share the duties of managing the first team, ostensibly creating a Curtis/Sillett type managership; the twist is that Phil Sharpe is a self-made millionaire whose only previous experience was a spell incharge of a Sunday side.

Bob Whittingham crosses against Halesowen
(Sutton Observer)

The committee were asking us to believe that the appointment was purely a footballing one, thus removing some more of their dwindling credibility, but the side improved considerably with the addition of some quality players. Meanwhile Eddie Caulfield found himself increasingly marginalised in the matter of team affairs as Phil Sharpe, aided by the existing coach, Chris Sharpe, wore his track-suit bottoms with more authority. As the transfer deadline approached the brilliant Lance Morrison was signed from Gloucester for £1500 - a club record fee and only the second time in Sutton's history that money has been paid to sign someone. Since gate receipts at the time were barely covering the cost of fielding the club's three teams, naive supporter wondered where the money was coming from.

Sutton ended the season firmly in midtable mediocrity and losing the Worcestershire Senior Cup Final to a Kidderminster club preoccupied with the Trophy but still mean enough to charge visiting supporters 50p to enter either of the Aggborough bars. Wicked soup though. The redundant Eddie Caulfield has gone back to Paget bitterly criticising the money obsession at Coles Lane which he, innocently or otherwise, helped to create.

The outlook for Sutton Coldfield Town and its small band of supporters is a mixed one. On the pitch you have to say it is bright because of the financial backing which is covertly available. But under the present regime it will be very easy to criticise any success that comes to Coles Lane as being bought by the cynical application of money. In the car park on match days midfielder Alan McLaren's Reliant Robin parks incongruously alongside the Porsches, Jaguars and Mercedes favoured by the club's underwriters.

There are still backroom staff such as secretary Gerry Shanahan and the newly elevated 'unofficial manager' Allan Hampton who cling to the values of men like Maurice Flint, Ron Timmings and Gerge Humpherson; men who gave the club respect and status. That can't be bought - it has to be earned.

Colin Peel

TERRACE TALK

BARNET

UPDATE

On the night of April 23rd Barnet drew 2-2 away to Stafford leaving us two points behind Altrincham, who had two games in hand. Yet again it seemed that Barnet were going to be the nearly men. However, it was Alty who cracked, losing to Barrow, Stafford and Northwich whilst Barnet won their final three games to ensure promotion to the Football League.

It was those final three games that truly epitomised Barnet's season. We struggled to beat Welling at Underhill despite leading 2-0 at one stage, relying on Gary Bull (inspirational throughout the season) to score a last gasp penalty and give us a 3-2 win. Our home form during the last half of the season was truly erratic as players' nerves began to show. On the Monday we travelled to Wycombe and outclassed the home side with one of the best performances of the season, showing what an excellent footballing team we can be. So it was that on Saturday May 4th we travelled to Fisher needing only a draw to ensure promotion. A crowd of around 4,200 (4,000 from Barnet) watched in disbelief as Fisher went 1-0 up and then 2-1 early in the second half. I don't think I've ever felt so low as I did at that point. Fortunately Barnet showed their ability to grit their teeth (a characteristic which gave us many an away win last season) and David Howell equalised after about sixty-five minutes. Gary Bull's double strike in the last five minutes (the first of which was probably the best goal of the season) ensured 4th Division status next year. Emotional scenes duly followed. After five years of knocking on the door Barnet had finally done it. It was a brilliant season all round with Barnet also winning the Herts. Senior Cup and reaching the third round of the F.A. Cup having beaten then 4th Division leaders Northampton on the way.

These are good times for Barnet F.C. We continue to sell players at exorbitant prices, having sold four last year for deals that in time will value over half a million pounds. We have gained League status and at the time of writing have managed to get the majority of the first team to sign new contracts.

However, next season may not be the bed of roses that people imagine. Despite the necessary ground improvements that are presently taking place Underhill will be one of the worst grounds in the League. Moreover, whilst we managed to score 103 goals in the Conference last year, 4th Division defences will prove much sterner, while in turn our own defence will need strengthening. Should Barnet not do well I have no doubt crowds will average around 1500 (half the amount we averaged as a successful non-league side). Last, but by no means least, it is my belief that watching non-league football is far more enjoyable than 4th Division football and I know that when I travel to Carlisle next year a little bit of me will cry inside when I go to change ends at half time and find a policeman and a ten foot fence barring my way.

I see our first year in the League as a learning process - a chance to find our feet in new surroundings. We may strike lucky and get promotion at the first attempt, but if we don't I won't really care - as long as we get six points out of Lincoln.

FOOTNOTE: Just after the season ended, Kevin Durham, a key member of Barnet's championship side, died of a heart attack. It would be wrong to write this article without mention of this matter. He will be sorely missed both on and off the football pitch. May he rest in peace.

Doran Garfunkel

INTRODUCTION TO THE DIRECTORY

Our team of contributors has now managed to visit about three quarters of the grounds in the GMVC and its three principal feeder leagues - and remain sober enough to come up with some kind of description. About half the details have been rewritten since last year, and all the photographs are new. Obviously for next season we'd like to change as much as possible and fill the remaining gaps, so if you've 'done' a substantial number of grounds either following your team or pursuing your vocation as a groundhopper we'd like to hear from you. We hope to include more about the next tier of feeder leagues aswell.

Main contributors to this year's information were: GMVC - Paul Godfrey, Peter Lewis; Diadora League - Ian Levene, DJ Robinson, Barry Swain, Duncan Towell; Beazer Homes League - Martin Lacey, Daniel Levene, D.C. Evans, Neil Wyatt, Rob & Richard Clark; HFS Loans League - Andy Dakin, Laurie Alder.

We have opted not to include names of photographers alongside each shot; if anyone is offended by this policy please accept our apologies. Thanks are due in this department to the following: Mick Cunningham, Barry Swain, DJ Robinson, Andy Stevens, Andy Dakin, Fingers Fruin, Neil Wyatt, Nick Robinson, Colin Peel, D. West, Simons Haircut, and Colin Burton, who climbed the floodlights at Boston United!

If we missed your name out, sorry!

Directory

THE FOOTBALL (VAUXHALL) CONFERENCE

ALTRINCHAM Moss Lane, Altrincham, Cheshire WA15 8AP Tel. 061-928 1045. Information 0898 664845.

5/10 minutes walk from Altrincham town centre, bus station and BR. No social club in ground but 'The Moss' just up the road serves this purpose. Main stand on halfway line holds 1000 and looks bigger due to upward sloping roof. Covered terrace with low roof to one side, grass bank to the other. Covered terrace running length of opposite side. Golf Road covered terrace at one end, open Chequers Bank at other end, used by away supporters at segregated matches. Club shop at this end. Crowds restricted to 3000 for safety reasons at end of last season.

BARROW, Holker Street, Barrow-in-Furness, Cumbria, Tel. 0229 820346/823061. Information 0898 888620.

5 minute walk from railway station, on main A590 into town. Best view is from social club above the sports hall at one end: unfortunately it's closed during matches! Main stand seating 1000 along most of one side, old but brightly painted. Large terrace along opposite side, roof removed a few years ago though new roof is planned. 'Holker End' terrace with rusty roof at one end, houses partisan home supporters, also an aggressive and racist tendency not popular with visiting supporters. Sports hall built on what used to be terracing at other end.

BATH CITY, Twerton Park, Bath, Avon, BA2 1DB. Tel. 0225 423087/313247. Information 0898 884474.

Shared with Bristol Rovers and completely inadequate for second division football, though spacious for City's crowds, depleted by the town's penchant for rugby. Main stand gutted by arson attack last season, now being rebuilt. Paddock in front of stand still open. Large covered terrace on opposite side. Good size open terrace behind one goal, temporary seating installed on part of it after the fire, which obstructs view. Very small terrace behind other goal. Little atmosphere. Ground 2-3 miles from city centre and station, just off A36 Lower Bristol Road. Large social club outside.

BOSTON UNITED, York Street, Boston, Lincs. Tel. 0205 365524/5. Information 0898 121539.

Until recently undisputed best ground in non-league football. 2000 seat main stand along length of one side, large covered terrace opposite. Old main stand behind one goal with 500 seats, directors box and press facilities. Small terrace in front. Huge covered and fenced in terrace behind opposite goal. Traditionally large crowds, though loyalty stretched by lack of recent success, consequently much barracking of their own team. Welcoming clubhouse outside ground, though better beer from the Waggon & Horses nearby.

CHELTENHAM TOWN, Whaddon Road, Cheltenham, Glos. GL52 5NA. Tel. 0242 513397. Information 0898 333096.

15 minutes walk from town centre and much further from station. Newly refurbished social club with seriously-taken skittles as entertainment at evening games. Main stand seating 1200 along three quarters length of one side with paddock in front, snack bar (good pies) and well stocked club shop to one side. Smallish terraces on remaining three sides, part covered at one end and roof planned for the side during close season. Never enough programmes so arrive early.

COLCHESTER UNITED, Layer Road, Colchester, Essex, CO2 7JJ. Tel. 0206 574042. Information 0839 664410.

Dreadfully neglected ground. Wooden main stand along three quarters of one side. Large covered terrace on opposite side, open terrace behind one goal, covered segregated terrace behind opposite goal. Fans segregated for all games. Police escort for visiting fans can ensure you don't arrive on time!

FARNBOROUGH TOWN, John Roberts Ground, Cherrywood Road, Farnborough, Hants. GU14 8UD. Tel. 0252 541469.

Very modest, though well kept ground. Small main stand, covered terrace on opposite side, small open terrace behind one goal and not much at opposite end. Clubhouse resembles a Harvester restaurant! Smallish crowds but very friendly supporters.

GATESHEAD, International Stadium, Neilson Road, Gateshead, NE10 0EF. Tel. 091-478 3883.

Huge athletics stadium, holds 12,000 all seated though only (!) 7000 seat main stand is open for matches. Venue does not serve the club well, as small attendances reflect the lack of atmosphere. Cheap, pleasant bar in ground, more ambiguous welcome in pub outside. Freezing in winter and pretty desolate at any time of year. Contrary to claims, there's still nobody collecting admission money if you arrive early!

KETTERING TOWN, Rockingham Road, Kettering, Northants. NN16 9AW. Tel. 0536 83028. Information 0898 888639.

Huge main stand running two thirs length of pitch. Story that it was supposed to go the full length but the club ran out of money would now appear to have substance as I've seen an old club brochure containing an 'artists impression'. Social club and shop to one side. Covered terrace on opposite side, good size open terrace behind one goal, smaller part covered terrace for away supporters at other end. Ground on A6003 about 1½ miles from town centre and station. Once a friendly enough place but success has attracted a notorious yob element.

KIDDERMINSTER HARRIERS, Aggborough, Hoo Road, Kidderminster, Worcs. DY10 1NB. Tel. 0562 823931. Information 0898 121 547.

Ground much improved recently with removal of

^ Farnborough Town v

Macclesfield

^ Redbridge Forest v

Witton Albion

Directory

Kettering Town ^^

^^ Stafford Rangers

Northwich Victoria ^^^

Merthyr Tydfil ▼▼▼

Runcorn

▲▲ Altrincham

Telford United ▲▲

Directory

Boston United

speedway track and new terracing behind goals, one end covered, one open. Slightly odd looking main stand seating 400 - extension or rebuilding planned for 1992. Low covered terrace on opposite side. Impressive club shop, good social club, though not always open to visiting supporters. Large car park. Ten minutes walk from station (BR and Severn Valley Railway steam trains!) or five minutes if you take your wellingtons and cut through the cattle market. Club best known for the soup, a legend in non-league circles.

MACCLESFIELD TOWN, Moss Rose Ground, London Road, Macclesfield, Cheshire, SK11 7SP. Tel. 0625 511545/24324. Information 0898 121546.

On A523 approx. 1 mile from town centre and BR. 600 seat main stand with area of flat standing to one side and small area of covered terrace to other. Covered terrace on opposite side, open terraces behind both goals, one newly built and equipped with segregation fences as a consequence of Chester City's groundsharing. New main stand planned. Good pub, The Star, outside ground.

MERTHYR TYDFIL, Penydarren Park, Merthyr Tydfil, Mid Gla. CF47 8RF. Tel 0685 4102. Information 0898 884533.

Ground almost rebuilt to accomodate European football after Merthyr won the Welsh Cup. Moderate size main stand, smaller 'family stand' behind one goal. Large covered terrace with perimeter and segregation fences along one side, large open terrace behind other goal. Clubhouse in ground, though visiting supporters not always welcome. Ten minutes walk from bus station and BR, though located on top of a mountain.

NORTHWICH VICTORIA, The Drill Field, Northwich, Cheshire, CW9 5HN. Tel. 0606 41450. Information 0898 664813.

Ground off A533 close to town centre and about 20 minutes walk from railway station. Reasonable clubhouse but try also The Volunteer next door and The Windmill, off M6 at J19. The world's oldest football ground in continuous use, which probably explains why it's seen better days, including league football last century! 600 seat main stand to one side of the halfway line with terracing in front and to sides. Tall, thin covered terrace on opposite side with grass banks fenced off either side. Narrow covered terrace behind one goal, flat standing behind other.

REDBRIDGE FOREST, Victoria Road, Dagenham, Essex, RM10 7XL. Tel. 081-592 7194/593 3864.

Low main stand along two thirds length of one side. Good sized covered terrace opposite, smallish open terraces behind both goals. Club exists as a result of mergers involving Leytonstone, Ilford and Walthamstow Avenue; now based at Dagenham F.C. with whom, surprise (!), they tried to merge, thwarted so far. Very few supporters - rather like Fisher, a club without tradition. Ten minutes walk from Dagenham East tube.

RUNCORN, Canal Street, Runcorn, Cheshire, WA7 1RZ. Tel. 0928 560076. Information 0898 664814.

Difficult to find, especially by car. Good social club but unimpressive ground. Smallish main stand with covered terrace to both sides. Low terrace, part covered on opposite side. Open terrace behind one goal, flat standing at other end. Supporters occasionally hostile, though rarely numerous.

SLOUGH TOWN, Wexham Park Stadium, Wexham Road, Slough SL2 5QR. Tel. 0753 23358. Information 0898 446885.

Ground built in the seventies, recent improvements for admission to the Conference. 400 seat main stand with terracing either side, small terraces on remaining three sides, one end and central section of side covered. Basic ground but good atmosphere. Well stocked club shop, seperate programme shop in supporters club office. 20 minutes walk from BR.

Northwich Victoria

STAFFORD RANGERS, Marston Road, Stafford ST16 3BX. Tel. 0785 42750. Information 0898 664839.

Ground to north of town centre and a good half hour walk from station. Comfortable social club outside ground. Steep main stand offering excellent view, tea bar and changing rooms to one side, well stocked club shop to other. Covered terrace along length of opposite touchline. Shallow, part covered terrace at one end, sand and gravel bank with segregation fences at other end, good for building sandcastles if the game's boring.

TELFORD UNITED, Bucks Head Ground, Watling Street, Wellington, Telford, Shropshire, TF1 2NJ. Tel. 0952 223838. Information 0898 121545.

Easy to locate from M54 or Wellington BR. Large clubhouse, also Bucks Head pub outside the ground and recommended chip shop down the road. Old main stand with terracing to both sides, one covered. New 'Maxell' stand seating 1000 on opposite side with open terraces to both sides. Terrace and cinder bank at both ends, one part covered. Big ground but very little atmosphere.

WELLING UNITED, Park View Road, Welling, Kent. Tel. 081-301 1196/5676. Information 0898 800654.

Old Bexley United ground. 10 minutes walk from Welling BR. Low wooden main stand along length of one side. Part covered terrace on opposite side and open terrace behind both goals. Cramped social club behind stand. French bread hot dogs recommended from tea bar.

WITTON ALBION, Wincham Park, Chapel Street, Wincham, Northwich, Cheshire CW9 6DA. Tel. 0606 43008.

New ground, built in 1989. Modest 500 seat stand, shallow terraces on remaining three sides, all part covered. 1½ miles from Northwich centre.

WYCOMBE WANDERERS, Adams Park, Hillbottom Road, Sands, High Wycombe, Bucks. HP12 4HJ. Tel. 0494 24567. Information 0898 446855.

Magnificent new ground opened in 1990. 1267 seat main stand along one side, covered terrace on remaining three sides. Half of side reserved for away supporters, though segregation not enforced at all matches. Excellent food from tea bar. Social club may or may not be open to visiting supporters. Miles from station, though buses run. Leave early if you want to avoid the 'mother of all traffic jams'.

YEOVIL TOWN, Huish Park, Boundary Road, Yeovil, Somerset, BA22 8YF. Tel. 0935 23662. Information 0898 333092.

Another ground opened in 1991, on industrial estate miles from town centre. Stands along both sides seat 5000. Terraces at both ends hold a further 4000, open at present but rooves planned. Away end is only open if there's enough away supporters. Excellent catering and club shop. Restaurant open but no bar for supporters. Atmosphere has been somewhat muted since the move. Activities of Yeovil's notorious yokel yobs have also apparently declined.

ISTHMIAN (DIADORA) LEAGUE

PREMIER DIVISION

AYLESBURY UNITED, The Stadium, Buckingham Road, Aylesbury, Bucks. HP19 3QL. Tel. 0296 436350/436525. Information 0898 446824.

Recently built ground. Good main stand and nice club shop. Terracing on remaining three sides, fairly narrow and shallow, covered opposite main stand. Clubhouse outside ground not always open to visitors but reasonable pub nearby. Home fans not the friendliest in this league. Longish walk from Aylesbury BR.

BASINGSTOKE TOWN, The Camrose Ground, Western Way, Basingstoke, Hants. RG24 6HW. Tel. 0256 461465.

Good stand with 840 seats and covered terracing on one side. Covered terrace on opposite side, open terraces behind goals. Excellent clubhouse with good food. Small club shop. Two miles from BR.

BISHOP'S STORTFORD, George Wilson Stadium, Rhodes Avenue, Bishop's Stortford, Herts. CM23 3JN. Tel. 0279 654140. Information 0898 333097.

23o seat stand with executive boxes, large bar behind. Shallow terrace opposite, covered terraces behind both goals. 10 minutes walk from BR. Look out for 'Cross Rhodes' fanzine.

BOGNOR REGIS TOWN, Nyewood Lane, Bognor Regis, West Sussex, PO21 2TY. Tel. 0243 822325.

Smallish main stand, covered terracing opposite and behind one goal, open terrace behind other goal. Short walk through cycle paths from station. Reasonable bar but more fun drinking in the town. Great place for a day out, especially in August.

BROMLEY, Hayes Lane, Bromley, Kent, BR2 9EF. Tel. 081-460 5291. Information 0898 122904.

Large main stand, closed for safety reasons part of last season. Substantial open terrace on opposite side. Part covered terrace behind one goal, covered area with bench seats, mostly broken, behind other goal. Dingy but friendly bar in ground. Twenty-five minutes walk from Bromley South BR.

CARSHALTON ATHLETIC, War Memorial Sports Ground, Colston Avenue, Carshalton, Surrey, SM5 2PW. Tel. 081-642 8658/770 3601. Information 0898 446849.

Reasonable sized stand, large terrace opposite which lost its roof in gales two years ago. Smaller terraces behind both goals, one end recently covered. Allegedly best clubhouse in league with excellent food. Small club shop. Close to BR.

CHESHAM UNITED, Meadow Park, Amy Lane, Amersham Road, Chesham, Bucks. HP5 1NE. Tel. 0494 783964.

Money-no-object club who finally got promoted, improving ground along with team. Seated stand one side, covered terrace opposite, open terraces behind goals.

DAGENHAM, Victoria Road, Dagenham, Essex, RM10 7XL. Tel. 081-592 7194/593 3864.

Original occupants of ground shared with Redbridge Forest.

ENFIELD, Southbury Road, Enfield, Middx. EN1 1YQ. Tel. 081-363 2858. Information 0898 122920.

850 seat main stand with open terrace on one side. Terraces on remaining three sides, all part covered. Away fans charged to enter bar. Impressive programme and well stocked club shop. Ten minutes walk from Enfield Town or Southbury BR.

GRAYS ATHLETIC, The Recreation Ground, Bridge Road, Grays, Essex, RM17 6BZ. Tel. 0375 391649.

Ground hemmed in by redevelopment. Covered area down one side with seats between two areas of terracing. Narrow terrace on opposite side and behind one goal. Large modern bar with sports hall underneath. Ten minutes walk from BR.

HARROW BOROUGH, Earlsmead, Carlyon Avenue, South Harrow, Middx. HA2 8SS. Tel. 081-422 5221.

Small main stand with small covered terraces either side. Narrow covered terrace opposite and open terraces behind both goals. Large clubhouse with four bars. Entrance hidden among suburban houses. 20 minutes walk from Northolt or South Harrow tube.

HAYES, Townfield House, Church Road, Hayes, Middx.

Directory

Bromley

Enfield

^ St Albans City >

^ Wivenhoe Town v

HENDON, Claremont Road, Cricklewood, London NW2 1AE. Tel. 081-455 9185. Information 0898 664254.

Big ground, legacy of amateur glory days. 500 seat stand, large covered terrace on opposite side, open terraces behind goals. Sloping pitch, superb tea bar.

KINGSTONIAN, Kingsmeadow Stadium, 422A Kingston Road, Kingston, Surrey, KT1 3PB. Tel. 081-547 3335. Information 0898 884441.

Third season at new ground. Large main stand and good size covered terrace opposite. Shallow open terraces behind both goals. Large clubhouse outside ground. Unpleasant smells waft from nearby sewage works.

MARLOW, Alfred Davis Memorial Ground, Oak Tree Road, Marlow, Bucks. SL7 3ED. Tel. 0628 483970.

300 seat main stand, covered terracing along half of opposite side, small open terraces behind goals.

ST. ALBANS CITY, Clarence Park, Hatfield Road, St. Albans, Herts. AL1 4PL. Tel. 0727 66819.

Pleasant ground in corner of park with trees growing all around (and in one case on) the terraces. Long, dingy main stand with small clubhouse up some stairs behind. Terraces on remaining three sides, small area opposite main stand covered. Excellent programme. Ten minutes walk from St Albans City BR.

STAINES TOWN, Wheatsheaf Park, Wheatsheaf Lane, Staines, Middx. TW18 2PD. Tel. 0784 455988.

Worst ground in division following relegation of Barking! Reasonable main stand and small covered terrace opposite.

SUTTON UNITED, Borough Sports Ground, Gander Green Lane, Sutton, Surrey, SM1 2EY. Tel. 081-644 4440/5120. Information 0898 121537.

Oval shape ground in municipal park. 1000 seat main stand along half length of one side with large clubhouse behind, small club shop to one side and curved terrace. Small covered terrace on opposite side. Flat standing and grass bank behind one goal, few steps of terracing and grass bank behind other goal. Friendly club but not much atmosphere. Close to West Sutton BR, though train service erratic at weekends.

WINDSOR & ETON, Stag Meadow, St. Leonards Road, Windsor, Berks. SL4 3DR. Tel. 0753860656.

Very open ground, pleasant in summer but desolate in winter. 350 seat main stand with small covered terrace opposite. Open terrace and grass bank round rest of ground. Fair walk from BR.

WIVENHOE TOWN, Broad Lane Ground, Elmstead Road, Wivenhoe, Essex, CO7 7HA. Tel. 0206 823416. Information 0898 884458.

Small main stand, reasonable size covered terraces behind both goals, covered terrace apparently under construction on opposite side last season. Could be an excellent ground if/when finished.

Staines Town

WOKING, Kingfield Sports Ground, Kingfield, Woking, Surrey, GU22 9AA. Tel 0483 772470/776126. Information 0898 122902.

Ground fails to live up to public acclaim generated by their cup run, though improvements underway last season. Main stand along one side, open terrace on opposite side, part covered terrace behind one goal, grass bank behind other goal. A minority of morons among 'supporters' attracted by recent success. Reasonable bar with cheap prices but not enough staff.

WOKINGHAM TOWN, Finchampstead Road, Wokingham, Berks. RG11 2NR. Tel. 0734 780253/772884.

Club shared at Reading at start of last season while ground improvements carried out, though still fairly unimpressive. Tiny main stand, covered terrace on one side, small open terrace behind both goals, large clubhouse outside ground.

FIRST DIVISION

ABINGDON TOWN, Culham Road, Abingdon, Oxon. OX14 3BT. Tel. 0235 521684/555566.

AVELEY, Mill Field, Mill Road, Aveley, Essex, RM15 4TR. Tel. 0708 865940.

400 seat main stand with open terracing on either side. Shallow covered terrace along half length of opposite

side, nothing behind goals. Awful floodlights, minimal support, clubhouse includes tea bar and is more like village hall. Plenty of parking space.

BARKING, Mayesbrook Park, Lodge Avenue, Dagenham, Essex, RM8 2JR. Tel. 081-595 6511.

Fairly new ground. One stand - half standing, half seated, minimal open terracing at one end of sloping pitch. Little support. Spacious clubhouse and plenty of parking.

BOREHAM WOOD, Meadow Park, Broughinge Road, Boreham Wood, Herts. WD6 5AL . Tel. 081 953 9883.

Main stand attached to clubhouse offering less than perfect view. Shallow covered terrace along opposite side and open terrace elsewhere. No club shop, tea bar hidden away.

CHALFONT ST. PETER, The Playing Fields, Amersham Road, Chalfont St. Peter, Bucks. SL9 9QX. Tel. 0753 885797.

Pleasant village setting. One small seated stand joining onto pleasant clubhouse. Good tea bar at back of clubhouse. Club shop inside. Minimal terracing behind one goal, grass verges elsewhere.

CROYDON, Croydon Sports Arena, Albert Road, South Norwood, London SE25 4QL. Tel. 081-654 3462/8555.

Desolate athletics arena. Good main stand and open terracing on one side. Walways around remaining three sides seldom used. Clubhouse often deserted. Two tea bars.

DORKING, Meadowbank, Mill Lane, Dorking, Surrey, RH4 1DX. Tel. 0306 884112.

Pretty basic ground for a seemingly ambitious club. Basic clubhouse joins onto wooden seated main stand. Good tea bar, no club shop. Other three sides are grass with a small covered shed on the far side, no sign of any terracing. Good pub in the car park. Close to town centre.

DULWICH HAMLET, Sandy Lane, Mitcham, Surrey, CR4 2HD. Tel. 081-648 3248.

Groundsharing at deadly rivals Tooting & Mitcham while once magnificent Champion Hill Ground is turned into a supermarket. Thankfully the plans allow for a more modest stadium on part of the site, so the club seem to have come out OK, and should be back on their own turf in a year or so.

HARLOW TOWN, Harlow Sports Centre, Hammarskjold Road, Harlow, Essex, CM20 2JF. Tel. 0279 421927/635100/428188.

One seated stand with three sides of steep grass banks. Athletics track round pitch, ski lift whirs above one end. Catering van is best in division, no club shop, enthusiastic supporters though very few of them! New ground at Royden Road should be ready mid-season, allegedly in the Kingstonian/Witton/Aylesbury indentikit style, though obviously a big improvement on present venue.

HEYBRIDGE SWIFTS, Scraley Road, Heybridge, Maldon, Essex, CM9 7BL. Tel. 0621 852978.

As generations of groundhoppers have no doubt discovered, there are TWO places called Heybridge in Essex, so make sure you go to the right one. If the other Heybridge ever get a team together there could be real problems. Rural setting, seated stand along one side, small open terrace at one end. Nice clubhouse, good tea bar, no club shop. Pleasant people.

HITCHIN TOWN, Top Field, Fishponds Road, Hitchin, Herts. SG5 1NU. Tel. 0462 459028/434483.

Seated stand two thirds length of one side with wooden terrace opposite, part covered. Terracing at both ends, one part covered. Good club shop, two tea bars, sweet shop and reasonable clubhouse. Well supported club.

Directory

Chalfont St. Peter

Whyteleafe

Hitchin Town ▾▾▾

LEYTON-WINGATE, 282 Lea Bridge Road, London E10 7LD. Tel. 081-539 6861.

Two small seated stands and very small covered terrace on one side, minimal terracing along opposite side and behind one goal. Small but friendly clubhouse outside. Better beer in the Hare and Hounds nearby.

MAIDENHEAD UNITED, York Road, Maidenhead, Berks. SL6 1SQ. Tel. 0628 36314/24739.

Small main stand backing onto railway. Open terrace and small covered area on opposite side with clubhouse behind. Small open terrace at one end, covered terrace at other. Pleasant ground, five minutes from station.

MOLESEY, Walton Road, West Molesey, Surrey, KT8 0JG. Tel. 081-979 4823/941 7989.

Pleasant if basic ground for ambitious club sadly not well supported. Good main stand with tea bar and club shop underneath. Small covered shed on far side, pathways behind goals with a few bits of terracing. Active but tatty social club, videos of recent Molesey matches shown!

STEVENAGE BOROUGH, Stevenage Stadium, Broadhall Way, Stevenage, Herts. SG2 8RH. Tel. 0438 367059.

Highly rated ground with good main stand. Small covered terrace on opposite side, open terrace behind one goal, pathway behind other. Well supported club though not very hospitable. No club shop, reasonable tea bar, busy but basic clubhouse.

TOOTING & MITCHAM UNITED, Sandy Lane, Mitcham, Surrey, CR4 2HD. Tel. 081-648 3248/685 9229.

Decaying relic of past glories. Main stand holds 1000 and still in reasonable condition, large open terraces on remaining three sides. Good club shop, two tea bars , one serving renowned burgers. Enthusiastic supporters, though numbers dwindling. Reasonable walk from Mitcham town centre, further from BR and bus definitely required from Tooting Broadway tube.

UXBRIDGE, Honeycroft, Horton Road, West Drayton, Middx. UB7 8HX. Tel. 0895 443557/445830.

Modern ground with basic main stand one one side and small covered terrace opposite. Open terrace behind one goal. Good tea bar and club shop, excellent clubhouse with superb food. Nowhere near Uxbridge.

VAUXHALL MOTORS, The Brache Estate, Park Street, Luton, Beds. LU1 3YT. Tel. 0582 23061.

Small seated stand and tiny terrace at clubhouse end. Good clubhouse and tea bar, no club shop or supporters.

WALTON & HERSHAM, Sports Ground, Stompond Lane, Walton-on-Thames, Surrey, KT12 1HF. Tel. 0932 245263/ 244967.

Athletics track. Nice seated stand and large covered terrace on opposite side. Open terrace behind one goal. Basic clubhouse, includes tea bar. Club shop near entrance.

WEMBLEY, Vale Farm, Watford Road, Sudbury, Middx. HA0 4UR. Tel. 081-904 8169/908 5461.

Decaying ground. Small wooden seated stand on clubhouse side, good size covered terrace opposite, nothing behind goals. Good pitch, floodlights and tea bar, no club shop, few supporters.

WHYTELEAFE, Church Road, Whyteleafe, Surrey, CR3 0AR. Tel. 081-660 5491/645 0422.

Picturesque setting to rival Welsh clubs! Small main stand with open terracing to either side, grass bank at one end. Nice clubhouse and good tea bar.

YEADING, The Warren, Beaconsfield Road, Hayes, Middx. Tel. 081-848 7362/7369.

Up and coming club still fresh from F.A. Vase glory. Small stand along half of one side, next to club house. Remaining three sides undeveloped. Nice clubhouse.

SECOND DIVISION

BANSTEAD ATHLETIC, Merland Rise, Tadworth, Surrey, KT20 5JG. Tel. 0737 350982.

BARTON ROVERS, Sharpenhoe Road, Barton-le-Cley, Bedford MK45 4NS. Tel. 0582 882607.

Compact ground with small main stand opposite shallow covered terrace. Open standing area behind both goals. Modern social club with two bars.

BERKHAMSTED TOWN, Broadwater, Lower Kings Road, Berkhamsted, Herts. HP4 2AA. Tel. 0442 862815.

Small, new ground. Very small seated area with adjacent covered standing, otherwise open hard standing.

BILLERICAY TOWN, New Lodge, Blunts Wall Road, Billericay, Essex, CM12 9SA. Tel. 0277 655177.

Bits-and-pieces ground. Two stands, one shaped like a Pac-man and large glass-fronted executive lounge. Plenty of uncovered standing room.

EGHAM TOWN, Tempest Road, Egham, Surrey, TW20 8HS. Tel. 0784 435226.

HAREFIELD UNITED, Preston Park, Breakspear Road North, Harefield, Middx. UB9 6BH. Tel. 0895 823474/ 822275.

HEMEL HEMPSTEAD, Vauxhall Road, Adeyfield, Hemel Hempstead, Herts. HP2 4HW. Tel. 0442 242081/259777.

Small main stand and covered terracing one side. Large social club with two bars.

HUNGERFORD TOWN, Bulpit Lane, Hungerford, Berks. RG17 0AY. Tel. 0488 682939/684597.

LEATHERHEAD, Fetcham Grove, Guildford Road, Leatherhead, Surrey, KT22 9AS. Tel. 0372 372634/377636.

LEWES, The Dripping Pan, Mountfield Road, Lewes, Sussex, BN7 1XN. Tel. 0273 472100/472574.

Amazing ground surrounded by grass banks with the main stand perched on top of one side. Clubhouse and all facilities behind one goal.

MALDEN VALE, Grand Drive, Raynes Park, London SW20 9NB. Tel. 081-542 2193.

METROPOLITAN POLICE, Imber Court, Ember Lane, East Molesey, Surrey, KT8 0BT. Tel. 081-398 1267/7358.

Superb seated stand along one side, covered terracing behind one goal, uncovered terracing on opposite side and behind other goal. Such facilities rather wasted when only a handful of spectators come to watch.

NEWBURY TOWN, Faraday Road, Newbury, Berks. RG13 2AD. Tel. 0635 40048/36601.

PURFLEET, Thurrock Hotel, Ship Lane, Grays, Essex, RM15 4HB. Tel. 0708 868901.

Magnificent social club overlooking ground, with reasonable size main stand attached. Covered standing opposite.

RAINHAM TOWN, as above- groundsharing with Purfleet.

RUISLIP MANOR, Grosvenor Vale, off West End Road, Ruislip, Middx. HA4 6JQ. Tel. 0895 637487/676168.

Small but tidy ground. Rickety main stand, compact covered standing in front of tea bar, can get very crowded.

SAFFRON WALDEN TOWN, Catons Lane, Saffron Walden, Essex, CB10 2DU. Tel. 0799 22789.

Pleasant ground in rural setting. Modest main stand with wooden box type seating. Small brick enclosure opposite with one or two wooden benches. Covered terrace behind one goal, pathway behind other. Good social club and hospitable locals.

SOUTHALL, Western Road, Southall, Middx. UB2 5HX. Tel. 081-574 1084.

SOUTHWICK, Old Barn Way, off Manor Hall Road, Southwick, West Sussex, BN4 4NT. Tel. 0273 591744.

Seated main stand on one side with small covered terraces to either side. Small seated stand on opposite side. Nothing behind goals, though a covered terrace planned. Clubhouse outside ground, very basic.

WARE, Buryfield, Park Road, Ware, Herts. SG12 0AJ. Tel. 0920 463247.

Basic main stand and small covered shed.

WITHAM TOWN, Spa Road, Witham, Essex, CM8 1UN. Tel. 0376 511198/500146.

Excellent social club but minimal spectator provision other than small main stand.

WORTHING, Woodside Road, Worthing, W. Sussex, BN14 7HQ. Tel. 0903 39575.

Impressive new stand and second seated stand opposite. Covered terrace at one end, open terrace at other end. Ground worthy of much higher level of football.

^ Saffron Walden Town v

Southwick

Berkhamsted Town

Barton Rovers

THIRD DIVISION

BRACKNELL TOWN, Larges Lane, Bracknell, Berks. RG12 3AN. Tel. 0344 412305.

CAMBERLEY TOWN, Krooner Park, Krooner Road, off Frimley Road, Camberley, Surrey, GU15 1SD. Tel. 0276 65392.

CHERTSEY TOWN, Alwyns Lane, Chertsey, Surrey KT16 8DN. Tel. 0932 561774.

CLAPTON, Old Spotted Dog Ground, Upton Lane, Forest Gate, London E7 9NP. Tel. 081-472 0822.

A real phenomenom. Clubhouse has been rebuilt three times recently, twice due to fires. Stand is falling apart but recently opened covered terrace provides salvation. Ugly, depressing ground with inexplicable charm.

COLLIER ROW, 'Sungate', Collier Row Road, Romford, Essex, RM5 2BH. Tel. 0708 722766.

Little covered standing but small stand containing

100 leather tip-up seats purchased from Butlins in Clacton. Reputed to be most comfortable in non-league football though tending to freeze solid in cold weather. Little space behind goals, but good clubhouse. Wonderful atmosphere during daylight.

COVE, Oak Farm, off Romayne Close, Cove, Farnborough, Hants. Tel. 0252 543615.

EASTBOURNE UNITED, The Oval, Channel View Road, Eastbourne, East Sussex, BN22 7LN. Tel. 0323 26989.

EDGWARE TOWN, White Lion Ground, High Street, Edgware, Middx. HA8 5AQ. Tel. 081-952 6799.

Pitch seems to have been hollowed out from the terraces. Large covered terrace opposite stand, steep grassy slope behind one goal. Main stand is so high you can just about make out the pitch through low cloud!

EPSOM & EWELL, West Street, Ewell, Surrey, KT17 1XU. Tel. 081-393 7077.

FELTHAM & HOUNSLOW BOROUGH, Feltham Sports Arena, Shakespeare Avenue, Feltham, Middx. TW14 9HX. Tel. 081-890 6119/6905/6241.

Newly merged club, playing at Feltham's ground, plastic pitch.

FLACKWELL HEATH, Wilks Park, Heath End, Flackwell Heath, High Wycombe, Bucks. HP10 9EA. Tel. 06285 23892.

HAMPTON, Beveree Stadium, Beaver Close, off Station Road, Hampton, Middx. TW12 2BX. Tel. 081-979 2456/941 4936.

HERTFORD TOWN, Hertingfordbury Park, West Street, Hertford, SG13 8EZ. Tel. 0992 583716.

Moderate main stand and covered standing on one side, covered terrace behind one goal.

HORNCHURCH, The Stadium, Bridge Avenue, Upminster, Essex, RM14 2LX. Tel. 04022 22307/20080.

Athletics stadium, not as bad as people make out but still a bit dead at times. Stoppage time can last several minutes to allow for retrieval of the ball if it misses the goal. Wooden seating in stand. Ground looks better since they replaced the tin baths which used to serves as dugouts.

HORSHAM, Queen Street, Horsham, West Sussex, RH13 5AD. Tel. 0403 55787/52310.

KINGSBURY TOWN, Silver Jubilee Park, Townsend Lane, Kingsbury, London NW9 0DE. Tel. 081-205 1645/5204.

Small ground in corner of large park. Minimal main stand and covered terrace to meet league requirements, otherwise grass banks and concrete hard standing.

PETERSFIELD UNITED, Love Lane, Petersfield, Hants. GU31 4BW. Tel. 0730 62177.

ROYSTON TOWN, Garden Walk, Royston, Herts. SG8 7HP. Tel. 0763 241204.

THAME UNITED, Windmill Road, Thame, Oxon. OX9 2DR. Tel. 084421 3017.

TILBURY, Chadfields, St. Chad's Road, Tilbury, Essex, RM18 8NL. Tel. 0375 843093.

Tatty ground despite recent minor improvements.

TRING TOWN, Pendley Sports Centre, Cow Lane, Tring, Herts. HP23 5NS. Tel. 044282 3075.

Rural setting with trees ringing the ground. One small stand for spectators.

SOUTHERN (BEAZER HOMES) LEAGUE

PREMIER DIVISION

ATHERSTONE UNITED, Sheepy Road, Atherstone, Warwickshire CV9 3AD. Tel. 0827 717929.

Delapidated ground (though improvements rumoured) on B4416 ½ mile north of town centre. Small main stand with covered terrace to one side and changing rooms in portakabin type thing on one side. Small covered terrace on opposite side, few steps of terracing plus grass banks behind both goals. Pleasant enough in summer but depressing in winter. Friendly supporters but the type of place where officials take exception if you shout more than "Rah rah come on team, play up!". No bar in ground though friendly, modern pub directly outside. What apparently used to be the bar is now large tea bar, good place to hide if the football's dull, faggots and mushy peas among the ethnic delicacies on offer. Announcer gives out interesting snippets of non-league news pre-match, which is more welcome than his musical taste (non-stop Hollies Greatest Hits!) There is a station at Atherstone, though nobody has ever heard of a train stopping there!

BASHLEY, Bashley Rec, Bashley Road, New Milton, Hants. BH25 5RY. Tel. 0425 620280.

Village club that have come up from nowhere, and attract reasonable attendances, all things considered. Lovely rural setting, pretty basic ground, though continuing improvements, with main stand extended along full length of pitch during summer. Pleasant bar behind one goal, open throughout the game. Friendly supporters. New Milton BR a mile or two away.

BROMSGROVE ROVERS, Victoria Ground, Birmingham Road, Bromsgrove, Worcs. B61 0DR. Tel. 0527 78260/76949.

Good size main stand with terracing in front. Terracing behind both goals, one end covered, clubhouse on opposite side. Good programme/souvenir shop. Two tea bars, good food from the one on main stand side, though big queues and prone to running out. Sporting supporters. BR nearby, but once again not many trains to anywhere

Directory

Crawley Town

Worcester City

Waterlooville

Cambridge City

useful!

BURTON ALBION, Eton Park, Princess Way, Burton-on-Trent, Staffs. DE14 2RU. Tel. 0283 65938.

Small but tidy main stand with clubhouse to one side. Enjoy a pitchside pre-match pint if the weather's good. Covered terrace along opposite side. Cinder bank, part covered behind one goal, grass bank, possibly due for development, at other end. Club with big potential generally unfulfilled on the pitch. A few racist loudmouths among the supporters. Brewing capital of Britain, so no shortage of pubs; brewing museum too if you're that way inclined. Long walk out of town from the station.

CAMBRIDGE CITY, City Ground, Milton Road, Cambridge, CB4 1UY. Tel. 0223 357973.

New ground built next door to old site for club which once competed on equal terms with neighbouring United. Initially only a main stand, but opposite side which used to be grass bank has now been terraced. Rather cramped nevertheless. Excellent clubhouse.

CHELMSFORD CITY, The Stadium, New Writtle Street, Chelmsford, Essex, CM2 0RP. Tel. 0245 353052.

Large main stand, grass on opposite side where there was once a terrace, terracing behind both goals, one end covered. Club has had financial problems forever, retains strong support despite failure to deliver the goods. Next to Essex County Cricket ground. Average clubhouse, good pub nearby.

CORBY TOWN, Rockingham Triangle Stadium, Rockingham Road, Corby, Northants. NN17 2AE. Tel. 0536 401007.

Athletics stadium with big main stand, miles from pitch. Supporters who object to sitting down can stand along the back. Small but vocal crowds, mostly with unintelligible Scottish accents. Bar outside ground with good view of pitch. Not surprisingly it closes at three on Saturdays, though might be worth a try for evening games!

CRAWLEY TOWN, Town Mead, Ifield Avenue, West Green, Crawley, Sussex, RH11 7HP. Tel. 0293 521800.

Very small, low main stand with small covered terrace to one side. Good size terrace behind one goal, part covered, two steps of terracing recently built on remaining two sides. Supporters tend not to change ends at half time, certainly not in inclement weather, but they're generally friendly. Good atmosphere and a club with obvious potential if they put a team together. Restrictions on visiting supporters in bar may now have been relaxed, though there's a decent pub on roundabout up the road anyway. Fifteen minutes walk through town centre from station. Well stocked club shop.

DARTFORD, Watling Street, Dartford, Kent, DA2 6EN. Tel. 0322 273639.

Ground shared with Maidstone United and painted in their colours. Supporters not surprisingly paranoid about a merger. Large main stand with good size bar behind. Substantial covered terrace opposite with leaky roof. Small open terrace behind one goal. Annoying opaque goalnets. Housing estate right behind other goal where there used to be a grass bank. Ridiculous number of police on duty at most matches, sometimes outnumber visiting supporters. Miles from the station and all uphill, though there's a couple of pubs en route.

DORCHESTER TOWN, The Avenue Stadium, Dorchester, Dorset, DT1 2RY. Tel. 0305 262451.

One year old ground which caused a stir with it's royalty-approved architecture. Next door to old ground which is now a supermarket. Ground, in fact, looks rather like a DIY store from the outside. Showpiece main stand, terracing on remaining three sides, one end covered. Publicity doubled average crowds last season despite mediocre team. Bar among the most luxurious in football, with marble and leather. Not surprisingly common supporters are not admitted - we only know about it because some Rushden supporters went there and there were so few of them they were mistaken for officials!

DOVER ATHLETIC, Crabble Athletic Ground, Lewisham Road, River, Dover, Kent. Tel. 0304 822373.

Ground almost totally rebuilt in unsuccessful attempt to get into the GMVC which caused much resentment. 700 seat main stand along length of one side with directors' portakabins perched on top. Covered terraces behind both goals, open on remaining side with 'Centre Spot' social club. Picturesque setting, surrounded by hills, from where you can get a reasonable view if you're too mean to pay. Long uphill walk from Dover Priory BR, but plenty of pubs en route (see feature in 'Terrace Talk' section). Always well supported club, supporters make plenty of noise away from home though fairly quiet at the Crabble. Success has brought the usual handful of unwanted hangers-on.

FISHER ATHLETIC, Surrey Docks Stadium, Salter Road, London, SE16 1LQ. Tel. 071-231 5144.

Least popular and least supported club in GMVC finally got relegated. Modern stadium, with tent-like main stand, smallish covered terrace on opposite side, small open terraces behind both goals. How 4000+ got in for Barnet's promotion-clincher here is one of the mysteries of our time - the place looks full with 400. Home supporters are often hard to spot. Excellent social club. Occasional yob element, inevitably pledging allegiance to nearby Millwall, but usually peaceful. Short walk from Rotherhithe tube.

GLOUCESTER CITY, Meadow Park, Sudmeadow Road, Hempsted, Gloucester, GL2 6HS. Tel. 0452 523883.

Newish ground, built on some kind of island in the River Severn, making it prone to spectacular floods (see cover of last year's 'Where's The Bar?') and almost as spectacular traffic jams after big games. Modest main stand with building housing changing rooms and upstairs social club to one side. Covered terrace along length of opposite side. Large, steep open terrace behind one goal, smaller open terrace, some way from goal, at other end. Club suffers from being the city's 'second' sport, but enthusiastically supported. Half hour walk from BR through city centre and 'Historic Docks'.

GRAVESEND & NORTHFLEET, Stonebridge Road, Northfleet, Kent, DA11 9BA. Tel. 0474 533796.

The garden of England? Industrial setting to rival Runcorn, with ships manouevring into Tilbury docks across the Thames, electricity wires crackling overhead and setting dominated by cement works - which would be a good place to bury some of the club's foul mouthed junior supporters. Otherwise hospitable club and potentially excellent ground. Good size main stand along length of one side, covered terrace on opposite side, huge covered terrace behind one goal and open terrace at other end. All slightly run down and crowds tend to be sparse. Also it always rains here.

HALESOWEN TOWN, The Grove, Old Hawne Lane, Halesowen, West Midlands. Tel. 021-550 2179.

Ground much improved in recent years to match elevation in status of club. Modest main stand, fair sized open terrace opposite, terracing behind both goals, one end covered and raised above pitch level. Good bar, but Waggon & Horses, two minutes away is highly recommended. Loyal supporters are a pleasant lot, though there is also a yob element of part-time Villa/WBA/Wolves supporters. Stewards are totally miserable. No. 9 bus from Birmingham or a long walk from Old Hill BR.

MOOR GREEN, The Moorlands, Sherwood Road, Hall Green, Birmingham B28 0EX. Tel. 021-777 2757.

Should have been the obvious candidates for relegation due to Southern League's new ground strictures, so presumably some improvements have been made. Pitch was turned through 90 degrees many years ago, causing incon-

Directory

Atherstone United ▲

▼ Dorchester Town ▲

Dover Athletic

gruous layout with small main stand in one corner behind the goal-line with small wooden terrace in front. Larger covered terrace which would once have been behind the goal now at side and miles from the pitch, only footpath and mud on remaining two sides as of December '90. Small but dedicated band of followers - had a nice line in customised Christmas carols when I visited! 15 minutes from Hall Green BR, but invest in an A-Z before you set out!

POOLE TOWN, The Stadium, Wimborne Road, Poole, Dorset, BH15 2BP. Tel. 0202 674747.

Speedway stadium with large main stand, strange scoreboard building at one end and not much else. Distant view of pitch.

TROWBRIDGE TOWN, Frome Road, Trowbridge, Wilts. BA14 0DB. Tel. 0225 752076.

Odd looking and ramshackle ground since main stand burnt down in 1985. Stand replaced by portakabin changing rooms and concrete hard standing. Low covered terrace on opposite side with some seats bolted in middle section, with social club behind. Small covered terrace at one end, grass bank with wooden cover at back at opposite end. Strong yokel following. Move to new ground has been planned for some time.

V.S. RUGBY, Butlin Road, Rugby, Warwickshire, CV21 3ST. Tel. 0788 543692.

Very small main stand, large but shallow open terrace on opposite side, small covered terraces at both ends. Tiny but well stocked club shop, good tea bar but big queues. Large bar, cheap prices, renowned hospitality. 15 minutes from BR.

WATERLOOVILLE, Jubilee Park, Aston Park, Waterlooville, Hants. PO7 7SZ. Tel. 0705 263867.

Large main stand with covered terrace to one side, opposite side undeveloped. Covered terrace behind one goal, small shallow open terrace at opposite end. Excellent bar outside ground, good shop and tea bar. Ground close to town centre but obscurely located on industrial estate.

WEALDSTONE, Vicarage Road, Watford, Herts. WD1 8ER. Tel. 0923 212916.

Having paid a reported £2½ million for a 50% share in Watford's ground Wealdstone might claim to have the best ground in non-league football. Despite this you'd be hard pressed to find a supporter who wouldn't rather be at Lower Mead. Main stand, South Terrace (The Rookery) and lower tier of Rous Stand (50p transfer from terrace) are open for Wealdstone games; most of crowd congregate in the latter as you could fit an average non-league stand into the gap between goal-line and terraces here, meaning atmosphere is nowhere near as hot as at Lower Mead, though not as bad as Stones fans feared. Bigger crowds are desperately needed and it will be a while before this feels like 'home' for the club. New buildings housing club offices and shop are planned but unlikely before 1992/3. Lack of shop is major drawback as the old Supporters Club shop was among the best. Social club behind main stand (outside ground) is good and open to all at Wealdstone fixtures. Short walk from Watford High Street BR, long walk from Watford Junction or tube.

WORCESTER CITY, St Georges Lane, Barbourne, Worcester, WR1 1QT. Tel. 0905 23003.

Sleeping giant club beset by permanent air of depression. Impressive main stand along full length of pitch. Smaller stand on opposite side with terracing in front and to side. Open terracing behind both goals. Good tea bar with burgers recommended. Supporters moan a lot. 15 minutes walk from Foregate Street BR or 25 from Shrub Hill.

Fisher Athletic

Dartford

Burton Albion

Halesowen Town

MIDLAND DIVISION

ALVECHURCH, Lye Meadow, Birmingham Road, Alvechurch Worcs. Tel. 021-445 2929.

Village club which actually won the Southern League back in 1981. Very small main stand with grass bank to one side, clubhouse on opposite side. Small covered terrace behind one goal, diagonally stepped to compensate for slope of pitch. Few supporters. You can get train from Birmingham but station is in the middle of nowhere.

BARRY TOWN, Jenner Park, Barry, South Glamorgan, CF6 7BG. Tel. 0446735858.

Athletics stadium, rather run down. 800 seat main stand with covered terracing opposite. Good though small bar inside ground, also good pub a little way uphill. Ground built on slope overlooking sea.

BEDWORTH UNITED, The Oval, Miners Welfare Park, Coventry Road, Bedworth, Warwickshire, CV12 8NN. Tel. 0203 314302.

Covered terrace along one side with seated section in the middle. Clubhouse on opposite side. Grass bank behind one goal, a long way from pitch, car park behind other goal. No club shop but good tea bar and friendly bar. Ten minutes walk from Bedworth BR.

BILSTON TOWN, Queen Street, Bilston, West Midlands, WV14 7EX. Tel. 0902 491498.

Bleak surroundings but friendly club. Large main stand on half way line with grass bank opposite. Flat standing at both ends. Large but drab bar outside serving Banks beer at good prices. Well stocked programme shop and friendly supporters. No. 78 bus from Wolverhampton.

BRIDGNORTH TOWN, Crown Meadow, Innage Lane, Bridgnorth, Shropshire, WV16 6PZ.

Country club with spartan ground, few supporters, no atmosphere but some charm. Steeply sloping pitch. Small covered terrace behind one goal with about 50 seats. Tea bar serves tea in real mugs, but no hot food. Excellent bar, Noggin bitter recommended. Irregular buses from Wolverhampton or occasional steam trains from Kidderminster on Severn Valley Railway. Ideal picnic spot.

DUDLEY TOWN, The Round Oak Stadium, John Street, Brierley Hill, West Midlands. Tel. 0384 263478.

Newish ground, fairly basic. Covered seating and open terrace on one side, raised above pitch level. Footpath round remaining three sides. Small bar, reasonably priced, programme/souvenir shop in bar area. Friendly supporters. 30 minutes walk from Cradley Heath BR or 245/246 buses from Stourbridge Town BR.

GRANTHAM TOWN, Trent Road, Grantham, Lincs. Tel. 0476 62011.

New ground just opened, reportedly up to GMVC standards, though running track round pitch may spoil atmosphere. 7000 capacity including 800 seat main stand and 1100 capacity covered terrace opposite. Rather inhospitable supporters.

HEDNESFORD TOWN, Cross Keys Ground, Hill Street, Hednesford, Staffordshire. Tel. 0543 422870.

Small covered seating areas on both sides, with open terraces to sides of each. Covered terrace at one end, not much at the other. Spartan but pleasant social club inside ground with reasonable beer and excellent juke box. Well stocked walk-in programme shop. Partisan supporters, make more noise than most in this division. Good tea bar offering burgers and chips. 20 minutes from BR (from Birmingham via Wallsall) or slow bus from Wallsall.

HINCKLEY TOWN, Leicester Road, Hickley, Leics. Tel. 0455 615062.

Fast rising club, though with few supporters. Ground is part of large sports complex, well out of town and miles from station. No pubs anywhere near. Huge social club. One permanent seated stand and piecemeal add-on developments. Hinckley Athletic, once the town's premier club, still have most of the supporters, though Town have the backing.

Directory

KINGS LYNN, The Walks Stadium, Tennyson Road, Kings Lynn, Norfolk, PE30 5PB. Tel. 0553 760060.

Huge main stand with covered terracing in front and opposite. Small open terraces at both ends. Small programme shop run by true enthusiast. Pricey catering trolley. Spacious bar but beer not highly rated! Club has fallen on hard times and considered withdrawing from Southern League to save on travelling expenses.

LEICESTER UNITED, United Park, Winchester Road, Blaby, Leicester LE43 3HN. Tel. 0533 778998.

Club known as Enderby Town before moving to Blaby five years ago. Main stand with covered terracing either side. Footpath around remaining three sides. Friendly and vociferous supporters, good club shop, best programme in the league by a long way. Good bar outside ground. Miles from BR, but Midland Fox buses from Leicester.

NEWPORT A.F.C., Somerton Park, Somerton Lane, Newport, Gwent, NP9 0HZ. Tel. 0633 271771.

The 'AFC' is added to distinguish from the old Newport County club, whose ground they now occupy. Still being restored to its former glory - if you could call it that, but big crowds despite finding the going tough on the field last season suggest they could eventually go higher than their predecessors.

NUNEATON BOROUGH, Manor Park, Beaumont Road, Nuneaton, Warwickshire, CV11 5HR. Tel. 0203 385738/ 342690.

Huge decaying ground was the millstone which got them relegated from the GMVC and troubles haven't ceased since.Good size, newish main stand with flat standing either side, covered terrace and grass bank opposite. Large, part-covered terrace at one end, small open terrace at other. Reasonable programme shop, fair tea bar, large social club inside ground. 20 minutes walk from BR, longer if you don't know the short cuts. Well supported club.

RACING CLUB WARWICK, Townsend Meadow, Hampton Road, Warwick. Tel. 0926 495786/493622.

Very basic ground, next to racecourse. Small main stand one side, small covered standing area opposite, remainder flat grass or footpath. Small, friendly bar inside ground, no club shop, small refreshment hut. Long walk through tourist-strewn town centre from BR.

REDDITCH UNITED, Valley Stadium, Bromsgrove Road, Redditch, Worcs. B97 4RN. Tel. 0527 67450.

Unusual main stand with bar on top floor. Covered terracing opposite, part-covered terrace behind one goal, open terrace at other end. Catering caravan serves good burgers. Club shop inside bar complex. Beware of local one-way system - you won't find Bromsgrove Road by following signs for Bromsgrove!

RUSHDEN TOWN, Hayden Road, Rushden, Northants. NN10 0HX. Tel. 0933 53375.

The only club to suffer the much-threatened sanction of relegation from the premier due to ground failings, for which Den Strudwick ought to be punished by being forced to stand in the mud behind the goal at Moor Green all season. Rushden's charm and hospitality was more of a credit to the Southern League than the smart but empty stands or

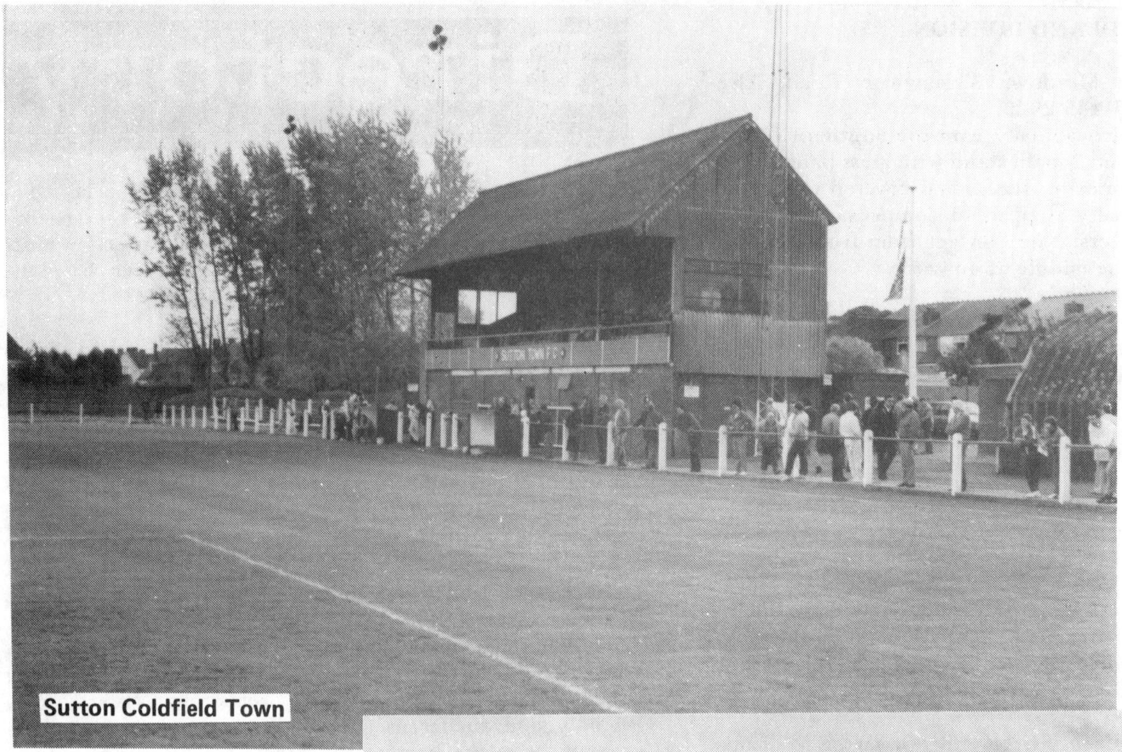
Sutton Coldfield Town

Newport A.F.C.

Nuneaton Borough (Nuneaton Evening Tribune)

Kings Lynn

Stroud

Bilston Town

Bedworth United

Alvechurch

safety-barriered terraces you'll find at some other grounds. Modest main stand with small open terraces either side, small covered terrace opposite, small open terrace one end, flat grass standing at other end. Sloping pitch, small bar, well stocked club shop, excellent burgers and tea in real mugs at tea bar. Nowhere near railway but buses from Wellingborough.

SOLIHULL BOROUGH, c/o Moor Green F.C., Sherwood Road, Hall Green, Birmingham B28 0EX. Tel. 021-777 2757.

Who??? Groundsharing at Moor Green, which isn't exactly a recommendation!

STOURBRIDGE, War Memorial Athletic Ground, High Street, Amblecote, Stourbridge, DY8 4EB. Tel. 0384 394040.

Denied promotion largely because one side of the ground forms part of a cricket pitch, which restricts potential for development. Main stand on other side with covered terraces to either side. Large covered terrace at one end, substantial grass bank at other end. Large bar inside ground with friendly staff and good beer at reasonable prices. Good programme/souvenir hut. 15 minutes walk from Stourbridge Town BR. Moorings Tavern, just off ring road, recommended for real ale fans.

STROUD, The Lawn, Nympsfield Road, Forest Green, Nailsworth, Glos. GL6 0ET. Tel. 045383 4860.

Formerly called Forest Green Rovers, but nobody knew where that was. Now called Stroud, which is where the club isn't! Small main stand with open terrace either side, flat standing opposite, part-covered, ideal for your own half-time kickabout, small part covered terrace at one end, flat standing at other. Friendly social club outside ground with reasonable beer. Small club shop. Pleasant ground and always a good day out. Four miles from Stroud town and BR.

SUTTON COLDFIELD TOWN, Central Ground, Coles Lane, Sutton Coldfield, West Midlands, B72 1NL. Tel. 021-354 2997/355 5475.

Pleasant ground in posh Birmingham suburb. 'Signal box' main stand with two small 'sheds' on opposite side. Remainder flat concrete or grass standing. Plush bar with large screen TV. Superb chips from hole-in-wall tea bar. Good programme/souvenir shop run by an expert. 20 min-

utes walk from Sutton Coldfield or Wylde Green BR.

TAMWORTH, The Lamb Ground, Kettlebrook, Tamworth, Staffs. B79 1HA. Tel. 0827 65798.

Small ground nearly overtaken by success of team. Small main stand along one side and covered terrace opposite. Open terrace behind one goal and grass bank at other end. Generally unwelcoming place with large and notorious yob element, especially for cup matches. 15 minutes walk round ring road from BR.

YATE TOWN, Lodge Road, Yate, Bristol BS17 5LE. Tel. 0454 228103.

Very basic ground. 200 seat main stand the only protection from the elements. Flat standing elsewhere. Good social club.

SOUTHERN DIVISION

ANDOVER, The Portway Stadium, West Portway Industrial Estate, Andover, Hants. SP10 3LF. Tel. 0264 333052.

ASHFORD TOWN, The Homelands, Ashford Road, Kingsnorth, Ashford, Kent, TN26 1NJ. Tel. 0233 611838.

New ground opened in 1989, after which club was promptly relegated. Miles from town centre, though a 'football special' bus runs from the station, rather slow and occasionally an intimidating experience when local yobs get on! Large main stand and not much else. Muddy car park.

BALDOCK TOWN, Norton Road, Baldock, Herts. Tel. 0462 895449.

Main stand appears to be made of petrol station canopy. Grass banking on other three sides. Reasonable social club.

BRAINTREE TOWN, Cressing Road, Braintree, Essex, CM7 6RD. Tel. 0376 45617.

BUCKINGHAM TOWN, Ford Meadow, Ford Street, Buckingham. Tel. 0280 816257.

Odd shape main stand, flat standing on remaining three sides. Excellent club shop across river, but bridge has been known to be guarded by an enormous duck! Good bar.

BURNHAM, Wymers Wood Road, Burnham, Slough, SL1 8JG. Tel. 0628 602697/602467.

Ground consists of pitch with metal rail round it and extremely small stand. Excellent social club and plenty of parking space.

BURY TOWN, Ram Meadow, Cotton Lane, Bury St. Edmunds, Suffolk. Tel. 0284 754721/754820.

Reasonable stand and covered accomodation on three sides. Above average crowds and good atmosphere. Good social club and programme.

CANTERBURY CITY, Kingsmead Stadium, Kingsmead Road, Canterbury, Kent, CT2 7PH. Tel. 0227 464732.

One of the worst grounds in BHL with virtually no seating or cover for spectators. Football takes second place to greyhound racing. Viewing is best from the mud banks opposite bar and restaurant. Very few supporters, though excellent bar and club shop.

DUNSTABLE, Creasey Park, Brewers Hill Road, Dunstable, Beds. Tel. 0582 606691.

Delapidated looking main stand with shallow terracing in front, grass banks behind the goals.

ERITH AND BELVEDERE, Park View, Lower Road, Belvedere, Kent, DA17 6DF. Tel. 081-311 4444.

Depressing, run down stadium. Virtually all spectators opt to sit in wooden main stand rather than risk crumbling, moss covered terraces. Adjoins Belvedere BR - views available from railway bridge or flyover behind one goal if you're too mean to pay!

FAREHAM TOWN, Cams Alders Stadium, Highfield Avenue, Fareham, Hants. PO14 1JA. Tel. 0329 231151.

A pitch, running track and hideously designed main stand. Broom cupboard-like social club.

GOSPORT BOROUGH, Privett Park, Privett Road, Gosport, Hants. Tel. 0705 583986.

Wooden main stand running length of one side, very small covered terrace opposite, grass at both ends.

HASTINGS TOWN, The Pilot Field, Elphinstone Road, Hastings, East Sussex, TN34 2AX. Tel. 0424 444635/430517.

Large grandstand dominating ground. Spectators seperated from pitch by disused asphalt track. Covered terracing behind one goal, uncovered grass standing on remaining two sides. Good crowds, small bar under stand.

HAVANT TOWN, Westleigh Park, Martins Road, Havant, Hants. PO9 5TH. Tel. 0705 470918.

HYTHE TOWN, Reachfields Stadium, Fort Road, Hythe, Kent, CT21 6JS. Tel. 0303 265658/264932.

Cramped ground, though covered on three sides, built over last three years thanks to millionaire chairman, attracting mixture of envy and suspicion from Kent rivals. Spacious bar but no club shop. Folkestone Central BR then bus or taxi.

MARGATE, Hartsdown Park, Hartsdown Road, Margate, Kent, CT9 5QZ. Tel. 0843 221769.

One of the better grounds in this division. Covered terracing behind both goals, though one roof is prone to disintegrate in high winds. Old wooden main stand with seats covered in pigeon droppings, pebble covered standing area on opposite side. Excellent social club and large tea bar.

NEWPORT I.O.W., St. Georges Park, St. Georges Way, Newport, Isle of Wight, PO30 2QH. Tel. 0983 525027.

Newish ground with 300 seat main stand, opposite side and one end covered. Large social club with good selection of food. Good crowds.

SALISBURY, Victoria Park, Castle Road, Salisbury, Wilts. SP1 3ER. Tel. 0722 336689.

Ground in middle of and barely distinguishable from large public park. Small wooden stand and covered terrace on one side. Grass on remaining sides. Social club resembles cricket pavilion.

SITTINGBOURNE, Central Park, Eurolink, Sittingbourne, Kent, ME10 3SB. Tel. 0795 475577/475547.

SUDBURY TOWN, Priory Stadium, Priory Walk, Sudbury, Suffolk. Tel. 0787 79095.

Attractive 300 seat main stand with large covered terrace opposite. Flat uncovered standing behind both goals. Good, partisan crowds contrary to image of sleepy market town.

WEYMOUTH, Wessex Stadium, Radipole Lane, Weymouth, Dorset, DT4 0TJ. Tel. 0305 785558.

Since building a stadium fit for the Football League club has careered helplessly in the opposite direction. Large main stand with open terracing either side. Shallow terracing on opposite side, part covered, covered terracing behind both goals. Three tea bars, large car park, two miles from town centre and station.

WITNEY TOWN, Marriotts Close, Welch Way, Witney, Oxon. OX8 5LZ. Tel. 0993 702549/705930.

Low, shallow covered terrace along one side with seated section in middle. Brick wall behind one goal and flat uncovered standing on remaining two sides. Cramped town centre site; move to a new ground has been planned for some time.

^ Hastings Town v

Newport I.O.W.

Havant Town

MARGATE

NORTHERN PREMIER (HFS LOANS) LEAGUE

PREMIER DIVISION

ACCRINGTON STANLEY, Crown Ground, Livingstone Road, Accrington, Lancs. Tel. 0254 383235.

Not actually related to the former Football League club. New breeze block and corrugated sheeting stand for 200 running half length of one side, directors and sponsors lounge next to it on half way line and covered terrace along rest of this side. Covered terrace on opposite side, flat hard standing behind both goals. Well run club shop with enthusiastic staff.

BANGOR CITY, The Stadium, Farrar Road, Bangor, Gwynedd. Tel. 0248 355852.

350 seat main stand. Large covered terrace opposite, terracing behind both goals, one end covered. Obtrusive fences erected to meet UEFA requirements after qualifying for Cup Winners Cup. Friendly programme shop. Local language is Welsh. Close to railway station.

BISHOP AUCKLAND, Kingsway, Bishop Auckland, Co. Durham. Tel. 0388 603686.

Small stand doubling as cricket pavilion, next to social club. Large wooden main stand opposite with steep terracing either side. Terracing at one end, grass at other. Partisan crowds, good social club.

BUXTON, The Silverlands, Buxton, Derbyshire. Tel. 0298 24733/23197.

Large main stand with terracing either side. Covered terracing opposite, one end covered, other end open. Good atmosphere created by enthusiastic fans. Very cold all year. Pies and burgers recommended. Good pubs in town centre.

CHORLEY, Victory Park, Duke Street, Chorley, Lancs. PR7 3DU. Tel. 0257 263406.

Large main stand along length of one side, shale bank opposite, good size covered terraces behind both goals. Large social club by main entrance. Small programme/souvenir shop. Ground hidden down backstreets.

DROYLSDEN, Butchers Arms, Market Street, Droylsden, Manchester. Tel. 061-370 1426.

Small 100 seat main stand and low covered area opposite. Narrow open terrace at one end, other end closed to spectators.

EMLEY, Emley Welfare Sports Ground, Emley, Huddersfield, W. Yorks. Tel. 0924 840087/848398.

Recently built stand for 300 alongside new dressing rooms etc. Low cover behind one goal and open hard standing at other end. Cricket pitch on opposite side. Clubhouse outside ground with hot food available. Ground in middle of nowhere and hard to find.

FLEETWOOD TOWN, Highbury Stadium, Park Avenue, Fleetwood, Lancs. Tel. 0253 876443.

Small, tidy main stand with covered terrace to one side. Covered terrace behind one goal, rest of ground open. Two social clubs. Beware local thug element who turn up for big matches or if Blackpool are away.

FRICKLEY ATHLETIC, Westfield Lane, South Elmsall, Pontefract, W. Yorks. Tel. 0977 642460.

500 seat main stand with terracing in front and to sides. Covered terracing on opposite side, grass banks behind goals. Ground surrounded by slagheaps and tightly packed terraced houses (club formerly Frickley Colliery). Good social club outside and friendly pub at top of road. Most locals friendly but a minority of nutters (mostly pledging allegiance to Leeds Utd.) who become a majority at big matches.

GAINSBOROUGH TRINITY, Northolme, North Street, Gainsborough, Lincs. Tel. 0427 613295.

Former Football League club still using same ground. Main stand on one side with social club (access from outside only). Covered terrace behind one goal and on opposite side, large open terrace at other end. Can be excellent atmosphere.

GOOLE TOWN, Victoria Pleasure Grounds, Carter Street, Goole, N. Humberside. Tel. 0405 762794.

Main stand on one side, covered terrace opposite, both ends open. Little loved Humber port town, allegedly full of 'Gooligans'!

HORWICH, Grundy Road, Victoria Hill, Horwich, Lancs. Tel. 0204 696908.

Quaint wooden stand on one side, covered terrace opposite, both ends open due to decay and wind damage. Excellent Lancashire hotpot from canteen. Good social club, not many fans.

HYDE UNITED, Tameside Stadium, Ewen Fields, Walker Lane, Hyde, Cheshire, SK14 5PL. Tel. 061-368 1031/1621.

Council owned stadium with plastic pitch. Modern 400 seat main stand. Spotless toilets, a rarity! Covered terrace alongside and opposite. Covered terrace behind one goal, grass bank at other end. Players change in a school. Social club behind stand. Good atmosphere but beware occasional loony.

LEEK TOWN, Harrison Park, Macclesfield Road, Leek, Staffs. ST13 8LD. Tel. 0538 399278.

Excellent though small ground, improved during the course of their !989/90 Trophy run. Small main stand with glass fronted directors box, covered terracing along two thirds of opposite side, cover behind both goals. Excellent pies.

MARINE, Rossett Park, College Road, Crosby, Merseyside. Tel. 051-924 1743/4046.

Cramped three sided ground. Main stand behind one goal, very small covered terrace along one side, changing rooms and covered terrace behind other goal. Nothing on other side due to proximity of houses. Very good social club outside ground, large well stocked programme shop inside.

MATLOCK TOWN, Causeway Lane, Matlock, Derbyshire. Tel. 0629 55362/583866.

Beautiful setting. Main stand and open terrace one side, old covered terrace opposite and newer covered terrace behind one goal. Opposite end adjoins cricket pitch, though standing there is allowed. Club shop in office block on main road. Social club adjacent to stand, several good pubs in town.

MORECAMBE, Christie Park, Lancaster Road, Morecambe, Lancs. LA4 5TJ. Tel. 0524 832230/411797.

Large main stand running most of length of one side, with terracing in front, social club underneath. Large covered terrace behind one goal, good club shop at back. Open terrace on remaining two sides. Second social club outside.

MOSSLEY, Seel Park, Market Street, Mossley, Lancs. Tel. 0457 832369.

Small recently built main stand with open terracing in front and to one side. Excellent covered terrace behind one goal, shallow terrace on opposite side, part covered, open behind other goal. Watch out for missiles thrown from adjoining school, especially around November 5th. Social club in one corner.

SHEPSHED ALBION, Charterhouse Park, The Dovecote, Loughborough Road, Shepshed, Leicestershire, LE12 9BN. Tel. 0509 502684.

Tiny main stand with social club beside. Small covered terraces opposite and at one end, flat standing at other end. Large bar but a bit spartan. Impossible to get to without a

Directory

Stalybridge Celtic

Workington

Gainsborough Trinity

Hyde United

car.

SOUTHPORT, Haig Avenue, Southport, PR8 6JZ. Tel. 0704 533422/530182.

2000 seat main stand dominates ground with social club adjoining. Nothing else remains from Football League days. Grass banks on remaining three sides.

STALYBRIDGE CELTIC, Bower Fold, Mottram Road, Stalybridge, Cheshire. Tel. 061-338 2828.

300 seat main stand and terrace one side, part covered terrace on opposite side, large covered terrace behind one goal, open at other end with old railway carriage serving as tea hut. Small programme shop. Good pies. Drink outside at nearby pub or Station Buffet at Stalybridge BR.

WHITLEY BAY, Hillheads Park, Hillheads Road, Whitley Bay, Tyne & Wear. Tel. 091-251 3680.

FIRST DIVISION

ALFRETON TOWN, North Street, Alfreton, Derbyshire. Tel. 0773 832819.

BRIDLINGTON TOWN, Queensgate, Bridlington, YO16 5LN. Tel. 0262 606879/400295.

CAERNARFON TOWN, The Oval, Marcus Street, Caernarfon, Gwynedd. Tel. 0286 5002.

Small, newish main stand with grass standing to either side. Open terrace opposite. New, part covered terrace behind one goal, older covered terrace at other end, fenced in for visiting supporters at cup ties. Social club outside ground. Sparse club shop.

COLWYN BAY, Llanllian Road, Old Colwyn, Clwyd. Tel. 0492 514581.

CONGLETON TOWN, Booth Street, Congleton, Cheshire. Tel. 0260 274460.

Old wooden black and white stand with bench seating, covered terrace to one side. Nothing on opposite side, covered terrace behind one goal, grass bank at other end. Good pies. Beware stone throwing juveniles at open end. Ground hidden down a side street.

CURZON ASHTON, National Park, Katherine Street, Ashton-Under-Lyne. Tel. 061-330 6033.

350 seat main stand with small open terraces either side and in front of clubhouse opposite. Hardstanding at both ends.

EASTWOOD TOWN, Coronation Park, Eastwood, Notts. Tel. 0773 715823.

Small main stand, large tarmac standing area opposite. Low cover behind one goal, very small open terrace at other end. Excellent catering, including bacon butties.

FARSLEY CELTIC, Throstle Nest, Newlands, Farsley, Pudsey, W. Yorks. LS28 5BE. Tel. 0532 561517.

GUISELEY, Nethermoor, Otley Road, Guiseley, Leeds, LS20 8BT. Tel. 0943 872872.

HARROGATE TOWN, Wetherby Road, Harrogate, N. Yorks. Tel. 0423 883671.

IRLAM TOWN, Silver Street, Irlam, Manchester. Tel. 061-775 5599.

Two small prefab stands either side of halfway line, low covered standing opposite including a few seats. Grass at both ends with paved walkway. Smallest crowds in league, team kept going by thriving social club.

KNOWSLEY UNITED, Alt Park, Endmoor Road, Huyton, Merseyside. Tel. 051-480 2529.

LANCASTER CITY, Giant Axe, West Road, Lancaster. Tel. 0524 382238.

NETHERFIELD, Parkside Road, Kendal, Cumbria. Tel. 0539 722469.

NEWTOWN, Latham Park, Park Lane, Newtown, Powys. Tel. 0686 626159.

Interesting stand for 200 perched on top of grass bank which tapers towards corner flag. Barn type covered terrace on opposite side. Flat standing behind both goals. Tremendous scenery and guaranteed friendly welcome.

RADCLIFFE BOROUGH, Stainton Park, Pilkington Road, Radcliffe, Manchester, M26 0PE. Tel. 061-725 9197.

Covered standing along most of clubhouse side, bench seating in covered area behind one goal. Rest of ground open gravel standing.

RHYL, Belle Vue, Grange Road, Rhyl. Tel. 0745 338327.

Main stand and grass bank on one side, open on opposite side. Sizeable open terrace behind one goal, covered terrace at other end. Social club and good programme shop outside.

ROSSENDALE UNITED, Dark Lane, Newchurch, Rossendale, Lancs. BB4 7UA. Tel. 0706 215119/213296.

Old wooden blue and white striped stand with overhanging roof covering paddock steps. Low covered standing along part of opposite side, few steps of terracing one end, other end open.

WARRINGTON TOWN, Common Lane, off Loushers Lane, Latchford, Warrington, WA4 2PS. Tel. 0925 31932.

Improvements undertaken for admission to Northern Premier. Not much covered accomodation. Superb pint of Boddingtons in social club.

WINSFORD UNITED, Barton Stadium, Wharton, Winsford, Cheshire, CW7 3EU. Tel. 0606 593021.

Stand consisting of three rows of seats in front of glass fronted viewing area which is part of social club. Very low covered terrace along length of opposite side. Both ends open and flat. Greyhound track round pitch.

WORKINGTON, Borough Park, Workington, Cumbria, CA14 2DT. Tel. 0900 602871.

Old main stand due for demolition, now minus roof and seats. Large covered area on opposite side with some bench seats. Good terraces behind both goals, one part covered.

WORKSOP TOWN, c/o Gainsborough Trinity, Northolme, Gainsborough, Lincs. Tel. 0427 613295.

Groundsharing at Gainsborough pending completion of new ground in Worksop.

LONDON SPARTAN LEAGUE - Premier Division

AMERSHAM TOWN, School Lane, Amersham, Bucks. Tel. 0494 727428.
BARKINGSIDE, 'Oakside', Station Road, Barkingside, Ilford, Essex. Tel. 081-555 3611.
BEACONSFIELD UNITED, Holloway Park, Slough Road, Beaconsfield, Bucks. Tel. 0494 676868.
BECKTON UNITED, Manor Way, East Ham, London E6. Tel. 071-476 4857.
BRIMSDOWN, Goldsdown Road, Enfield, Middx. Tel. 081-804 5491.
BROOK HOUSE, Farm Park, Kingshill Avenue, Hayes, Middx. Tel. 081-845 0110.
CHESHUNT, The Stadium, Theobalds Lane, Cheshunt, Herts. Tel. 0992 26752.
COCKFOSTERS, Chalk Lane, Cockfosters, Barnet, Herts. Tel. 081-449 5833.
CORINTHIAN CASUALS, King Georges Recreation Ground, Hook Lane, Tolworth, Surrey. Tel. 081-397 3368.
CROYDON ATHLETIC, N.F.C. Sports, off Mayfield Road, Thornton Heath, Surrey. Tel. 081-684 4951.
ELTHAM TOWN, Footscray Road, Eltham, London SE9. Tel. 081-850 0695.
HANWELL TOWN, Reynolds Field, Perivale Lane, Perivale, Greenford, Middx. Tel. 081-998 1701.
HARINGEY BOROUGH, Coles Park, White Hart Lane, Wood Green, London N17. Tel. 081-881 9184.
HILLINGDON BOROUGH, Breakspear Road, Ruislip, Middx. Tel. 0895 639544.
NORTH GREENFORD UNITED, Berkeley Fields, Berkeley Avenue, Greenford, Middx. Tel. 081-422 8923.
NORTHWOOD, Chestnut Avenue, Northwood, Middx. Tel. 09274 27148.
SOUTHGATE ATHLETIC, Tottenhall Road Sports, Tottenhall Road, Palmers Green, London N13. Tel. 081-888 1542.
WALTHAM ABBEY, 'Capershotts', Sewardstone Road, Waltham Abbey, Essex. Tel. 0992 711287.
WALTHAMSTOW PENNANT, Wadham Lodge, Brookscroft Road, Walthamstow. Tel. 081-527 2444.

COMBINED COUNTIES LEAGUE

ASH UNITED, Youngs Drive, Ash, Surrey. Tel. 0252 20385.
ASHFORD TOWN, Short Lane, Stanwell, Middx. Tel. 0784 245908.
BEDFONT, The Orchard, Hatton Road, Bedfont, Middx. Tel. 081-890 7264.
CHIPSTEAD, High Road, Chipstead, Surrey. Tel. 0737 553250.
COBHAM, Leg O'Mutton Field, Downside Bridge Road, Cobham, Surrey. Tel. 0932 865959.
CRANLEIGH, Snoxall Playing Fields, Knowle Lane, Cranleigh, Surrey. Tel. 0483 275295.
DITTON, Long Ditton Recreation Ground, Windmill Lane, Long Ditton, Surrey. Tel. 081-398 7428.
FARLEIGH ROVERS, Parsonage Field, Green Lane, Warlingham, Surrey. Tel. 0883 626483.
FARNHAM TOWN, Memorial Ground, West Street, Farnham, Surrey. Tel. 0252 715305.
FRIMLEY GREEN, Recreation Ground, Frimley Green Road, Frimley Green, Surrey. Tel. 0252 835089.
GODALMING TOWN, Weycourt, Meadrow, Godalming, Surrey. Tel. 0483 417520.
HARTLEY WINTNEY, Memorial Playing Fields, Green Lane, Hartley Wintney, Hants. Tel. 025126 3586.
HORLEY TOWN, The Defence, Smallfield Road, Horley, Surrey. Tel. 0293 786075.
MALDEN TOWN, Manor Park, Malden Road, New Malden, Surrey. Tel. 081-942 6521.
MERSTHAM, Merstham Recreation Ground, Albury Road, Merstham, Surrey. Tel. 0737 644046.
SANDHURST TOWN, Memorial Ground, Yorktown Road, Sandhurst, Berks. Tel. 0252 873767.
STEYNING TOWN, The Shooting Field, Steyning, West Sussex. Tel. 0903 812228.
VIKING SPORTS, Avenue Park, Western Avenue, Greenford, Middx. Tel. 081-578 2706.
WESTFIELD, Woking Park, Kingfield, Woking, Surrey. Tel. 0483 771106.

EASTERN COUNTIES LEAGUE - Premier Division

BRANTHAM ATHLETIC, New Village, Brantham, Manningtree, Essex. Tel. 0206 392506.
BRIGHTLINGSEA UNITED, North Road, Brightlingsea, Essex. Tel. 0206 304199.
CHATTERIS TOWN, West Street, Chatteris, Cambs. Tel. 03543 2139.
CLACTON TOWN, Rush Green Bowl, Rush Green Road, Clacton-on-Sea, Essex. Tel. 0255 432590.
CORNARD UNITED, Blackhouse Lane Sports Field, Great Cornard, Sudbury, Suffolk. Tel. 0787 76719.
FELIXSTOWE TOWN, Dellwood Avenue, Felixstowe, Suffolk. Tel. 0394 282917.
GORLESTON, Emerald Park, Gorleston, Norfolk. Tel. 0493 602802.
GREAT YARMOUTH TOWN, Wellesley Road, Great Yarmouth, Norfolk. Tel. 0493 843373/842936.
HALSTEAD TOWN, Rosemary Lane, Halstead, Essex. Tel. 0787 472082.
HARWICH & PARKESTON, Royal Oak, Main Road, Dovercourt, Harwich, Essex. Tel. 0255 503649.
HAVERHILL ROVERS, Hamlet Croft, Haverhill, Suffolk. Tel. 0440 702137.
HISTON, Bridge Road, Impington, Cambridge. Tel. 0223 232301.
LOWESTOFT TOWN, Crown Meadow, Lowestoft, Suffolk. Tel. 0502 573818.
MARCH TOWN UNITED, GER Sports Ground, Robin Goodfellows Lane, March, Cambs. Tel. 0354 53073.
NEWMARKET TOWN, New Cheveley Road, Newmarket, Suffolk. Tel. 0638 663637.
NORWICH UNITED, Plantation Road, Blofield, Norfolk. Tel. 0603 716963.
STOWMARKET TOWN, Greens Meadow, Bury Road, Stowmarket, Suffolk. Tel. 0449 612533.
THETFORD TOWN, Mundford Road, Thetford, Norfolk. Tel. 0842 766120.
TIPTREE UNITED, Chapel Road, Tiptree, Essex. Tel. 0621 815213.
WATTON UNITED, Dereham Road, Watton, Norfolk. Tel. 0953 881281.
WISBECH TOWN, Fenland Park, Lerowe Road, Wisbech, Cambs. Tel. 0945 584176.
WROXHAM, Trafford Park, Skinners Lane, Wroxham, Norfolk. Tel. 0603 783538.

SOUTH MIDLANDS LEAGUE — Premier Division

BIGGLESWADE TOWN, Fairfield Road, Biggleswade, Beds. Tel. 0767 312374.
BRACHE SPARTA, Foxdell Sports Ground, Dallow Road, Luton, Beds. Tel. 0582 20751.
BUCKINGHAM ATHLETIC, Stratford Fields, Stratford Road, Buckingham. Tel. 0280 816945.
HARPENDEN TOWN, Rothamsted Park, Harpenden, Herts. Tel. 0582 715724.
HODDESDON TOWN, Lowfield, Park View, Hoddesdon, Herts. Tel. 0992 463133.
LANGFORD, Forde Park, Langford Road, Henlow. Tel. 0462 816106.

LEIGHTON TOWN, Bell Close, Lake Street, Leighton Buzzard, Beds. Tel. 0525 373311.
LETCHWORTH GARDEN CITY, Baldock Road, Letchworth, Herts. Tel. 0462 684691.
LEVERSTOCK GREEN, Pancake Lane, Leverstock Green, Hemel Hempstead, Herts. Tel. 0442 246280.
MILTON KEYNES BOROUGH, Manor Fields, Bletchley, Bucks. Tel. 0908 375256.
NEW BRADWELL ST. PETER, Recreation Ground, Bradwell Road, New Bradwell, Milton Keynes. Tel. 0908 315766.
OXFORD CITY, Pressed Steel, Roman Way, Cowley, Oxford.
PIRTON, Pirton Recreation Ground, Walnut Tree Road, Hitchin, Herts. Tel. 0462 712531.
PITSTONE & IVINGHOE, Pitstone Recreation Ground, Leighton Buzzard, Beds. Tel. 0296 661271.
POTTERS BAR TOWN, Parkfield Centre, The Walk, Potters Bar, Herts. Tel. 0707 54833.
SHILLINGTON, Playing Fields, Shillington, Hitchin, Herts. Tel. 0462 711757.
THE 61 F.C., Kingsway, Beverley Road, Luton, Beds. Tel. 0582 582965.
TOTTERNHOE, Totternhoe Recreation Ground, Dunstable, Beds. Tel. 0582 606738.
WELWYN GARDEN CITY, Herns Lane, Welwyn Garden City, Herts. Tel. 0707 328470.
WINGATE AND FINCHLEY, Summers Lane, Finchley, London N12. Tel. 081-446 0906.
WINSLOW UNITED, Winslow Recreation Ground, Elmfields Gate, Winslow, Bucks. Tel. 029671 3057.
WOLVERTON, The Park, Old Wolverton Road, Wolverton, Milton Keynes. Tel. 0908 312264.

KENT LEAGUE — Division One

ALMA SWANLEY, Green Court Road, Crockenhill, Swanley, Kent. Tel. 0322 666120.
BECKENHAM TOWN, Eden Park Avenue, Beckenham, Kent. Tel. 081-650 1066.
CHATHAM TOWN, Maidstone Road, Chatham, Kent, ME4 6ES. Tel. 0634 812194.
CORINTHIAN, Gay Dawn, Fawkham Road, Fawkham, Dartford, Kent. Tel. 04747 7559.
CRAY WANDERERS, Oxford Road, Sidcup, Kent. Tel. 081-300 9201.
CROCKENHILL, Wested, Eynsford Road, Crockenhill, Swanley, Kent. Tel. 0322 662097.
DANSON, Crook Log, Brampton Road, Bexleyheath, Kent. Tel. 081-303 6052.
DARENTH HEATHSIDE, Horton Road, South Darenth, Dartford, Kent. Tel. 0322 863554.
DEAL TOWN, The Charles Sports Ground, Mill Road, Deal, Kent. Tel. 0304 375623.
FAVERSHAM TOWN, Salters Lane, Faversham, Kent. Tel. 0795 532738.
GREENWICH BOROUGH, Harrow Meadow, Eltham Green Road, Eltham, London SE9. Tel. 081-850 3098.
HERNE BAY, Winch's Field, Stanley Gardens, Herne Bay, Kent. Tel. 0227 374156.
KENT POLICE, Sutton Road, Maidstone, Kent. Tel. 0831 510030.
METROPOLITAN POLICE (HAYES), The Warren, Croydon Road, Hayes, Kent. Tel. 081-462 1266.
RAMSGATE, Southwood, Prices Avenue, Ramsgate, Kent, CT11 0AN. Tel. 0843 591662.
SHEPPEY UNITED, Botany Road, St. Georges Avenue, Sheerness, Kent. Tel. 0795 665299.
SLADE GREEN, The Small Glen, Moat Lane, Slade Green, Erith, Kent. Tel. 0322 349018.
THAMES POLYTECHNIC, Kidbrooke Lane, Eltham, London SE9. Tel. 081-850 1221.
THAMESMEAD TOWN, Bayliss Avenue, Thamesmead, London SE28. Tel. 081- 311 4211.
TONBRIDGE, Longmead Stadium, Darenth Avenue, Tonbridge, Kent, TN10 3JW. Tel. 0732 358868/352417.
TUNBRIDGE WELLS, Culverden Stadium, Culverden Down, Tunbridge Wells, Kent. Tel. 0892 20517.
WHITSTABLE TOWN, Belmont Road, Whitstable, Kent. Tel. 0227 266012.

CENTRAL MIDLANDS LEAGUE — Supreme Division

ARNOLD TOWN, King George V Playing Fields, Gedling Road, Arnold, Nottingham. Tel. 0602 263660.
BLIDWORTH WELFARE, Welfare Ground, Mansfield Road, Blidworth, Notts. Tel. 0623 798724.
BORROWASH VICTORIA, Asterdale Club, Spondon Leisure Centre, Borrowash Road, Spondon, Derby. Tel. 0332 669688/668656.
HARWORTH COLLIERY INSTITUTE, Scrooby Road, Harworth, Doncaster, S. Yorks. Tel. 0302 750614.
HEANOR TOWN, The Town Ground, Mayfield Avenue, Heanor, Derbys. Tel. 0773 713742/715815.
HUCKNALL TOWN, Watnall Road, Hucknall, Notts. Tel. 0602 641292.
LINCOLN UNITED, Ashby Avenue, Hartsholme, Lincoln. Tel. 0522 690674.
LOUTH UNITED, Park Avenue, Louth, Lincolnshire. Tel. 0507 607351.
MELTON TOWN, Egerton Park, Melton Mowbray, Leicestershire. Tel. 0664 60350.
NETTLEHAM, Mulsanne Park, Field Close, Nettleham, Lincoln. Tel. 0522 750007.
OAKHAM UNITED, Mansfield Hosiery Mills Sports Ground, Mansfield Road, Sutton-in-Ashfield, Notts. Tel. 0623 552376
PRIORY (EASTWOOD), Birnam Park, Eastwood, Notts.
SHEFFIELD AURORA, Aurora Sports & Social Club, Bawtry Road, Brinsworth, Rotherham,Tel. 0709 372613.
SHIREBROOK COLLIERY, BRSA Club, Langwith Road, Shirebrook, Mansfield, Notts. Tel. 0623 742535.
STANTON ILKESTON, Hallam Fields Sports Ground, Stanton Club, Nr. Ilkeston, Derbys. Tel. 0602 323244.
WOMBWELL TOWN, Wombwell Sporting Centre, Station Road, Wombwell, Barnsley. Tel. 0226 752128.

NORTHERN COUNTIES EAST LEAGUE

Premier Division
ARMTHORPE WELFARE, Church Street, Armthorpe, Doncaster, S. Yorks. Tel. 0302 831247.
BELPER TOWN, Christ Church Meadow, Bridge Street, Belper, Derbys. Tel. 0773 825549.
BRIGG TOWN, The Hawthorns, Hawthorn Avenue, Brigg, S. Humberside. Tel. 0652 52767.
DENABY UNITED, Tickhill Square, Denaby Main, Doncaster, S. Yorks. Tel. 0709 864042.
ECCLESHILL UNITED, Plumpton Park, Kingsway, Wrose, Bradford BD2 1PN. Tel. 0274 615739.
GLASSHOUGHTON WELFARE, Leeds Road, Glasshoughton, Castleford, W. Yorks. Tel. 0977 518981.
HARROGATE RAILWAY ATHLETIC, Station View, Starbeck, Harrogate, N. Yorks. Tel. 0423 885539/883104.
LIVERSEDGE, Clayborn Ground, Quaker Lane, Hightown Road, Cleckheaton, W. Yorks. Tel. 0274 862108.
MALTBY M.W., Muglet Lane, Maltby, S. Yorks. Tel. 0709 812462.
NORTH FERRIBY UNITED, Church Road, North Ferriby, N. Humberside. Tel. 0482 634601.
NORTH SHIELDS, Appleby Park, Hawkeys Lane, North Shields, Tyne & Wear. Tel. 091-257 0513/0282.
OSSETT ALBION, Dimple Wells, Ossett, W. Yorks. Tel. 0924 273618/280450.

OSSETT TOWN, Ingfield, Ossett, W. Yorks. Tel. 0924 272960.
PONTEFRACT COLLIERIES, Skinner Lane, Pontefract, W. Yorks. Tel. 0977 702180.
SHEFFIELD, Don Valley Stadium, Worksop Road, Sheffield 9. Tel. 0742 435355.
SPENNYMOOR UNITED, Brewery Field, Durham Road, Spennymoor, Co. Durham DL16 6JN. Tel. 0388 811934.
SUTTON TOWN, Lowmoor Road, Kirkby-in-Ashfield, Notts. Tel. 0623 752181.
THACKLEY, Dennyfield, Ainsbury Avenue, Thackley, Bradford. Tel. 0274 615571.
WINTERTON RANGERS, West Street, Winterton, Scunthorpe, S. Humberside. Tel. 0724 732628.
Division 1
BRADLEY RANGERS, Warrenside, Deighton, Huddersfield, W. Yorks. Tel. 0484 542044.
BRODSWORTH M.W., Welfare Ground, Woodlands, Doncaster, S. Yorks. Tel. 0302 728380.
GARFORTH TOWN, Brierlands Lane, Aberford Road, Garforth, Leeds. Tel. 0532 864083.
HALL ROAD RANGERS, Dene Park, Dene Close, Dunswell, Hull. Tel. 0482 850101.
HALLAM, Sandygate Road, Crosspool, Sheffield 10. Tel. 0742 309484.
HATFIELD MAIN, Dunscroft Welfare Ground, Dunscroft, Doncaster, S. Yorks. Tel. 0302 841326.
IMMINGHAM TOWN, Woodlands Avenue, Immingham, S. Humberside. Tel. 0469 575724.
PICKERING TOWN, Malton Road, Pickering, N. Yorks. Tel. 0751 73317.
R.E.S. PARKGATE, Roundwood Sports Ground, Green Lane, Rawmarsh, Rotherham, S. Yks. Tel. 0709 523471.
ROSSINGTON MAIN, Welfare Ground, Oxford Street, Rossington, Doncaster, S. Yorks. Tel. 0302 865524.
SELBY TOWN, Flaxley Road, Selby, N. Yorks.
STOCKSBRIDGE PARK STEELS, Bracken Moor Lane, Stocksbridge, Sheffield. Tel. 0742 882045.
TADCASTER ALBION, The Park, Ings Lane, Tadcaster, N. Yorks. Tel. 0937 834119.
WORSBROUGH BRIDGE M.W., Park Road, Worsbrough Bridge, Barnsley, S. Yorks. Tel. 0226 284452.
YORK R.I., New Lane, Acomb, York. Tel. 0904 798930.
YORKSHIRE AMATEUR, Bracken Edge, Sycamore Avenue, Leeds LS8 4DZ. Tel. 0532 624093.

WESTERN LEAGUE – Premier Division

BIDEFORD, Sports Ground, Kingsley Road, Bideford, Devon. Tel. 0237 474974.
BRISTOL MANOR FARM, The Creek, Portway, Sea Mills, Bristol. Tel. 0272 683571.
CHARD TOWN, Dening Sports Field, Zembard Lane, Chard, Somerset. Tel. 0460 61402.
CHIPPENHAM TOWN, Hardenhuish Park, Bristol Road, Chippenham, Wilts. Tel. 0249 650400.
CLEVEDON TOWN, Teignmouth Road, Clevedon, Avon. Tel. 0275 871636/874276.
DAWLISH, Playing Fields, Exeter Road, Dawlish, Devon. Tel. 0626 863110.
ELMORE, Horsdon Park, Tiverton, Devon. Tel. 0884 252341.
EXMOUTH, King George V Ground, Southern Road, Exmouth, Devon. Tel. 0395 263348/279085.
FROME TOWN, Badgers Hill, Frome, Somerset. Tel. 0373 464087.
LISKEARD ATHLETIC, Lux Park, Liskeard, Cornwall. Tel. 0579 42665.
MANGOTSFIELD, Cossham Street, Mangotsfield, Bristol. Tel. 0272 560119.
MINEHEAD, Irnham Road, Minehead, Somerset. Tel. 0643 704989.
OTTERY ST. MARY, Washbrook Meadows, Butts Road, Ottery St. Mary, Devon. Tel. 040 481 3539.
PAULTON ROVERS, Athletic Ground, Winterfield Road, Paulton, Avon. Tel. 0761 412907.
PLYMOUTH ARGYLE, Home Park, Plymouth. Tel. 0752 562561/2/3.
SALTASH, Kimberley Stadium, Callington Road, Saltash, Cornwall. Tel. 0752 845746.
TAUNTON TOWN, Wordsworth Drive, Taunton, Somerset, TA1 2HG. Tel. 0823 278191.
TIVERTON TOWN, Ladysmead, Bolham Road, Tiverton, Devon. Tel. 0884 252397.
TORRINGTON, Vicarage Field, School Lane, Torrington, Devon. Tel. 0805 22853.
WELTON ROVERS, West Clewes, North Road, Midsomer Norton, Avon. Tel. 0761 412097.
WESTON-SUPER-MARE, Woodspring Park, Winterstoke Road, Weston-super-Mare, Avon. Tel.0761621 618/635665.

UNITED COUNTIES LEAGUE – Premier Division

ARLESEY TOWN, Lamb Meadow, Arlesey, Beds. Tel. 0462 731448.
BOSTON, Tattershall Road, Boston, Lincs. Tel. 0205 365470.
BOURNE TOWN, Abbey Lawn, Abbey Road, Bourne, Lincs. Tel. 0778 422292 ext. 3290.
BRACKLEY TOWN, St. James Park, Churchill Way, Brackley, Northants. Tel. 0280 704077.
COGENHOE UNITED, Compton Park, Cogenhoe, Northants. Tel. 0604 890521.
DAVENTRY TOWN, Elderstubbs, Leamington Way, Daventry, Northants. Tel. 0327 706286.
DESBOROUGH TOWN, Waterworks Field, Braybrooke Road, Desborough, Kettering, Northants. Tel. 0536 761350.
EYNESBURY ROVERS, Hall Road, Eynesbury, St. Neots, Cambs. Tel. 0480 474041.
HAMLET STEWARTS & LLOYDS, Occupation Road, Corby, Nothants. Tel. 0536 401497.
HOLBEACH UNITED, Carters Park, Holbeach, Spalding, Lincs. Tel. 0406 24761.
IRTHLINGBOROUGH DIAMONDS, Nene Park, Irthlingborough, Northants. Tel. 0933 650345.
KEMPSTON ROVERS, Hillgrounds Road, Kempston, Bedford. Tel. 0234 852346.
LONG BUCKBY, Station Road, Long Buckby, Northampton. Tel. 0327 842682.
MIRLEES BLACKSTONE, Lincoln Road, Stamford, Lincs. Tel. 0780 57835/65789.
NORTHAMPTON SPENCER, Kingsthorpe Mill, Studland Road, Northampton. Tel. 0604 718898.
PETERBOROUGH CITY, South Bretton Playing Fields, Ringwood, Peterborough. Tel.
POTTON UNITED, The Hollow, Biggleswade Road, Potton, Beds. Tel. 0767 261100.
RAUNDS TOWN, Kiln Park, Raunds, Wellingborough, Northants. Tel. 0933 623351.
ROTHWELL TOWN, Cecil Street, Rothwell, Northants. Tel. 0536 710694.
SPALDING UNITED, Halley Stewart Field, Winnrey Avenue, Spalding, Lincs. Tel. 0775 761153/724957.
STAMFORD, Wothorpe Road, Stamford, Lincs. Tel. 0780 63079.
STOTFOLD, Roker Park, Stotfold, Hitchin, Herts. Tel. 0462 730421.
WELLINGBOROUGH TOWN, Dog and Duck, London Road, Wellingborough, Northants. Tel. 0933 223536.
WOOTTON BLUE CROSS, Weston Park, Wootton, Beds. Tel. 0234 767662.

GROUNDS OF THE NORTH-WEST COUNTIES LEAGUE: Left, top to bottom - Burscough, Skelmersdale United, Maine Road, Penrith, Salford City; Right, top to bottom - Prescot, Knowsley United (now HFS Loans League), Vauxhall GM, Ashton United, Formby.

NORTH WEST COUNTIES LEAGUE

The North West Counties League, formed in 1982 from the old Cheshire League and Lancashire Combination, has quickly gained a reputation for good facilities and friendly atmospheres. As from 1991/2 floodlights will be compulsory for all clubs in the first division, and such is the progressive nature of the league that no club has been automatically relegated due to lack of lights, unlike its sister league, the Northern Counties East. In fact more and more division two clubs are now purchasing lights.

The NWCL Committee has been in the past accused of being too strict with regard to ground standards although any problems appear now to have been ironed out, the one possible exception being Maghull, who stubbornly remain in division two despite having no covered accomodation whatsoever, while regulations state that both seating and covered standing are required. Notable expulsions in the meantime, Newton and Padiham, both had more than adequate facilities.

Attendances at NWCL games tend to vary and quite often are higher for midweek games. In Colne Dynamoes championship season 1,679 fans saw the virtual decider against Rossendale United, yet last season's champions, Knowsley, struggled on occasions to attract 50 people. Colwyn Bay and Ashton United have a larger following, although beware the big game involving the Welsh side; they seem to attract a fair size moron following.

Programmes must be issued, though allowances are made for hastily arranged end of season games. Most clubs put together a good prog, and all are very reasonably priced, making use of an excellent league newsletter to fill in pages. Refreshments in the grounds are tremendous value, certainly better than Football League both in price and quality, with real mugs of tea, chip butties and hotpot. The clubhouse bars are in the main old fashioned large timber sheds, which add to the friendly atmosphere despite somewhat spartan facilities.

Certain grounds, especially in Division One, have the facilities to progress to the HFS Loand League without much improvement. Top of the list is Ashton United, whose new stand and terracing would shame more than a few clubs at a higher level. Leyland DAF SGL, Nantwich Town and Vauxhall GM all have good standard grounds, as do Penrith and Atherton LR. Prescot's Hope Street stadium has a large stand although most of the seats have been removed, while St. Helens Town, Skelmersdale and newly promoted Great Harwood Town all have potential to be at a higher level.

Despite all this the NWCL is equally about clubs like Westhoughton Town, Formby and Blackpool Mechanics, the bread and butter clubs in a league where standards may vary but the enjoyment of involvement at all levels within the clubs is on the up and up. Long may it continue.

Andy Dakin

First Division

ASHTON UNITED, Surrey Street, Hurst Cross, Aston-under-Lyne, Tameside. Tel. 061-339 4158.
ATHERTON LABURNAM ROVERS, Crilly Park, Spa Road, Atherton, Greater Manchester. Tel. 0942 883950.
BACUP BOROUGH, West View, Cowtoot Lane, Blackthorn, Bacup, Lancs. Tel. 0706 878655.
BLACKPOOL ROVERS, School Road, Marton, Blackpool, Lancs. Tel. 0253 60570.
BOOTLE, Bucks Park, Northern Perimeter Road, Netherton, Merseyside. Tel. 051-526 1850/527 1851.
BRADFORD PARK AVENUE, McLaren Field, Town Street, Leeds, W. Yorks. Tel. 0532 564842/578504.
CLITHEROE, Shawbridge, Clitheroe, Lancs. Tel. 0200 23344.
DARWEN, Anchor Ground, Anchor Road, Darwen, Lancs. Tel. 0254 705627.
EASTWOOD HANLEY, Berryhill Fields, Trentmill Road, Hanley, Stoke-on-Trent. Tel. 0782 274238.
FLIXTON, Valley Road, Flixton, Manchester. Tel. 061-748 2903.
GREAT HARWOOD TOWN, The Showground, Wood Street, Great Harwood, Lancs. Tel. 0254 883913.
MAINE ROAD, Manchester County F.A. Ground, Brantingham Road, Chorlton-cum-Hardy, Manchester. Tel. 061-862 9619.
NANTWICH TOWN, Jackson Avenue, off London Road, Nantwich, Cheshire. Tel. 0270 624098.
PENRITH, Southend Road Ground, Penrith, Cumbria. Tel. 0768 63212.
PRESCOT, Hope Street, Prescot, Merseyside. Tel. 051-430 0507.
ST. HELENS TOWN, Hoghton Road, Sutton, St. Helens, Merseyside. Tel. 0744 817225/812721.
SKELMERSDALE UNITED, White Moss Park, White Moss Road, Skelmersdale, Lancs. Tel. 0695 22123.
VAUXHALL G.M., Rivacre Road, Ellesmere Port, Cheshire. Tel. 051-327 2294.

Second Division

ASHTON TOWN, Edge Green Street, Ashton-in-Makerfield, Wigan, Greater Manchester. Tel. 0942 719168.
ATHERTON COLLIÈRIES, Alder Street, Atherton, Greater Manchester. Tel. 0942 884649.
BAMBER BRIDGE, Irongate, Brownedge Road, Bamber Bridge, Preston, Lancs. Tel. 0772 627387.
BLACKPOOL MECHANICS, Back Common Edge Road, Blackpool, Lancs. Tel. 0253 61721.
BURSCOUGH, Victoria Park, Mart Lane, Burscough, Ormskirk, Lancs. Tel. 0704 893237.
CASTLETON GABRIELS, Butterworth Park, Chadwick Lane, off Heywood Road, Castleton, Rochdale. Tel. 0706 527103.
CHADDERTON, Andrew Street, Chadderton, Oldham, Lancs. Tel. 061-624 9733.
CHEADLE TOWN, Park Road, Cheadle, Cheshire. Tel. 061-428 2510.
FORMBY, Brows Lane, Formby, Merseyside. Tel. 0704 872603.
GLOSSOP, Surrey Street, Glossop, Derbyshire. Tel. 0457 855469.
HOLKER, Rakesmoor Lane, Hawcoat, Barrow-in-Furness, Cumbria. Tel. 0229 828176.
KIDSGROVE ATHLETIC, Hollinwood Road, Kidsgrove, Stoke-on-Trent, ST7 1BQ. Tel. 0782 782412.
MAGHULL, Old Hall Field, Hall Lane, Maghull, Merseyside. Tel. 051-526 7320.
NEWCASTLE TOWN, Lyme Valley Parkway Stadium, Lilleshall Road, Clayton, Newcastle-under-Lyme, Staffs. Tel. 0782 662351/662350.
OLDHAM TOWN, Nordens Road, off Middleton Road, Chadderton, Oldham, Lancs. Tel. 061-624 0914.
SALFORD CITY, Moor Lane, Kersal, Salford, Manchester. Tel. 061-792 6287.
SQUIRES GATE, School Road, Marton, Blackpool, Lancs. Tel. 0253 798584.
WESTHOUGHTON TOWN, New Sirs, St. James Street, Westhoughton, Bolton, Lancs. Tel. 0942 818544.

WEST MIDLANDS LEAGUE – Premier Division

BLAKENALL, Red Lion Ground, Somerfield Road, Leamore, Bloxwich, Walsall, West Midlands WS3 2EJ. Tel. 0922 405835.
CHASETOWN, The Scholars Ground, Church Street, Chasetown, Walsall, W. Midlands. Tel. 05436 2222.
HINCKLEY ATHLETIC, Middlefield Lane, Hinckley, Leicestershire. Tel. 0455 613553.
LYE TOWN, Stourbridge Road, Lye, Stourbridge, West Midlands. Tel. 0384 422672.
MALVERN TOWN, Langland Stadium, Langland Road, Malvern, Worcestershire, WR14 2EQ. Tel. 0684 574068.
OLDBURY UNITED, The Cricketts, York Road, Rowley Regis, Warley, West Midlands. Tel. 021-559 5564.
OLDSWINFORD, The Dell Sports Stadium, Bryce Road, Pensnett, Brierley Hill, West Midlands. Tel. 0384 77289.
PAGET RANGERS, Springfield Road, Walmley, Sutton Coldfield, West Midlands, B76 8SJ. Tel. 021-351 1563.
PELSALL VILLA, The Bush Ground, Wallsall Road, Pellsall, Wallsall, West Midlands. Tel. 0922 682018/692748.
ROCESTER, Riverfield Mill Street, Rocester, Staffs. Tel. 0889 590463.
RUSHALL OLYMPIC, Dales Lane, off Daw End Lane, Rushall, Wallsall, West Midlands. Tel. 0922 641021.
STOURPORT SWIFTS, Walshes Meadow, Harold Davies Drive, Stourport-on-Severn, Worcs. Tel. 02993 5188.
WEDNESFIELD, Cottage Ground, Amos Lane, Wednesfield, Wolverhampton, West Midlands. Tel. 0902 735506.
WEST BROMWICH TOWN, Willenhall Town F.C., Noose Lane, Willenhall, West Midlands. Tel. 0902 605132.
WESTFIELDS, Thorn Lighting, Holme Lacy Road, Rotherwas, Hereford. Tel. 0432 266670/268131.
WILLENHALL TOWN, Noose Lane, Willenhall, West Midlands. Tel. 0902 636586/65132.
CRADLEY TOWN, Beeches View Avenue, Halesowen, West Midlands. Tel. 0384 69904.
GRESLEY ROVERS, The Moat Ground, Moat Street, Gresley, Burton-on-Trent, Staffs. Tel. 0283 216315.
HALESOWEN HARRIERS, Park Road, Colley Gate, Halesowen, West Midlands. Tel. 0384 896748.

NORTHERN LEAGUE – First Division
BILLINGHAM SYNTHONIA, The Stadium, Central Avenue, Billingham, Cleveland. Tel. 0642 552358.
BLYTH SPARTANS, Croft Park, Blyth, Northumberland. Tel. 0670 354818.
BRANDON UNITED, Welfare Ground, Rear Commercial Street, Brandon, Co. Durham. Tel. 091-378 2957.
CONSETT, Belle Vue Park, Ashdale Road, Consett, Co. Durham. Tel. 0207 503788.
EASINGTON COLLIERY, C.W. Park, Easington, Co. Durham. Tel. 091-527 3047.
FERRYHILL ATHLETIC, Darlington Road, Ferryhill, Co. Durham. Tel. 0740 651937.
GRETNA, Raydale Park, Gretna, Cumbria. Tel. 0461 37602.
GUISBOROUGH TOWN, King George V Playing Fields, Howlbeck Road, Guisborough, Cleveland. Tel. 0287 636925.
LANGLEY PARK WELFARE, Welfare Ground, Low Moor Road, Langley Park, Durham. Tel. 091-373 1526.
MURTON, Murton Park, Church Lane, Murton, Seaham, Co. Durham. Tel. 091-517 0814.
NEWCASTLE BLUE STAR, Wheatsheaf Sports Ground, Woolsington, Newcastle-on-Tyne. Tel. 091-286 0425.
NORTHALLERTON TOWN, Ainderby Road, Romanby, Northallerton, North Yorkshire. Tel. 0609 772418.
PETERLEE NEWTOWN, Eden Lane, Peterlee, Co. Durham. Tel. 091-586 3004/4415.
SEAHAM RED STAR, Seaham Town Park, Stockton Road, Seaham, Co. Durham. Tel. 091-581 2540/513 0880.
SHILDON, Dean Street, Shildon, Co. Durham. Tel. 0388 773877.
SOUTH BANK, Normanby Road, South Bank, Middlesbrough, Cleveland. Tel. 0642 453193.
TOW LAW TOWN, Ironworks Road, Tow Law, Co. Durham. Tel. 0388 731443.
WEST AUCKLAND TOWN, Darlington Road, West Auckland, Co. Durham. Tel. 0388 834403.
WHICKHAM, Glebe Ground, Rectory Lane, Whickham, Newcastle-on-Tyne. Tel. 091-488 3054.
WHITBY TOWN, Turnbull Ground, Upgang Lane, Whitby, North Yorkshire. Tel. 0947 604847.

Second Division
ALNWICK TOWN, St. James Park, Alnwick, Northumberland. Tel. 0665 603162.
ASHINGTON, Portland Park, Ashington, Northumberland. Tel. 0670 812240.
BEDLINGTON TERRIERS, Welfare Park, Park Road, Bedlington, Northumberland. Tel. 0670 825485.
BILLINGHAM TOWN, Bedford Terrace, Billingham, Cleveland. Tel. 0642 560043.
CHESTER-LE-STREET TOWN, Moor Park, Chester Moor, Chester-le-Street, Co. Durham. Tel. 091-388 3363.
CROOK TOWN, Millfield Ground, West Road, Crook, Co. Durham. Tel. 0388 762959.
DARLINGTON CLEVELAND BRIDGE, Neasham Road, Darlington. Tel. 0325 469735.
DUNSTON FEDERATION BREWERIES, Federation Park, Wellington Road, Dunston, Gateshead. Tel. 091-493 2935.
DURHAM CITY, Ferens Park, The Sands, Durham, DH1 1JY. Tel. 091-386 9616.
ESH WINNING, West Terrace, Waterhouses, Co. Durham. Tel. 091-373 3872.
EVENWOOD TOWN, Welfare Ground, Stones End, Evenwood, Bishop Auckland, Co. Durham. Tel. 0388 832281.
HEBBURN, Hebburn Sports & Social Ground, Victoria Road West, Hebburn, Tyne & Wear. Tel. 091-483 5101.
HORDEN COLLIERY WELFARE, Welfare Park, Park Road, Horden, Peterlee, Co. Durham. Tel. 091-518 0248.
NORTON & STOCKTON ANCIENTS, Station Road, Norton, Stockton-on-Tees, Cleveland. Tel. 0642 530203.
PRUDHOE EAST END, Kimberley Park, Broomhouse Road, Prudhoe, Northumberland. Tel. 0661 35900.
RYHOPE COMMUNITY, Meadow Park, Ryhope, Sunderland. Tel. 091-523 6555.
SHOTTON COMRADES, Station Road, Shotton Colliery, Co. Durham. Tel. 091-526 2859.
STOCKTON, Teesdale Park, Acklam Road, Thornaby, Cleveland. Tel. 0642 606803.
WASHINGTON, Albany Park, Spout Lane, Concord, District 11, Washington, Tyne & Wear. Tel. 091-417 7779.
WILLINGTON, Hall Lane, Willington, Co. Durham. Tel. 0388 746221.

SUSSEX COUNTY LEAGUE – First Division

ARUNDEL, Mill Road, Arundel, Sussex. Tel. 0903 882548.
BEXHILL TOWN, The Polegrove, Bexhill, Sussex. Tel. 0424 220732.
BURGESS HILL TOWN, Leylands Park, Burgess Hill, Sussex. Tel. 0444 242429.
CHICHESTER CITY, Oaklands Park, Chichester, Sussex. Tel. 0243 785978.
EASTBOURNE TOWN, The Saffrons, Eastbourne, Sussex. Tel. 0323 23734.
HAILSHAM TOWN, The Beaconsfield, Western Road, Hailsham, Sussex. Tel. 0323 840446.
HAYWARDS HEATH TOWN, Hanbury Park Stadium, Haywards Heath, Sussex. Tel. 0444 412837.
LANGNEY SPORTS, Priory Lane, Eastbourne, Sussex. Tel. 0323 766265.

LITTLEHAMPTON, The Sportsfield, Littlehampton, Sussex. Tel. 0903 713944.
NEWHAVEN, Fort Road Recreation Ground, Newhaven, Sussex. Tel. 0273 513940.
OAKWOOD, Oakwood Sports & Social Club, Tinsley Lane, Three Bridges, Crawley, Sussex. Tel. 0293 515742.
PAGHAM, Nyetimber Lane, Pagham, Sussex. Tel. 0243 266112.
PEACEHAVEN & TELSCOMBE, Pddinghoe Avenue, Peacehaven, E. Sussex. Tel. 0273 582471.
RINGMER, Caburn Ground, Anchor Field, Ringmer, E. Sussex. Tel. 0273 812738.
SHOREHAM, Middle Road, Shoreham, Sussex. Tel. 0273 454261.
THREE BRIDGES, Jubilee Field, Three Bridges, Crawley, Sussex. Tel. 0293 530540.
WHITEHAWK, Enclosed Ground, East Brighton Park, Brighton, E. Sussex. Tel. 0273 609736.
WICK, Crabtree Park, Coombes Way, Wick, Littlehampton, W. Sussex. Tel. 0903 713535.

MIDLAND COMBINATION — Premier Division

ALCESTER TOWN, Conway Playing Fields, St. Faiths Road, Alcester, Worcs. Tel. 0789 763356.
ARMITAGE 90, Rugeley Road, Kings Bromley, Burton-on-Trent, DE13 7SG. Tel. 0543 491077.
BARLESTONE ST. GILES, Barton Road, Barlestone, Nuneaton, Warwickshire. Tel. 0455 291392.
BLOXWICH TOWN, Abbey Park, Glastonbury Crescent, Mossley Estate, Bloxwich, Wallsall. Tel. 0922 477640.
BOLDMERE ST. MICHAELS, Church Road, Boldmere, Sutton Coldfield, West Midlands. Tel. 021-373 4435.
BOLEHALL SWIFTS, Rene Road, Bolehall, Tamworth, Staffs. Tel. 0827 62637.
CHELMSLEY TOWN, The Pavilion, Coleshill Road, Marston Green, West Midlands. Tel. 021-779 5400.
COLESHILL TOWN, Pack Meadow, Packington Lane, Coleshill, Birmingham, B46 3JQ. Tel. 0675 463259.
EVESHAM UNITED, Common Road, Evesham, Worcs. Tel. 0386 442303.
HIGHGATE UNITED, The Coppice, Tythe Barn Lane, Shirley, Solihull, West Midlands, B90 1PH. Tel. 021-744 4194.
HINCKLEY, Middlefield Lane, Hinckley, Leicestershire. Tel. 0455 613553.
KINGS HEATH, The Glen, Tilehouse Lane, Shirley, Solihull, West Midlands. Tel. 021-745 7219.
KNOWLE, Hampton Road, Knowle, Solihull, West Midlands. Tel. 0564 779807.
MILE OAK ROVERS, Recreation Ground, Price Avenue, Mile Oak, Tamworth, Staffs. Tel. 0827 289614.
NORTHFIELD TOWN, Shenley Lane Community Association, Shenley Lane, Selly Oak, Birmingham 29. Tel. 021-478 3900.
PERSHORE TOWN, King George V Playing Fields, High Street, Pershore, Worcs. Tel. 0386 556902.
SANDWELL BOROUGH, Oldbury Sports Centre, Newbury Lane, Oldbury, Warley, West Midlands. Tel. 021-544 4013.
STAPENHILL, Edge Hill, Maple Grove, Stapenhill, Burton-on-Trent. Tel. 0283 62471.
STRATFORD TOWN, Masons Road, off Alcester Road, Stratford-upon-Avon, Warwickshire. Tel. 0789 297479.
WALSALL WOOD, Oak Park, Lichfield Road, Wallsall Wood, Wallsall. Tel. 0543 361084.
WEST MIDLANDS POLICE, Sports Ground, Tally Ho, Pershore Road, Edgbaston, Birmingham. Tel. 021-472 2944.

ESSEX SENIOR LEAGUE

BASILDON UNITED, Gardiners Close, Gardiners Lane, Basildon, Essex, SS14 3AW. Tel. 0268 520268.
BOWERS UNITED, Crown Avenue, off Kenneth Road, Pitsea, Basildon, Essex, SS13 2BE. Tel. 0268 555583.
BRENTWOOD, Larkins, Ongar Road, Pilgrims Hatch, Brentwood, Essex, CM15 9JB. Tel. 0277 210464.
BRIGHTLINGSEA UNITED, North Road, Brightlingsea, Colchester, Essex, CO7 0PL. Tel. 020630 4199.
BURNHAM RAMBLERS, Leslie Field, Springfield Road, Burnham-on-Crouch, Essex, CM0 8TE. Tel. 0621 784383.
CANVEY ISLAND, Park Lane, Canvey Island, Essex, SS8 7PX. Tel. 0268 682991.
CONCORD RANGERS, Thames Road, Canvey Island, Essex, SS8 0HP. Tel. 0268 691780.
EAST HAM UNITED, Ferndale Sports Ground, Pennyroyal Avenue, off East Ham Manorway, London E6 4NA. Tel. 071-476 5514.
EAST THURROCK UNITED, Rookery Hill, Corringham, Stanford-le-Hope, Essex, SS17 9LB. Tel. 0375 641009/644166.
ETON MANOR, Roding Lane, Buckhurst Hill, Essex. Tel. 081-504 9937.
FORD UNITED, Rush Green Road, Rush Green, Romford, Essex, RM7 0LU. Tel. 0708 745678.
HULLBRIDGE SPORTS, Lower Road, Hullbridge, Hockley, Essex, SS5 6BJ. Tel. 0702 230420.
MALDON TOWN, Fambridge Road, Maldon, Essex. Tel. 0621 853762.
SAWBRIDGEWORTH TOWN, Crofters End, West Road, Sawbridgeworth, Herts, CM21 0DE. Tel. 0279 722039.
SOUTHEND MANOR, Southchurch Park Arena, Lifstan Way, Southend-on-Sea, Essex. Tel. 0702 615577.
STAMBRIDGE, Rochford Road, Great Stambridge, Southend-on-Sea, Essex, SS4 2AX. Tel. 0702 258988.
STANSTED, Hargrave Park, Cambridge Road, Stansted, Essex. Tel. 0279 812897.
WOODFORD TOWN, 265 Snakes Lane, Woodford Green, Essex, IG8 7JJ. Tel. 081-504 0831.

HELLENIC LEAGUE — Premier Division

ABINGDON UNITED, Northcourt Road, Abingdon, Oxon. Tel. 0235 520255.
ALMONDSBURY PICKSONS, Oakland Park, Gloucester Road, Almondsbury, Glos. Tel. 0454 612220/201343.
BANBURY UNITED, The Stadium, off Station Approach, Banbury, Oxon. Tel. 0295 263354.
BICESTER TOWN, Sports Ground, Oxford Road, Bicester, Oxon. Tel. 0869 241036.
BISHOPS CLEEVE, Stoke Road, Bishops Cleeve, Glos. Tel. 024267 6257.
CARTERTON TOWN, Kilkenny Lane, Carterton, Oxon. Tel. 0993 842410.
CINDERFORD TOWN, Causeway Ground, Hilldene, Cinderford, Glos. Tel. 0594 822039.
CIRENCESTER TOWN, Tetbury Road, Cirencester, Glos. Tel. 0285 654783.
DIDCOT TOWN, Station Road, Didcot, Oxon. Tel. 0235 813212.
FAIRFORD TOWN, Cinder Lane, London Road, Fairford, Glos. Tel. 0285 712071.
HEADINGTON, Barton Recreation Ground, Oxford. Tel. 0865 60489.
KINTBURY RANGERS, Inkpen Road, Kintbury, Newbury, Berks. Tel. 0488 57001.
MILTON UNITED, High Street, Milton. Tel. 0235 832999.
MORETON TOWN, London Road, Moreton-in-Marsh, Glos. Tel. 0608 50861.
PEGASUS JUNIORS, Essex Arms Sports Ground, Widemarsh Street, Hereford. Tel. 0432 268705.
RAYNERS LANE, Tithe Farm Social Club, 51 Rayners Lane, Harrow, Middx. Tel. 081-866 9659.

SHORTWOOD UNITED, Meadowbank, Shortwood, Nailsworth, Glos. Tel. 045383 3936.
SWINDON ATHLETIC, Southbrook Recreation Ground, Pinehurst Road, Swindon, Wilts. Tel. 0793 513789.

WESSEX LEAGUE

The Wessex League is a relative newcomer to the non-league scene, formed in 1986/7 with seventeen competing clubs, mostly from Hampshire but including Steyning (Sussex), Thatcham (Berks.) and Bournemouth (Dorset). The first season was dominated by three sides, Bashley, Road Sea and A.F.C. Totton, eventually finishing in that order. However, two clubs, Road Sea and Portals Athletic both folded at the end of the inaugural season. New entrants were East Cowes Vics, Christchurch and Folland Sports from the Hampshire League together with Wimborne Town from the Great Mills Western League. Bashley were champions in 1987/8, also reaching the semi-final of the F.A. Vase before succumbing to Emley. Steyning withdrew at the end of the season and Wellworthy Athletic lost their ground but amalgamated with Lymington. For 1988/9 sponsorship was secured through Medisport and the league was accepted into the pyramid. Bashley won the championship for the third successive season, and promotion to the Beazer Homes League. Three new clubs joining were B.A.T., Fleet Town and Bemerton Heath Harlequins, and the 1989/90 season was the most competitive to date with six sides in contention to the end. Romsey Town won the title on the last Saturday of the season, but runners-up Newport I.O.W. were promoted as the facilities at Romsey were not up to the requirements of the higher grade. 1990/1 kicked off with new sponsors, Jewson, and two newcomers, Ryde Sports and Swanage Town and Herston. The season was again highly competitive with Bournemouth, Havant and Swanage involved towards the end. Havant Town were promoted as champions. Facilities at most of the Wessex League grounds are quite basic, but more than adequate for the level of football played.

AEROSTRUCTURES SPORTS & SOCIAL, Folland Park, Kings Avenue, Hamble, Southampton. Tel. 0703 452173.
A.F.C. LYMINGTON, Lymington Sports Ground, Southampton Road, Lymington, Hants. Tel. 0590 671305.
A.F.C. TOTTON, Testwood Park, Testwood Place, Totton, Southampton. Tel. 0703 868981.
B.A.T., B.A.T. Sports Ground, Ringwood Road, Totton, Southampton. Tel. 0703 862143.
BEMERTON HEATH HARLEQUINS, Western Way, Bemerton Heath, Salisbury, Wilts. Tel. 0722 331925.
BOURNEMOUTH, Victoria Park, Winton, Bournemouth. Tel. 0202 515123.
BROCKENHURST, Grigg Lane, Brockenhurst, Hants. Tel. 0590 23544.
CHRISTCHURCH, Avon Causeway, Christchurch, Hants. Tel. 0202 473792.
EAST COWES VICTORIA ATHLETIC, Beatrice Avenue, East Cowes, Isle of Wight. Tel. 0983 297165.
EASTLEIGH, Ten Acres, Stoneham Lane, East Stoneham, Eastleigh, Hants. Tel. 0703 613361.
FLEET TOWN, Calthorpe Park, Crookham Road, Fleet, Hants. Tel. 0252 623804.
HORNDEAN, Five Heads Park, Five Heads Road, Horndean, Hants. Tel. 0705 591363.
PORTSMOUTH ROYAL NAVY, Navy Stadium, HMS Temeraire, Burnaby Road, Portsmouth. Tel. 0705 822351 ext. 24235.
ROMSEY TOWN, The Bypass Ground, South Front, Romsey, Hants. Tel. 0794 512003.
RYDE SPORTS, Smallbrook Stadium, Ashey Road, Ryde, Isle of Wight. Tel. 0983 812906.
SHOLING SPORTS, Birch Lawn, North East Road, Sholing, Southampton. Tel. 0703 449381.
SWANAGE TOWN & HERSTON, Days Park, off De Moulham Road, Swanage, Dorset. Tel. 0929 424673.
THATCHAM TOWN, Lancaster Close, Thatcham, Berks. Tel. 0635 62016.
WIMBORNE TOWN, The Cuthbury, Cowgrove Road, Wimborne, Dorset. Tel. 0202 884821.

Bournemouth;

A.F.C. Lymington;

SURVEY

Our second annual non-league survey was not much more successful than the first. Although we had some 50% more questionnaires completed than last year, the spread of teams supported by the respondents was narrower, and with Wealdstone, Dover and Moor Green supporters the most numerous there was a danger it would turn into a survey of the BHL Premier Division rather than the game generally. In addition, a combination of egotism and inadequate wording on the forms meant most participants voted for themselves as best travelling supporters and their own players as most highly rated. The 'least popular non-league player/personality' category, perhaps not an advisable question in the first place, was used as an excuse for the Wealdstone and Dover supporters, particularly the latter, to abuse each other. This feud also coloured the 'least hospitable club' voting, with the vast majority of the votes for Wealdstone and Gloucester coming from Dover fans. We're working on a better questionnaire and better means of distribution for 1992. In the mean time we've collated the votes in the four categories which were answered reasonably sensibly, and here's the results:

BEST GROUND	YOUR FAVOURITE GROUND	MOST HOSPITABLE CLUB	LEAST HOSPITABLE CLUB
1. WYCOMBE WAND.	1. WYCOMBE WAND.	1. FARNBOROUGH T.	1. TAMWORTH
2. Boston United	2. Weymouth	2.Rushden Town	2. Gloucester City
3. Weymouth	3. Farnborough Town	3. Bashley	3.= Halesowen Town
4. Dorchester Town	4.= Bashley	4. V.S. Rugby	Yeovil Town
5. Gravesend & N.	Gloucester City	5. Merthyr Tydfil	5. Fisher Athletic
		6.= Bromsgrove Rovers	6. Enfield
		Dover Athletic	7. Dartford
		Weymouth	8. Crawley Town
		9. Gloucester City	9.= Chelmsford City
		10. Kidderminster H.	Wealdstone

MOST HOSPITABLE CLUB
FARNBOROUGH

EL TEL WAS A SPACE ALIEN - THE BEST OF THE ALTERNATIVE FOOTBALL PRESS VOLUME 1. Britain's first ever compilation of football fanzines, first published in 1989 and recently reprinted to satisfy continuing demand. The best of fourteen different fanzines covering different teams. 210 pages A4, ISBN 1 872204 00 7, Price £5.95 (+£1.50 p+p if ordering direct).

GET YOUR WRITS OUT - ANOTHER DOSE OF THE ALTERNATIVE FOOTBALL PRESS. Volume 2 of the above, published 1991, a selection from a further 15 magazines covering teams in all four divisions of the English Football League. 210 A4 pages, ISBN 1 872204 02 3, Price £6.95 (+ £1.50 p+p).

WHERE'S THE BAR? (first edition) : First edition of this book still available if you want to complete the set. Originally £2.25, now £1.50 post free. If you are sending for this book only £1.50 in stamps will be acceptable. ISBN 1 872204 01 5.

THE LAST DAY. Pictorial record of Wealdstone's final Southern League match at Lower Mead, plus press cuttings, reminiscences etc. 44 page A5 booklet, ISBN 1 872204 04 X, £2.50 (+£0.30 p+p).

ALL OUR BOOKS ARE AVAILABLE FROM SPORTSPAGES AND SOCCER BOOKSHELF AS WELL AS SOME BRANCHES OF WATERSTONES AND W.H. SMITH. ALTERNATIVELY THEY CAN BE ORDERED FROM ANY BOOKSHOP QUOTING THE ISBN NUMBER.

Juma Printing and Publishing
First Floor
Trafalgar Works
44 Wellington Street
Sheffield S1 4HD
Tel. (0742) 720915
Fax 786550.